UNQUOTED COMPANIES

This study provides the first ever in-depth analysis of a group of firms that make an important contribution to the UK economy. Much has been said and written by policy-makers about the importance of small firms. But little is known about those small firms which are successful and grow, while remaining essentially private, family firms. These larger unquoted companies are the focus of attention in this book.

A series of interviews with owners and managers provided a detailed picture of the legal framework, the operating characteristics and objectives, and the fiscal and financial constraints, of a small sample of these companies. A number of interesting characteristics emerged: the emphasis on family involvement and family continuity, the objective of building up the company taking precedence over profits, the relation of the private tax affairs of the owners to the operations of the company, and the apparent lack of financial constraints.

The interview evidence then formed the basis for detailed quantitative analysis of the performance and financial characteristics of unquoted companies, in comparison with their quoted counterparts. These analyses confirmed the conclusions drawn from the interviews, and added some new insights. In particular, on virtually every performance comparison, the evidence indicates that unquoted companies outperform quoted companies.

These conclusions (together with evidence presented to show how very substantial is the share of the unquoted sector in UK output) suggest that the sector should receive rather more attention from policy-makers than it has in the past. The major constraint the sector faces is the threat to the continuation of a company as an independent business if a principal shareholder dies and capital transfer tax becomes payable.

This is a major study of interest to all who are concerned with the operations of private business in the United Kingdom – researchers and students in business and industrial economics, banks and financiers, policy-makers, and, not least, the owners and managers of the firms themselves.

Donald A. Hay is Fellow and Tutor in Economics at Jesus College, Oxford. He is co-author of *Industrial Economics* and managing editor of *Journal of Industrial Economics*.

Dr Derek J. Morris is Fellow and Tutor in Economics at Oriel College, Oxford, and, on secondment (1981–4), Economic Director of the National Economic Development Office. He is co-author of *Industrial Economics* and editor of *The Economic System in the United Kingdom*.

Unquoted Companies

Their contribution to the United Kingdom economy

DONALD A. HAY
and
DEREK J. MORRIS

Foreword by Lord Lever of Manchester

First published 1984 by
THE MACMILLAN PRESS LTD
London and Basingstoke
Companies and representatives
throughout the world

ISBN 0 333 36335 3

Printed and bound in Great Britain at
The Camelot Press Ltd, Southampton

To our parents

Contents

Foreword

Lord Lever of Manchester

A precondition for a healthy private enterprise sector is a large element under sturdy owner-management. The businesses involved can be very small or very large. What has tended artificially to restrict the size of owner-managed enterprises and their extent has been, and to an important degree still is, a system of taxation which is at worst heavily prejudiced against this principle and at best indifferent to its needs. Indeed, it is a tribute to the virility of owner-managed enterprises that so many of them have survived in a hostile fiscal and financial climate.

When I had government responsibility for this sector in the last Labour Government, I came to the conclusion that two taxes, in particular capital gains tax and capital transfer tax, were major instruments damaging the performance and perpetuation of our most successful owner-managed enterprises. I was and am convinced that the abolition of capital gains tax on unquoted shares would be a powerful incentive to investment in this area. The results would many times compensate for the trifling loss of revenue. And the loss of revenue itself is small compared with the tax incentives given to invest elsewhere.

The most damaging tax, however, for the unquoted business is capital transfer tax, especially in its operation at death. The discriminating impact of this tax on owner-managed business should be obvious. If a man dies leaving £2 million in ICI shares, the level of tax exacted on a transfer at his death will have no effect upon the workings of that company. But if a man leaves a similar fortune to his children in an owner-managed business the results can be disruptive and disastrous to the business itself.

Although I welcome the further encouragement and reliefs that the Conservative Government has given to the unquoted sector, I myself believe that the abolition of capital transfer tax and capital gains tax in relation to the shares of unquoted companies would be more beneficial than some of the devices that have so far been deployed.

Unquoted Companies by Donald Hay and Derek Morris is of great value because it begins to cast light on the important question of the relative performance of quoted and unquoted companies. This is an area which hitherto has been dominated by ignorance and prejudice rather than by information and analysis.

All the lessons of recent history teach us that the modern world needs a thriving and effective private enterprise sector, not only to produce a high level of wealth creation and innovation, but also as part of the necessary structure of a free society. There is a legitimate place for state-owned corporations and for large private companies run by managers. But there is also a crucial role to be played by the owner-managed enterprise, which is a highly flexible instrument. Some businesses are owned completely by the people running them, others have knowledgeable investors with a limited part in the management. A whole range of situations can be dealt with. It is no surprise that the research in this book suggests that, within the private sector, it has been firms of the unquoted, owner-managed type that have tended to be the more efficient. By implication, the biggest question raised is whether we have been wise to allow so much of our entrepreneurial enterprise to come under the control of salaried managers or state bureaucrats.

I am sure that this book will be warmly welcomed. It is valuable in itself as a study of what will be a central economic and political issue in the future. It should also be a stimulus to further research and discussion as to the best balance of organisations within our economy and society.

HAROLD LEVER
The Rt Hon. Lord Lever of Manchester, PC

Preface

Most companies in the United Kingdom are not quoted on any Stock Exchange. There is therefore no effective market for their shares. While the vast majority are small, many medium-sized companies and a significant number of large ones are unquoted. Yet very little is known about their behaviour, performance or contribution to the UK economy. Previous studies are few and not recent.

One major reason for the lack of information and analysis concerning this important sector of industry has been that the accounts of unquoted companies were not publicly available until 1967. But since then all companies, whether quoted or not, have had to file their annual accounts at Companies House and thereby make them available for public inspection. As a result it is now possible to examine data on such companies over at least a ten-year span.

But it is not just the provision of statistics that prompts such a study. In recent years the economic analysis of industry and the study of company financial behaviour, previously pursued largely in isolation, have become much more closely linked. Seminal work by Marris has provided the basis for new theories of firms' behaviour which integrate pricing, financial behaviour and expenditure decisions of companies. Theories of merger, takeover and stock market behaviour have become part of the mainstream of industrial economic analysis and raise many important and interesting issues about the determinants of industrial efficiency. How effective are financial markets at supplying funds, monitoring performance and allocating resources? What has been the impact of the widespread divorce of the management of industrial resources from their ownership?

These and many related questions can best be studied (and in some cases probably only be studied) by consideration of quoted and unquoted companies as distinct classes of industrial organisation. For although in terms of the product markets in which they operate they may be similar, in terms of finance, ownership and management they are fundamentally different. By examining the consequences of this, much can be learnt about the behaviour of industry in developed western economies.

Recent years have seen a great increase of interest in small firms and policy initiatives designed to help them; and all small firms are unquoted. But the distinction between small and large firms differs both conceptually and in practice from the distinction between quoted and unquoted companies. We need to know what happens to successful 'small' companies which grow out of that classification but none the less remain unquoted, as typically is the case. It becomes of interest whether the strengths and weaknesses of small companies are correctly associated with their size or whether they are not in fact a function of their status as unquoted companies. This can only be examined by consideration of larger unquoted companies.

There are therefore numerous factors that make the study of unquoted companies as a group of particular interest. Given the lack of knowledge about them, we have attempted to provide as comprehensive a view as space, resources and data have allowed. We have utilised the most comprehensive data bases currently available of both quoted and unquoted companies. We have compiled directly from company accounts an inevitably much smaller but more detailed data base on unquoted companies. We have interviewed directors and managers, generally at the most senior levels, in a number of unquoted companies in different industries. This has revealed much about the characteristics of unquoted companies, and permitted us to make estimates both of their performance in relation to quoted companies and of their overall contribution to the UK economy. Much must remain provisional, and on many issues we cannot claim to provide definitive results. But if this book encourages other researchers to explore further and to develop analyses which can give greater insights into this important group of companies, then it will have achieved one important aim.

It is our hope that this subject will also be of general interest to those in industry and the financial world, to government ministers and politicians and to their advisers who are concerned with industrial performance. We have therefore endeavoured to make the book accessible to a wide readership, and in particular have provided an initial chapter which summarises the rest of the book including the main results. This can be omitted by those intending to read the other chapters, but may prove helpful as an initial guide to the subject-matter.

Preparation of this book, starting as we did with little upon which to build, would not have been possible without very substantial help from a number of sources. First and foremost we would like to record our great appreciation to all those owners and managers of unquoted companies who generously gave us their time and co-operation. They were subjected to a considerable amount of detailed questioning about all aspects of their companies; without exception they showed great forbearance and could not have been more helpful. We hope that they in particular will feel, on reading this book, that their efforts were worth while.

We would like to thank Ralph Leake and his colleagues at Jordan & Sons Ltd for assisting us with statistical data on the United Kingdom's larger unquoted companies. Their co-operation in letting us use their data was much appreciated. We are also most grateful to Christabel Biggs of ICFC for her help and encouragement at an early stage of our work, and acknowledge with thanks the permission of Dr G. Meeks, Mr A. Goudie, Professor G. Whittington and the Esmée Fairbairn Charitable Trust to use their databank of quoted company accounts.

We are heavily indebted to Malcolm Paget, who acted as research assistant throughout the project, deriving a large part of the data, processing the information, preparing sections of the analysis and reviewing related literature; also to the Oxford University Institute of Economics and Statistics for providing a room and facilities for the project. Our thanks also to Clive Payne, Giuseppe Mazzarino and Nick Pomiankowski who between them carried out all the extensive computer work, overcoming in the process major obstacles which would have defeated any less determined and persistent specialists in this field. We also wish to record our gratitude to Valerie Williams, Janet Wastie and Gillian Coates for their help in typing the book and providing invaluable secretarial assistance. Notwithstanding the important parts played by all these people, we naturally remain fully responsible for all errors of fact or analysis.

Finally, we would like to express, certainly not for the first time and probably not for the last time, our continuing appreciation for the support given to us by Elizabeth Hay and Susie Morris, for their toleration of many weeks when we worked in the evenings and at weekends, and their sympathetic understanding at all stages of our efforts to produce this book.

DONALD HAY
Jesus College

DEREK MORRIS
Oriel College

1 Introduction and Summary

1.1 INTRODUCTION

The research reported in this book has sought the answer to three questions about unquoted companies in the United Kingdom today:

1. What are the particular characteristics of unquoted companies and how are these characteristics shaped by the legal and institutional framework within which they operate?
2. What is the aggregate contribution of unquoted companies to the UK economy?
3. How do unquoted companies compare with their better-known quoted counterparts, especially in respect of their efficiency?

Some answers to these questions can be found in Chapters 2–7. There we present the result of research which was carried out in 1979–81 into the unquoted sector in the United Kingdom. Such work inevitably faces certain limitations. It is only relatively recently that sufficient data have become available to make the attempt worth while, and the data which are available frequently present difficulties. Moreover much of the data are from company accounts, which bear only a very imprecise relation to the underlying decisions and activities with which we would most wish to be concerned. For these reasons it has been necessary to use various data sources, to note the limitation of each, and to look at individual issues from several standpoints in order to derive any reasonably firm conclusions.

We believe this to be the most appropriate approach, and, in view of the very limited information currently available on unquoted companies as a class, probably the only feasible one. However the presentation of such work does make for technical detail which the general reader may prefer to avoid. As we believe our results to be of some significance, with potentially wide implications, we are anxious to overcome this problem. This initial chapter therefore seeks to provide a short summary of the work, leaving the technical details on one side. At each point, we will make reference to the appropriate source in the subsequent chapters. We hope that some readers will have their interest sufficiently aroused to want to read at least some of those later chapters.

The three questions at the beginning of this chapter will form the basic framework for our summary. However it is necessary to set them in context by suggesting some of the reasons for wishing to examine unquoted companies (see Chapter 2).

(1) The past twenty years have seen an unprecedented wave of takeovers and mergers in UK industry, which have led to a dramatic increase in industrial concentration and to the creation of very large quoted companies in most sectors. Indeed the major source of growth of some of these companies has been through takeovers. At the same time, the UK economy has experienced only limited growth, and the hoped-for dynamism of large companies, able to compete successfully in international markets, has proved elusive. There has in recent years been a growing public and political interest in the role of small and medium-sized firms in the economy, in the hope that they can provide superior internal efficiency and dynamism, and make a major contribution to the regeneration of UK industry.

The particular focus of attention has been *small* firms, notably in the Report of the Bolton Committee of Inquiry on Small Firms (1971). That report (see Chapter 3) noted the particular contribution of small firms as a challenge to the monopolistic tendencies of large firms, as a breeding ground for entrepreneurial talent and innovation, and as specialist suppliers to large firms. However, if *small* firms (defined for the purposes of the Bolton Inquiry as manufacturing firms with less than 200 employees and retailing firms with turnover of less than £50000 p.a. at 1970 prices) have this important role in the economy, one hopes and expects that some will be successful and grow beyond the status of 'small' firms. Very little attention has been focused on what happens to them next. One possible destiny, highlighted by recent work on mergers in the United Kingdom, is to be taken over by large quoted companies. Presumably their beneficial effects on the economy may then be dissipated.

The focus of this work therefore is on the larger unquoted companies, and particularly on the phenomenon of being unquoted. This does not mean that our work has no relevance to the issues of small firms, since they are all unquoted too, and will be affected to a greater or lesser extent by the problems and opportunities that we discuss below.

(2) A second reason for focusing on unquoted companies is that there

are good *a priori* reasons to believe that unquotedness has a fundamental effect on the behaviour and performance of such firms, compared to their quoted counterparts. The most obvious differences arise from the legal and fiscal framework within which such companies operate. By definition, such companies are cut off from one important source of outside finance – new equity capital. They are thus dependent on retentions and borrowing to finance their growth and development. In practice too most unquoted firms are family firms, or firms owned by a small group of major shareholders. The result is that the personal taxation position of these individuals is an important consideration determining the behaviour of the firm. This has been particularly the case since 1975, with the application of capital transfer tax to both lifetime gifts and inheritance. The major problem for substantial shareholders in an unquoted company is that of raising the cash to meet this liability.

Recent developments in industrial economics have provided a framework within which the implications of these legal and fiscal characteristics may be studied. The seminal work of Robin Marris, *The Economic Theory of Managerial Capitalism*[1] presented the first systematic integration of financial and managerial aspects of company behaviour into the explanation of growth, profitability and other performance characteristics of firms. Development of this framework has indicated that the objectives of managers, and the legal and fiscal environment, are likely to have marked effects on behaviour. It is precisely these effects that the present work seeks to elucidate, and an analytic approach to the subject, such as that developed by Marris, is required for the evaluation of policy towards such firms. Unless we can identify fairly precisely the relations between particular characteristics of unquoted companies and their behaviour and performance, then suggestions for reform, e.g. of taxation, are likely to be based on weak foundations, with uncertain and unpredictable effects.

(3) Fortunately, the increased interest in unquoted companies has coincided with considerable improvements in the availability of information about them. Since 1967 such companies have been required to file accounts which are open to inspection by the public. Since the early 1970s, summary accounting information about the largest 1000 private companies in the United Kingdom has been published by Jordan & Sons Ltd. This is a vast improvement on the situation ten years ago. However, major difficulties of data availability remain, mainly because the

---

[1] R. Marris, *The Economic Theory of Managerial Capitalism* (Macmillan, 1963).

distinction between quoted and unquoted companies is not a feature of any official statistics except for the *Business Monitor* M3 series. We hope to show in this book that the distinction is sufficiently important that consideration should be given to identifying quoted and unquoted firms in future official statistics, e.g. in reports on the Census of Production, but for the moment we have to make do with the rather more limited information at present available.

1.2 THE CHARACTERISTICS OF UNQUOTED COMPANIES

The formal characteristics of unquoted companies can be briefly summarised (see Chapter 2), making clear the distinction between them and their quoted counterparts. First, the vast majority will be private companies, meeting three legal conditions. In the articles of association the transfer of shares must be restricted and invitations to the public to subscribe for shares prohibited.[2] Up to 1967 these restrictions were matched by the privilege of not having to make public, information about the company, but the Companies Act of 1967 required all companies to file accounts with their annual return. Second, an unquoted firm does not have to submit to certain constraints that quotation brings. These are that at least 25 per cent of any class of equity capital should be in the hands of the public (i.e. people who are not in association with the directors or major shareholders), that the shares may be traded without restriction, and that information about the firm should be disclosed in line with the regulations of the Stock Exchange Council. The most stringent of these requirements concerns the disclosure of information. Third, the majority of unquoted companies are defined as close companies for purposes of taxation. The main element of the definition is that the company is ultimately owned and controlled by its directors, though the rules have become exceedingly complex in response to the discovery of loopholes in the initial legislation. The purpose of the definition is to identify companies where the concentration of ownership in the hands of a few individuals gives an opportunity to adjust their personal tax liability via the use of the company as a separate legal entity. In the context of the present study, the major effect of this distinction arose from the so-called shortfall provision. This allowed the Inland Revenue to regard funds retained in a close company, over and above those necessary for the maintenance and

---

[2] Until 1980, during the period analysed in this book, membership of private companies was limited to a maximum of fifty shareholders.

development of the business, as being distributed to shareholders for the purpose of assessing taxation. Shareholders could not therefore avoid personal income tax liability by excess accumulation of funds within the company. The shortfall provision on trading income was abolished in 1980, but formed a part of the environment of unquoted companies during the period of our study (mainly the 1970s).

However, the listing of these formal characteristics of unquoted companies tells us very little about the real characteristics of the larger unquoted company. For this reason a major part of the research undertaken was a series of interviews with key personnel in nineteen unquoted companies (see Chapter 5). In all but one case the most senior person interviewed was a director. In the majority of cases he was also chairman or managing director, and a major shareholder. The interviews were structured to obtain information about ownership, management, financial behaviour, taxation and company objectives. What emerged was a fairly consistent and comprehensive description of what it is to be an unquoted company.

(1) *Ownership.* All except four of the companies interviewed were strictly family businesses, and had remained so for a long period (since before the first world war in a majority of cases). All except one are close companies for purposes of taxation. Our particular inquiry was directed towards the pattern of shareholding, and how far the ultimate control of the company was retained by a small family group. The inquiry was complicated in the majority of the firms interviewed by the existence of trusts holding sizeable shareholdings. Three main types of trust were identified: (a) beneficial, where the intended beneficiary has a right to the benefit, and is so treated for tax purposes, (b) discretionary, where the trustees have the discretion to make benefits available, (c) accumulation and maintenance, which are settlements for the benefit of minor children or grandchildren. In practice, we found that beneficial and accumulation and maintenance trusts were invariably under the direct control of the major family shareholders, and hence posed no threat to the control of the business. Discretionary trusts tended to be more heterogeneous: some were for individuals (e.g. a surviving spouse), others for the benefit of branches of the family with a substantial number of potential beneficiaries. Given that the trustees need not be members of the immediate family or board, discretionary trusts can constitute a limitation to the control of the family management group. However only in four cases was this even a remote possibility, and in only one case did the existing family managers perceive a threat to their control. The reasons for the lack of concern were evident. In each case the 'other'

shareholders were still family members, albeit not from the immediate family. The 'other' shareholdings were dispersed, so that no one beneficiary of the discretionary trust had a major interest in the company. The board usually had to give permission for the transfer of shares, so it would be difficult for any 'other' shareholder to build up a concentrated holding. Finally, the 'other' shareholders usually lacked the information and expertise to generate alternative policies for the firm. The conclusion was therefore that discretionary trusts generally were no threat to the control of the major family group.

Having 'allocated' beneficial, discretionary and accumulation and maintenance trusts to those major shareholders who effectively control them, we were able to discern two broad patterns of shareholding. The first pattern, which we termed 'concentrated', is where five or fewer major shareholders effectively control 80 per cent or more of the shares. Seven companies fell into this category. These shareholders were invariably on the board of the company, and in most cases were executive directors. The second pattern, 'quasi-concentrated', applied to ten companies. One could identify a small group of shareholders (up to eight persons) with a substantially concentrated holding. However there was also a penumbra of small shareholders, usually still family members, but with numbers between twelve and 250. Taking both patterns together, three or fewer shareholders had effective control of the company in three-quarters of the firms for which the information is available. In practice, then, given that these shareholders agreed about the company strategy, there was little prospect that any other groups of shareholders could challenge them. However that did not mean that the interests of minority shareholders were systematically ignored by the controlling shareholders. A consistent theme was the need to have regard to the interests of such minorities in the matter of dividends, especially where the individuals concerned were dependent on dividends for income.

(2) *Management.* Having established the pattern of ownership of the companies, we next considered how that ownership was translated into effective management control. Despite great variation in the organis-ational detail, all the companies had a 'senior' board (main board, holding company board) with one or more subsidiary boards. On average, the senior boards had 3.7 family members (2.9 with executive roles) and 2.9 non-family members (2.6 with executive roles). However the averages concealed two distinct groups with rather different management structures. In one group, the senior board is composed of family members plus one or two non-family executives, e.g. a finance

director. Business operations are generally managed at subsidiary board level. In the other group, decision-taking is more centralised at senior board level, so that a fairly large group of non-family professional managers is present on the board. The structure of subsidiary boards is even more variable, but on average they had 1.8 family members and 4.2 non-family professionals, indicating a clear preponderance of the latter.

However, the formal structure of organisation is not necessarily a good indication of who effectively takes decisions, so the interviews sought to establish in each case whether or not it was a group with a family majority that had responsibility for strategic management decisions and for operational decision-taking. The evidence suggested that responsibility for strategic decisions was vested in a group with a family majority in only half the companies, and for operational decisions in only one-third of the companies. The interviews also sought to establish who it was, within each group, that in reality was in control. In more than half the cases the majority of key decision-takers were identified as family members. In the other cases, it was generally agreed that no board would take a decision against the views of a key family member. Finally, we were able to identify the close relationship between ownership and control in these companies. In most cases it was the same family individuals who are both major shareholders, *and* members of the effective controlling group, *and* members of the subsidiary boards. Family control only appeared to be threatened in two cases: one where the firm was close to collapse, the other where ownership and management was in the process of being transferred between generations.

The fact that the major shareholders are closely identified with the management of the company in most cases raises an important question about management continuity and expertise. If the firm is to retain this characteristic, then the family must be able to provide at each generation individuals with the ability and the readiness to run the company. This was a preoccupation of about three-quarters of the firms interviewed. Five had found a solution to the problem in the form of an individual within the family. Seven were keen to recruit within the family, but could not identify anyone with the requisite qualifications. Three had reservations about the managerial qualities of family candidates and were intent on reorganising their management structure to accommodate these individuals while retaining management expertise with professionals from outside the family. In every case there was a tacit recognition that good management was essential to the long-run survival of the firm, and that this should have priority over family interests. But at the same time there was clear apprehension at the possible effects of having a professional management divorced from the family shareholders, with the scope for conflict that this could bring.

(3) *Motivation*. Having established the fact that the major shareholders are in practice those who take the important decisions, the logical sequence requires us to ask what are the objectives of such shareholders. For all the family firms in the sample, the primary answer was unequivocal. They desire to maintain control, and to pass on a secure and sound business to the next generation. The desire to maintain independent control appears to be less a characteristic of the particular individuals interested in running such businesses, but more the inevitable outcome of the management/ownership nexus. Given that a major proportion of his personal assets is at stake, any individual will require either direct control of those assets or a ready market for them. The latter is not generally available as far as the shares of unquoted companies are concerned. Therefore the former is essential. This *necessary* connection between the ownership of unquoted companies and a predominant drive to retain independent management control is of great significance. It suggests very severe constraints on the extent to which companies, other than the small number large enough to obtain a quotation, can be expected to function efficiently except with the ownership/control structure described. To the extent that the performance of unquoted companies is superior, limitations on the maintenance of independent control are a still more serious threat to the United Kingdom's industrial efficiency.

When asked to translate the general motives of control and security into more concrete objectives for the management of the business, eleven out of the nineteen companies gave a higher priority to long-term growth, implying an overriding concern with very long-term survival, and investment related mainly to long-term needs rather than shorter-term profitability. For many the strategic time-scale was intergenerational. In contrast only three companies regarded profitability as the key objective. For five companies no clear classification of objectives could be provided.

For reasons which we discuss below, little attempt was made by the owners to extract their wealth from the company, either in the form of dividends or in the form of realisations. The objective of security was met by conservative financial policies, especially with respect to long-term borrowing. However this was not necessarily matched by a conservative business policy. Indeed seven of the companies recognised that they were operating in very risky markets. They were willing to take risks because it was their own money at stake, rather than borrowed money. The nature of management control also implied a degree of flexibility in taking decisions that enabled a more risky market strategy to be pursued.

Given the objective of maintaining family control, it is worth noting here some of the forces acting against this. The first is the dispersion of shareholdings over time as the number of descendants of the original family gets larger at each generation. The main preventive mechanism against such dispersion is the activity of a family group, with continuing associations with the firm, which buys up minority shareholdings whenever a distant member of the family wants to sell. The second threat to family control, which we discuss in detail below, is the need to sell a sizeable proportion of the company in order to meet the tax liability arising on the death of a major shareholder. The effective options are either to sell the company as a whole to some competitor, or to sell a proportion to a financial institution. The second option may enable the family to retain control for one or more generations, but clearly it progressively weakens their effective control, and may make them vulnerable to certain pressures from non-family shareholders. It therefore constitutes a serious long-term threat to the survival of these family companies. The full effects of the taxation problem, being based on legislation dating from 1975, have yet to be felt.

(4) *Financial behaviour.* The only formal restriction on the financing of unquoted private companies is that they cannot offer equity for subscription by the general public. If they are also close companies they were until 1980 subject to the possible restrictions in their use of funds arising from the shortfall provisions. The interviews we conducted provided an opportunity, in the context of a discussion of financial behaviour, to evaluate the effect of these constraints as perceived by the owners and managers.

In the absence of equity sources for the finance of growth and development, one might expect these companies to substitute long-term debt. However the evidence was that ten out of the nineteen carried no long-term debt at all. A further three only did so as a funding of the permanent core of what had been short-term rolling debt with the banks, and that normally at the behest of the banks, rather than out of a desire on the part of the company to obtain long-term funding. The reason for the strong preference for conservative financial policies was the risk to the independence of the firm involved in accepting the commitment to long-term debt finance, and the fear that this would restrict the freedom of the firm in making decisions.

Short-term financing, almost entirely from the clearing banks, was generally set at a level commensurate with the activity and stockholding of the firm, though seven firms restricted themselves to a more conservative level. None of the companies reported any difficulty in obtaining whatever level of financing they required. All had a very close relationship with their bankers.

The consequence of this external financing pattern is that the companies were heavily reliant on retained earning for their investment plans. One would expect this to be reflected in dividend policy, and indeed it was. Only four companies paid dividends above a minimal level. In three of these cases there was a definite policy of paying out between a third and a quarter of net profits as dividends. The fourth had a dividend-per-share target. The other fifteen firms gave various reasons for paying low dividends. Six out of the fifteen needed the funds for expansion and maintenance of the business, and indeed felt some constraint from lack of investment finance. Seven out of fifteen mentioned the high personal marginal tax rates which were a disincentive to increasing dividends. Ten out of fifteen noted that dividends were the basis for valuation of the shares for capital taxation purposes, and for this reason wished to keep dividends low.

The reasons given raise the immediate question as to why the shortfall provisions had not operated to require the companies to pay out more, given that eighteen out of nineteen were 'close'. Thirteen had never had to discuss the matter with the Inland Revenue beyond the provision of the necessary information. Five had had more detailed discussions, but none had suffered from an apportionment. The explanation of this was that the firms could normally justify retentions by the financing needs of the business. Specifically, the fact that the firm could not raise equity, the need to remain liquid to respond to new investment opportunities, and the extent of existing short-term debt obligations were accepted as sufficient justification for high retentions. Profitable investment opportunities were always available, though less than half the companies have ever felt their activities to be constrained by lack of finance. Despite this evidence that the shortfall provisions were never a serious problem for these companies, the abolition of the provisions in 1980 was uniformly welcomed, as removing a source of uncertainty in the companies' financial affairs, since in some cases the shortfall provisions had given rise to discussions with the Inland Revenue protracted over several years.

Finally, we may note the response of this sample of companies to the question as to whether they would consider going public and obtaining a quotation. Fifteen had never seriously considered the possibility, since it was seen to be contrary to their long-term objective of maintaining a family firm. They had no doubt that it would lead to eventual loss of control by the family. They also feared that a likely buyer would be a competitor or customer, who would then be able to influence company policy and begin to undermine the independent existence of the company. If a public issue of shares could not be avoided, then non-voting preference shares were the favoured solution, though the element of gearing involved was not viewed with any enthusiasm, for the same reasons that long-term debt was not favoured.

(5) *Taxation.* No description of unquoted companies would be complete without consideration of the particular capital taxation problems faced by the major shareholders in such companies. From a formal point of view these are personal tax problems, not problems of the company *per se*, but in practice these problems cannot be considered in isolation from the behaviour and objectives of the firm. Since 1975 the transfer of shares *inter vivos* involves the payment of both capital gains tax (since the transfer is treated as a realisation), and capital transfer tax on the values of shares transferred. On death only the latter is payable. In the case of shares in a quoted company, the liability can be met by selling a proportion of the shares. This option is not open to a shareholder in an unquoted company. If the shareholding is relatively minor, the problem can be dealt with by arranging an informal market among existing members of the family to buy up any shares that have to be sold to meet a tax liability. Several of our sample companies maintained such an informal market, with regular valuations being made by the board for this purpose. But if the shareholding is substantial (e.g. in the case of the death of a major shareholder), then the difficulty may be severe, despite the existence of reliefs and allowances, since other shareholders may not have the means to purchase the shares. With no market for shares in such companies and frequently only competitors or larger companies attempting to enter the industry interested in buying such shareholdings, the existence of successful independent companies is threatened as a result of the personal tax system.

All the family firms were exceedingly concerned about this question. It cannot be over-emphasised that although capital transfer tax was introduced in 1975, its impact on the unquoted sector will emerge only very slowly as the existing generation of owners dies. The impact is no less severe because of this. Indeed, the fact that so far the effect has largely been avoided, through the absence of significant lifetime transfers, may encourage the view that it does not pose a major threat to such companies. Yet in its present form it is a form of personal taxation which over time implies an increasing concentration of production in quoted companies, relatively small companies and one-generation intermediate-sized companies. In addition, it already operates as a direct disincentive to growth in that, beyond a certain size, further expansion implies eventually a larger capital tax liability than can be met other than by selling the company and terminating its existence as an independent organisation. Whether this is desirable in part depends on the relative performance of unquoted, particularly larger unquoted, companies, and on whether other means are available for achieving desired ends with regard to the objectives of personal taxation. But in view of the overall performance of the UK economy, the consequences for industrial structure of this form of taxation must be given substantial weight.

A number of partial solutions to the problem had been explored. Seven firms were in the process of passing on shares to the next generation in small parcels, up to the tax exemption limit. But that limit is sufficiently restrictive that only three saw this as a long-term solution to the problem. In another six companies the principal shareholder had taken out life insurance policies to provide a capital sum on death. The difficulty here is that if the capital sum required is substantial, then the premiums required represent a very large call on the individual's current income, so it may only offer a solution where the individual has other income or wealth apart from the company. However in that case the problem is much diminished, as there is something else to sell to meet the liability.

An alternative solution pursued by some companies was to make a bonus issue of preference shares to existing shareholders which could then be sold to institutions, or even quoted. This put cash in the hands of shareholders who needed it, e.g. to provide for a future tax liability. There are however a number of objections to this operation. First, it effectively gears up the income of the company, and so increases financial risk. It will also increase the average pay-out ratio of the company, and so less retentions will be available for future growth. Second, there are various legal restrictions on such preference share issues, which tend to mean that the operation can only be carried out once, or at least very infrequently. Third, the interest on preference shares has to be paid out of post-tax corporate income, unlike debt interest which can be set against tax. This means that the company has the disadvantage of being geared without any of the tax advantages that debt confers.

If none of these expedients is acceptable, or sufficient, to meet the problem, the individual has no alternative but to sell some or all of his equity holding. Financial institutions such as insurance companies, pension funds and merchant banks have bought sizeable minority holdings in unquoted companies, to hold as investments. Control then remains with the family group. The difficulty is that such investments are not particularly attractive from the point of view of the institution. The dividend is likely to be low, and capital gains are difficult to realise, so the institution is 'locked in'. This is not too much of a problem while the firm performs well, but poor performance may demand some intervention by the institution to protect their investment.

A financial institution may be more willing to come in if it sees a prospect of building up a majority holding over time, as successive shareholders die or transfer their shares. This is then a much more marketable asset. However it is clear that such a development would threaten the family control of the business. The majority shareholding could be sold over their heads to a quoted competitor, and their personal control would be at risk.

The alternative to a financial institution is a direct sale to another company. However another company is unlikely to see this as an attractive proposition, *unless* it brings some involvement in the decision-making of the firm. This can be arranged as far as normal business operations are concerned, but if there are differences over strategic decisions the minority shareholder can neither determine the decisions nor readily sell his shares. He is 'locked in' but without influence.

To complete the picture, we need to consider the basis on which the shares of an unquoted company are valued for capital taxation purposes. A majority of our sample companies had had to have such a valuation, and the pattern was reasonably clear for transfers involving minority holdings. None of the companies had had experience of valuation when a controlling shareholding is transferred. In this case, the prevailing opinion was that the Capital Taxation Office would apply a valuation based on the assets per share.

For the transfer of minor holdings, the basis was always the dividend stream of the share. The procedure was to determine the average dividend yield on a roughly comparable group of quoted companies in the same sector. To this yield was added a premium, to account for the lack of marketability of unquoted shares. This premium varied substantially, but was of the order of 20–30 per cent. The resulting yield plus premium is then applied to the dividend to arrive at a valuation. However this was then subject to negotiation in a number of cases. For example, restrictions on share transfer in the firm's articles of association were given as a reason for reducing the valuation. Transfers of small holdings, involving less than 5 per cent of the equity, were given a more nominal value. The liquidity of the company was taken into account in determining whether the dividend was reasonable. High dividend cover could be made the basis for a higher valuation, unless the company could show particular reasons for it, e.g. a high proportion of internal financing.

The effect of these methods of valuation is to give the private unquoted company an additional incentive to avoid paying more than minimal dividends, and to reduce the amount of capital taxation on the transfer of small parcels of shares from one generation of the family to the next. However the basic problem of how to avoid loss of control by sale of shares on the death of a principal shareholder remains, and is a major preoccupation of the companies we interviewed.

We may now summarise our findings as to the principal characteristics of the larger unquoted companies in our sample:

1. The majority of the companies were family businesses, and had been so over a number of generations.
2. Ultimate control of the companies rested with a small family group of major shareholders, though minority shareholdings could be widely dispersed, usually among more distant branches of the family.
3. The major family shareholders exercised effective control over the management of the companies by their presence on the company boards at both senior and subsidiary level, and by executive involvement.
4. The overriding objective was to remain a family company and to hand on a secure business to the next generation. It was recognised that this could bring managerial problems where the next generation lacked either the ability or the inclination to run the firm.
5. Because of the desire to retain family control over the business, the firms were highly dependent on retained earnings to finance growth and expansion. They generally sought to avoid any long-term financing which might be thought to threaten their independence.
6. The personal capital taxation problems of major shareholders are now a definite threat to the continued existence of these firms, and none had found a completely satisfactory method of dealing with it. Indeed on many occasions it was remarked that the only real hope was a major change in the basis for taxation.

1.3 THE AGGREGATE CONTRIBUTION OF UNQUOTED COMPANIES TO THE UK ECONOMY[3]

The contribution of unquoted companies to the UK economy can be considered in two related ways. First, one can ask questions about their share in national output and their share in the use of factors of production such as labour and capital. Second, one can go on to ask how efficient they are in using those factors to produce national output. Fully satisfactory answers to these questions are severely hampered by the absence of a distinction between quoted and unquoted companies in official statistics. However, we believe that the estimates which we discuss here are not likely to mislead to any significant degree.

Two preliminary points need to be made about the sources and methods. First, we were able to obtain estimates for the year 1975, which thus became the benchmark for our study. Second, the contribution of the unquoted sector can only be estimated *indirectly*, by estimating first the contribution of the private sector as a whole, and then subtracting from this the part attributable to the quoted sector, for which a fairly comprehensive data base exists.

We used national income concepts as the framework for the estimates. The two main sources of national income arising in the private sector are wages and profits. We also made a distinction between national income, which includes overseas earnings of UK residents, especially profits arising from the overseas operations of UK-based companies, and domestic income, which is only that income arising from activities in the United Kingdom, and which corresponds more directly to the product of the UK economy. The results are most easily summarised in tabular form, showing the contribution of unquoted companies to the *private* sector under each heading (see Table 1.1).

The main points of interest in Table 1.1 are the following:

1. The contribution of the unquoted companies to income and output in the *private* sector is very substantial.[4] On all criteria, except for that of gross national income from profits, the proportion is more than half. This implies that when the whole of the public sector is also allowed for, the unquoted sector is contributing between 25 and 30 per cent of national employment income, and of gross domestic income. These figures serve to emphasise our contention that the unquoted company

---

[3] See Chapter 4.
[4] Note that the primary sectors (agriculture and mining) are excluded from these calculations.

TABLE 1.1   Contribution to Private-sector National Income of the Unquoted
Company Sector, 1975 (per cent)

Sector	Gross National Income: Profits	Gross Domestic Income: Profits	Employ- ment Income	Gross National Income	Gross Domestic Income
Manufacturing	20	30	39	34	38
Services*	61	81	76	73	77
Manufacturing and Services	36	51	55	50	54

* The services sector includes Sectors 50–88 of the Standard Industrial Classification, but excludes the financial sector, for which estimates could not be made.

Source: All calculations and methods are fully described in Chapter 4.

sector constitutes a major sector in its own right, and one which is worthy of particular study and consideration.

2. Moreover, it must be stressed that the lesser contribution of the unquoted sector to gross national income, shown in Table 1.1, is largely a result of our unsatisfactory assumption that *all* profit remitted from abroad should be credited to the quoted sector. Since we know that many unquoted companies do enjoy substantial overseas income there is clearly a bias in this attribution, but there was no satisfactory basis for making another allocation.

3. The unquoted sector makes a greater contribution to employment income than to income from profits. This largely reflects the more labour-intensive nature of these companies, which is associated partly with their size (smaller firms are on average more labour-intensive) and partly with their sectoral distribution (especially in services).

4. The unquoted sector is much more strongly represented in services, where the contribution lies at 75 per cent or more, but it also provides more than a third of national or domestic income arising in the manufacturing private sector.

Assessing the contribution of the unquoted sector in terms of factor use, both employment and capital, brought further problems of estimation which are fully discussed in Chapter 4.

The employment share of unquoted companies in private-sector employment was estimated at 38 per cent in manufacturing and 72 per cent in non-financial services. The sectoral preponderance in services is clear, but once again the contribution to the manufacturing sector's employment is substantial. Overall the contribution of unquoted companies is similar to that of quoted companies. All these figures are very close to the estimates made by Merrett and Lehr[5] for 1966. This indicates considerable stability in the contribution of unquoted companies to the UK economy at a level approximately equal to that of quoted companies.

It was not possible to make an estimate of the proportion of capital stock accounted for by unquoted companies, but we made an estimate of their contribution to investment and corporate saving in the private sector in 1975. The proportions were of the order of 50 and 40 per cent in manufacturing. The figure for investment is surprisingly high, given that the employment share of unquoted companies was less than 40 per cent in private-sector manufacturing in that year. However the explanation is probably that quoted companies cut back on investment in a recession more sharply than unquoted, which are able to take a longer view of investment decisions (see below).

1.4 COMPARISONS OF THE PERFORMANCE AND EFFICIENCY OF THE QUOTED AND UNQUOTED COMPANY SECTORS[6]

Comparative studies of performance and efficiency are fraught with difficulties, conceptually and empirically. We have sought to overcome these difficulties by using three different data sources (though each source is based fundamentally on the published accounts of individual companies), and by looking at three kinds of efficiency comparison.

The three data sources were the following:

1. The *Business Monitor* M3 series, *Company Finance*, provided aggregate information relating to large samples of quoted and the larger unquoted companies for the period 1971–7. This information is presented as an aggregate balance-sheet, and income and appropriation account for all the sample companies in each sector; it therefore only permits an aggregate comparison.
2. The second set of comparisons utilised two data sources. One is the data bank of the published accounts of individual quoted companies, maintained at the University of Cambridge by Dr G. Meeks. The other is the summary results for the largest 1000 unquoted companies

[5] A. J. Merrett and M. E. Lehr, *The Private Company Today* (Gower, 1971).
[6] See Chapter 6.

published by Jordan & Sons Ltd. These two sources provide the largest coverage generally available of companies from which to make performance comparisons based on the information for individual firms. Such comparisons are likely to give a more detailed and reliable picture than aggregate comparisons. The disadvantage is that the published data on the unquoted companies are inevitably selective, and analysis is thus limited.

3. For the third set of comparisons we constructed our own data base for sixty unquoted companies over a period of fourteen years. The information was taken directly from the accounts of these companies. Comparison was made with a matched sample of 180 quoted companies from the Meeks data base.

The comparison of quoted and unquoted companies focused on:

  i. Productivity comparisons, based on measures of value-added per employee, and value-added per fixed assets.
 ii. Rate of return on assets, as an indicator of the efficiency of use of capital.
iii. Rate of growth of the firm, as an indicator that a company has the ability required to survive in the market-place, and to meet customer wants successfully.

In each case, there are severe difficulties of measurement and interpretation, which are examined in Chapter 6. However the picture which emerged was sufficiently consistent to justify some fairly firm conclusions, which we describe below.

Detailed comparisons of *productivity differences* between quoted and unquoted companies were made for nineteen sectors in 1975 using company data for 783 quoted and 1054 unquoted companies. Measures of value-added per employee, and value-added per fixed assets were derived for each company. Then within industrial sectors, sector averages were calculated for both quoted and unquoted firms. The differences in these averages were computed, and tested for their statistical significance. The first surprising result was that mean value-added per employee was higher for the unquoted companies in twelve out of the nineteen sectors. Our expectation was that quoted firms, being larger, would be more capital-intensive. Each employee, having more capital to work with, would be able to produce more, on average. But this expectation was only fulfilled in seven sectors. We should also note that most of the differences were small and not statistically significant (i.e. we were unable to reject the hypothesis that they could have arisen by chance). The measure of value-added per fixed assets was higher for unquoted companies in eighteen out of the nineteen sectors, and the differences were statistically significant in fifteen cases. Taking these results in conjunction with those for value-added per employee, we can reach the following conclusions. There are two sectors, retail distribution and miscellaneous services, where the two productivity measures point in opposite directions, so we cannot make any comment on total productivity. In three sectors, timber and furniture, wholesale distribution and transport and communication there are no significant differences on either measure. In the other fourteen sectors the higher productivity of fixed assets of the unquoted firms is combined with labour productivity that is not significantly lower than that of quoted companies. We therefore conclude that the unquoted firms in these sectors are obtaining more output (in value terms) per unit input from their resources than the quoted firms. In other words, they are more efficient. Analysis of a smaller sample of unquoted companies for 1973 suggested that these figures for 1975 were not a freak result.

All three data sources enabled us to make comparisons of *the return on assets* of the quoted and unquoted sectors.

The *Business Monitor* data permitted aggregate comparisons for the period 1971–7. The unquoted company sample consistently recorded a higher rate of return on net assets, of the order of two to three percentage points. This was the product of a lower profit margin (ratio of profit to turnover), and a higher ratio of turnover to net assets, the latter more than compensating for the former. The differences in profit margins may arise from the monopolistic pricing of large quoted companies, or from their lower costs through economies of scale, permitting a higher profit margin for a given price. The ratio of turnover to assets reflects in part the more labour-intensive nature of production in the smaller unquoted companies. However this does not detract from the fact that in aggregate the unquoted company sample was generating a higher rate of return on its assets, and this is more plausibly attributed to efficiency in use of factors than to monopoly power in the markets in which they operated.

To consider this conclusion further we looked at the performance of individual firms, using the other data sources noted above. Comparison of the Jordan unquoted companies with the Meeks quoted companies yielded mainly inconclusive results for differences in returns on assets in 1975. On average unquoted companies performed better in thirteen out of nineteen sectors, but in only three cases were differences statistically significant. The difficulty is that rates of return calculated in only one year show very considerable variation between firms in the same sector, for reasons internal to the specific experience of each firm. These specific differences swamp systematic differences in average returns arising from the status (i.e. quoted or unquoted) of the companies. This difficulty can only be overcome by taking comparisons over a number of years.

This was precisely what was done with the third set of comparisons. In each of fifteen sectors we were able to compare the performance of nine quoted companies with three large unquoted companies over a period of fourteen years. The 180 companies were sampled in such a way as to exclude any company which was highly diversified. We used a statistical technique (analysis of variance) to determine the degree to which observed differences in profit rates could be attributed to the distinction between quoted and unquoted companies. The conclusion was that for four important measures of pre-tax profitability, the status of the company was highly important and significant. For post-tax profitability the distinction was less important. The estimated differences were as follows:[7]

Profit measure	*Unquoted minus quoted* (%)
Gross operating profit rate	+ 5.3
Gross profit rate	+ 5.5
Profit net of depreciation	+ 4.5
Profit net of depreciation and interest	+ 4.3
Profit net of depreciation, interest and tax	+ 1.3

We should note that these differences are established after controlling for differences in profit rates between sectors, and for variations with business cycles over the fourteen years. We may therefore regard it as being reasonably well established that the unquoted companies were more profitable than their quoted counterparts over this period. The aggregate picture given by the *Business Monitor* series is confirmed. The most plausible explanation of the greater profitability of the unquoted companies is that they were more efficient.

The third indicator of performance considered in the study was *growth rates* of the firms.

Aggregate comparisons of the quoted and unquoted sectors, based on the *Business Monitor* data showed that not only did the unquoted companies earn a higher rate of return on their assets, but also they added to these assets at a faster rate than quoted companies in every single year between 1971 and 1977. The difference in aggregate was of

[7] See Table 6.10, p. 174.

the order of three or four percentage points. It is consistent with the higher share of unquoted companies in manufacturing fixed investment in 1975 noted above. The difference may reflect sectoral differences, with unquoted companies having a disproportionate stake in fast-growing sectors, and this point was considered in the analysis of individual firms reported next. However it is also plausible that it reflects the commitment of the owners of unquoted companies to the building up of their firms.

Analysis of the large sample drawn from Jordan's and Meeks's data was severely hampered by lack of information over time for the unquoted companies. We calculated growth rates between 1973 and 1975 in terms of fixed assets, sales and employment. For the first two the requisite data were available for only 280 unquoted companies, and for employment for only 186. Furthermore the information was concentrated in a few sectors, where unquoted firms are most important. Hence statistically valid comparisons with quoted firms were only possible in eleven or twelve of the twenty-two sectors. The most striking feature of the employment changes observed in 1973–5 is the shedding of labour by the quoted companies. In all but two sectors, quoted firms, on average, reduced their labour force. By comparison, the average recorded change in employment in unquoted companies is positive in fourteen sectors and negative only in six (there were no unquoted firms in the other two sectors). Although the differences are not statistically significant at sector level, the evidence supports the view that the unquoted sector was more successful at maintaining or increasing employment at a time when quoted firms were shedding labour.

Nor can the experience of the quoted firms be explained by a faster rate of capital accumulation, and the substitution of capital for labour. On the contrary, in the eleven sectors for which comparisons were possible, the average growth rate of fixed assets in unquoted companies exceeded that of quoted companies in ten sectors. Nine of these differences were statistically significant, and represented a very substantial difference in growth experience. The unquoted firms were both investing more, and taking on more labour, while quoted firms were investing at a lower rate and shedding labour in this period. Not surprisingly, the expansion of the unquoted firms is reflected in the growth rate of sales. In the twelve sectors for which comparisons were possible, the unquoted firms had, on this measure, grown more. Finally, we note that comparisons of the growth rate of capital employed, using our third data source, confirmed the superior growth record of unquoted firms over a fourteen-year period. The difference is of the order of six percentage points, even after excluding exceptionally high growth rates of unquoted companies in the food sector. To summarise, there is abundant evidence that the unquoted sector was altogether more dynamic in this period than the quoted sector. This is consistent with the view of unquoted firms as a 'seed-bed' for fast-growing firms and products.

Two further conclusions of the analysis of Chapter 6 are worthy of particular note here:

1. It is always possible that observed differences between quoted and unquoted companies, in terms of performance, should be more properly attributed to differences in size, and not to differences in status. Our analysis was able to reject this hypothesis. Size does have a negative correlation with profitability in the statistical analysis of our small sample, but this does not undermine the significance of company status as a determinant of profitability. No relationship between size and growth was discernible.

2. The comparisons of profitability and growth reported above indicate that the unquoted companies are distinguished, as a group, by both higher profits and higher growth rates. However we could find no statistically significant evidence that they differed from their quoted counterparts in terms of the emphasis given to these two indicators of performance. An analysis of the ratio of profitability to growth could detect no differences attributable to the type of firm. Our suggestion is that in this respect the objectives of unquoted firms do not differ from those of quoted companies.

1.5 FINANCIAL CHARACTERISTICS OF QUOTED AND UNQUOTED COMPANIES

The interviews led us to expect some marked differences in the financial characteristics of quoted and unquoted companies. They also suggested that financial behaviour might have a considerable effect on the overall performance of the two groups of companies. Here we report on an empirical investigation which sought to quantify the differences, and which evaluated these differences in the context of some simple models of the financial flows of firms.

Aggregate comparisons were based on the *Business Monitor* M3 series referred to above. These gave aggregate balance-sheets and profit-and-loss accounts for large samples of UK-owned quoted and unquoted companies for the period 1971–7. We used these published data to construct flow-of-funds analyses for the two aggregate sectors on an annual basis, tracing sources and uses per £100 of profit earned. The first major difference was in respect of dividends and loan interest, with quoted companies paying out at twice the rate of unquoted, with the consequence that the unquoted sector each year retains a substantially higher proportion of its profit. The higher pay-out of the quoted companies is compensated by their greater use of new issues. At the beginning of the period, unquoted companies were committing more of their gross profits to new capital assets, but this difference had disappeared by the end of the period.

Analysis of balance-sheets demonstrated a very different pattern of long-term gearing, measured either as the ratio of long-term debt to shareholding equity, or as the ratio of long-term debt to net assets. Long-term borrowing is a much smaller part of the liabilities of unquoted than of quoted companies.

The aggregate analysis is open to the objection that the observed differences may reflect differences in the sectoral distribution of the firms in the two groups. This possibility was investigated for the other samples (135 quoted and forty-five unquoted companies) utilising accounting information over fourteen years from 1967. These samples were described previously: their great advantage was that they enabled us to account systematically for differences between sectors, and over the business cycle, as well as between quoted and unquoted companies. The analysis largely confirmed the aggregate comparisons, but was able to fill in some interesting details, and to identify some long-term trends in the financial characteristics of the two sectors. Unquoted companies make more use of reserves and deferred taxation to finance their operations, relying much less on new equity issues than quoted companies. They also make less use of long-term debt: but this only reflects a difference in the term-structure of their debt, with unquoted companies making more use of short-term finance. The largest difference is the much greater use of debtors and creditors by unquoted companies, though this difference has diminished over time. Indeed, there is evidence of a convergence in the financial structure of the two groups of firms. On the asset side of the balance-sheet, unquoted companies have a higher proportion of stocks and a lower proportion of fixed assets. This is most plausibly related to less capital-intensive production methods in unquoted companies. Our conclusion is that unquoted companies have a much more flexible structure on both the asset and liability sides of the balance-sheet, in that a higher proportion of both are short-term. This gives the unquoted company more freedom and flexibility in responding to changing business conditions, a point which was emphasised in the interviews. The analysis confirmed that the differences between the two groups of firms are best interpreted in terms of the distinction between quoted and unquoted, and not between large and small firms. Size effects were shown to be significant, especially in explaining the structure of assets, but they can only explain a part of the observed differences.

Some more elaborate statistical analyses of the flow of funds through quoted and unquoted companies were performed in order to examine the extent to which each group might be regarded as facing overall constraints on expenditure. The results can only be tentative but suggest two general conclusions. First, while unquoted companies finance more of their investment internally, they are less constrained by fluctuations in internal funds. In part this may reflect conservative financing policies, but mainly indicates easy access to funds, notably short-term ones, because of higher profitability and shorter-term asset structure. Second, absence of access to the stock market does not appear to put unquoted companies at a financial disadvantage; in fact they appear more, rather than less, able to pursue chosen financial policies in the face of fluctuations in internally generated cash flow. While considerably more analysis is needed, we believe these results to be interesting indicators of the efficacy of the financing arrangements of unquoted companies.

1.6 CONCLUSIONS

Looking at our results as a whole, the picture is rather disturbing. We see a form of business organisation which is the only viable alternative to large companies with quoted shares and thus divorce of ownership from management. The unquoted company is generally more profitable and faster-growing and contributes more to maintaining employment; it also appears to be able to finance itself adequately. Because there is no market for individual shareholdings owner-managers are to a considerable extent 'locked in', i.e. they cannot just sell their assets if performance deteriorates as can shareholders in quoted companies. The incentive to good long-term performance is therefore likely to be stronger and the investment greater.

Yet the development of this form of business organisation is jeopardised because it has not been possible to separate the unquoted company from the personal taxation system applicable to its owners.

This is in sharp contrast to the situation of a quoted company, the development of which is independent of the personal taxation system applied to shareholders. The role of small companies has been better understood in recent years, and in consequence they have received considerable help. But those which grow successfully still face severe tax disincentives to further expansion, thereby constraining companies which appear, as a group, to be particularly efficient.

For many companies, coping with these tax disincentives is not just a tactical matter to be incorporated into financial planning. It is central to longer-term development of the companies concerned and inimical to their growth. The fact that most larger unquoted companies have coped so far reflects only that the problem can usually be postponed for the remaining active life of the existing generation of owner-managers. However, the strong disincentive to growth, arising from the fact that the continued existence of unquoted companies as independent organisations is threatened, already operates and is antipathetic to improved industrial performance.

How best to deal with this complex problem needs detailed attention, but in practice only three possible solutions present themselves.

Either an active market in the shares of such companies must be generated, or business reliefs must be extended substantially, or personal capital taxation must be more directly tied to realisation of assets rather than ownership or transfer of them. While there is some scope for the first solution, we have seen that it is unlikely to be large. In addition it weakens the commitment to good performance that arises from owner-managers being largely 'locked into' their companies. Whether necessary tax changes can be achieved while maintaining the egalitarian objectives of the taxation system remains to be seen, and we have not been in a position to pursue this. But the position of the UK economy, and the relative role of unquoted companies within it, suggest that this is a high priority in the attempts to reverse the United Kingdom's long history of relatively poor industrial performance.

2 Issues for Investigation

2.1 INTRODUCTION

The vast majority of companies in the United Kingdom are unquoted. That is to say, their equity shares are not quoted in any Stock Exchange listing, and cannot therefore be traded in a Stock Exchange as are the shares of quoted companies. This difference could have far-reaching consequences for the ownership, management control, financing and development of unquoted companies, as well as potentially important implications for their efficiency. Yet very little is known about the behaviour and performance of these companies, or about their contribution to the UK economy as a whole. Surprisingly little has been written which specifically focuses on their functioning, and few comparisons with quoted companies exist. There is virtually no recent work.

The purpose of this book is to record the results of a fairly detailed examination of unquoted companies undertaken during 1979–81. It seeks to understand the advantages and disadvantages of unquoted companies, to identify their specific difficulties and opportunities, to compare them with quoted companies both in aggregate and at a disaggregated level and to assess their contribution to the United Kingdom's industrial base.

The behaviour of unquoted companies, and in particular large unquoted ones, is of particular significance for academic research into industrial economic behaviour. Economists in this field therefore constitute one readership for whom this book is designed. The description of the data bases and of their deficiencies, and of the statistical and econometric techniques used, reflect this. But we believe that the issues with which we are concerned are of wider and more general interest, relating as they do to the determinants of industrial efficiency, the workings of the financial system, managerial motivation, behaviour and performance, and the impact of the system of taxation in the United Kingdom. For the wider audience of industrialists, politicians, those in the financial sector and many others, as well as students of economics, all of whom we hope will find something of value in this study, we have attempted as far as possible to explain the techniques used, their reliability and the significance or otherwise of the results derived. While therefore this is first and foremost a contribution to economic research, we very much hope that the non-economist will not be dissuaded on that account from reading it.

2.2 DEFINITIONS

There are five main categories of business organisation in the United Kingdom. These are sole traders, partnerships, unincorporated associations, UK incorporated companies and UK branches of overseas companies.[1] Only one, though the most important one, will concern us here, namely UK incorporated companies.[2]

These are legal entities distinct from the people who are their members at any time and are capable of continued existence despite complete change of their members. Nearly all are incorporated by registration[3] and may be unlimited, limited by guarantee or limited by shares. With regard to an unlimited company there is no limit on the liability of members to meet its debts, and it is a rarely used form of business organisation. The advantage is that it is exempt from many information disclosure requirements; in particular it does not have to file a copy of its accounts with the Registrar of Companies and the accounts do not therefore become available for public inspection. Members of companies limited by guarantee are liable only up to the amount guaranteed by each. This form of organisation is generally used by charities and professional and trade associations because there will be no profits of which members will wish to claim a share. For almost all business purposes a company limited by shares is the form of organisation used.

The Companies Acts, which regulate the forms of organisation,

---

[1] None of the first three are incorporated organisations and therefore do not have the protection of limited liability. Partnerships are in effect communal sole traders who are jointly and unlimitedly liable. Both their costs and profits are pooled. Unincorporated associations are generally used for charitable purposes.

[2] Legally they are known as corporations, but in common usage this term has come to mean large incorporated companies. Other forms of organisation are sometimes commonly known as companies, but we shall reserve the term only for incorporated associations.

[3] The alternatives, incorporation by Crown Charter and by Statute of Parliament, are rarely used.

distinguish between public and private companies. In common parlance this distinction is often regarded as synonymous with that between quoted and unquoted companies. While there is a high degree of correlation between the classification of companies on these two bases it must be stressed that *per se* the distinctions are themselves quite distinct. To qualify as a private company three main conditions must be met. In the articles of association, membership must be limited to a maximum of fifty, the transfer of shares must be restricted and invitation to the public to subscribe for shares prohibited. All other companies are public companies. The basic reason for this distinction being made was the belief that smaller concerns would not require all the legislative safeguards necessary in the case of large organisations obtaining share capital from a large and dispersed group of shareholders. The main advantages for private companies were the ability to make loans to directors and freedom from any obligation to file accounts with the Registrar of Companies. The Companies Act of 1948 introduced a distinction between exempt and non-exempt private companies, only exempt companies continuing to enjoy these advantages. This arose from the wish to prevent some companies, the shares of which the public could buy, operating in effect as private companies via subsidiaries. This distinction proved unsatisfactory however and the Companies Act of 1967 abolished the status of exempt private companies. All limited companies now have to file their accounts with their annual return, thus making them available for public inspection, and in general no company may make loans to directors. In addition information disclosure requirements were increased[4] and exemption from the requirement that the company's auditors be independent and qualified (which exempt private companies had previously enjoyed) was removed.[5]

At present therefore the only remaining differences of economic significance between private and public companies are the restriction on share transfers and the prohibition of share issue to the public to which private companies are subject. EEC regulations however increasingly differentiate between public and private companies, and international obligations have required stricter definitions and requirements in relation to public limited companies.

[4] This mainly concerned the details of holding companies, subsidiary and associated companies, emoluments of individual directors, turnover, loans and the evaluation of fixed assets.

[5] These changes followed recommendations by the Jenkins Committee on Company Law, Cmnd 1749 (1965). Only some 1600 out of nearly 400 000 exempt private companies in 1967 opted to become unlimited, thereby continuing to avoid the need to publish their accounts. See Board of Trade, *Companies in 1967* (1968).

A quoted company is one which has been admitted to the listing of securities of a recognised Stock Exchange.[6] This requires at least 25 per cent of any class of equity capital (or securities convertible into equity capital) to be in the hands of the public (i.e. people who are not in association with the directors or major shareholders).[7] A quoted company will therefore invariably be a public company, while the vast majority of unquoted companies are private. However it is possible for a public company, with the freedom of unrestricted share issue and transfer, none the less to be unquoted, and a number of such companies do exist. In general we will be concerned with the results that flow both from restriction on share issue and transfer, *and* from the absence of Stock Market constraints, but companies operating under only the second of these are also of note and therefore our interest will be focused on the unquoted company sector as a whole.

Quotation in itself entails three main characteristics: (i) shares of the company are held by the public, (ii) these shares may be traded without restriction, (iii) the company is subject to the regulations of the Stock Exchange Council. While these regulations are extensive and detailed, the main formal requirement is that of disclosure of information. The Stock Exchange listing agreement tries to ensure as far as practicable that all shareholders receive all relevant information promptly and simultaneously. Company results must be published at least every six months. Specified events concerning the company's capital structure and directorate as well as an extensive list of accounting and business operations information must be notified immediately. The aim is to avoid the establishment of a 'false market', and a model code of conduct to this end has been established.

The Stock Exchange Council lays down requirements with respect to accountants' reports and auditing. However the conventions employed are not different from those normally accepted by the accounting profession, though scrutiny may be more intensive. Finally the Council is particularly concerned to regulate activity in relation to mergers and takeovers to ensure equity of treatment for all shareholders.

Unquoted companies differ in principle only in the three respects listed above, yet the consequences are far-reaching. Conditions of supply of funds are obviously different. More importantly, the pattern of ownership and control develops differently. The constraints and opportunities facing management are different, and efficiency may be influenced. With no market trading in a company's shares, personal and

---

[6] For convenience, discussion will be restricted to the London Stock Exchange.
[7] A lower percentage may be allowed for very large issues.

company finance become much more interlinked. Valuation of assets is a considerably more complex process, and the impact of taxation differs, to name only a few of the effects.

Reference to one further definitional distinction must be made, namely that between *close* and *non-close* companies. This is solely a distinction for tax purposes. The main element of the definition of a close company is that it is ultimately under the control of its directors. Being a subsidiary of a non-close company, or having 35 per cent or more of the shares in public hands, make a company non-close. The specific definition is extremely complex, largely as a result of attempts to prevent loopholes appearing in the definition of the ultimate controllers of a company. The purpose of the definition is to identify companies where the concentrated nature of ownership prevents opportunities for the individuals concerned to reduce their tax liability via use of the company as a separate legal entity. Much of the tax legislation with reference to close companies refers to treatment of payments and loans made between companies on the one hand and directors and owners as individuals on the other. However the major implication for close companies, nearly all of which are both private and unquoted, arose from the so-called shortfall provision, until it was abolished in respect of trading income in 1980. This allowed the Inland Revenue to regard funds retained in a close company, over and above those viewed as necessary to the maintenance and development of the business, as being distributed to the shareholders for tax purposes and taxed accordingly. Shareholders could not therefore avoid personal income tax liability by excess accumulation of funds in the company. The impact of these provisions is considered in Chapter 5.

These in brief are the main legal distinctions with which we will be concerned. Nearly all of what follows is concerned with predominantly small and medium-sized, but also some large unquoted companies. Nearly all are also both private and close, but being unquoted entails neither of these characteristics.

2.3 REASONS FOR THE INVESTIGATION

Very little is generally known about unquoted companies as a group. A number of reasons exist for believing that it is important to fill this gap now. These reasons provide what is in effect a blueprint for the issues with which we will be concerned and it will therefore be useful to identify them at the start.

(a) *Data availability*

One of the most forbidding reasons for this gap in our knowledge about the industrial and commercial base in the United Kingdom has been the extreme difficulty of obtaining reliable, systematic and comparable data on the sector. With barely any exceptions, official statistics do not recognise the distinction between quoted and unquoted companies. As noted above, until 1967 such companies did not have to file accounts in a form which could then be examined by researchers, and while extensive data bases containing information from most quoted company accounts are now available, no such comparable data base is accessible for unquoted companies. Nor is it clear that the latter is a practical proposition with over one million such companies now in existence, many surviving for only a realtively short period of time.

In recent years however the position has changed substantially. The requirement to file accounts imposed in 1967 means that there is now a series of about twelve years of accounts available for as many unquoted companies as the researcher's data processing capabilities will permit. Summary data on the United Kingdom's largest 1000 private companies have been available for most of the 1970s and for the largest 2000 since 1980.[8] In addition the data on all quoted companies, and official statistics on the economy as a whole, are now much more comprehensive and detailed, making estimation of the contribution of the unquoted sector as the difference between the two, more straightforward.

For the analyst the present situation is still far from ideal. No remotely comprehensive computerised data bank exists for unquoted companies, as in the case for quoted ones. In addition company accounts reveal only part, albeit an important part, of the behaviour of companies. There is also a wider diversity of accounting conventions amongst companies not subject to Stock Exchange information requirements. General statistical problems are therefore reviewed in detail later as appropriate. None the less the considerable expansion of available information during the 1970s makes detailed study of the sector possible and appropriate.

(b) *Unquoted companies versus small companies*

A second reason for lack of attention to the unquoted sector in the past has been the fact that the vast majority of the companies it comprises are

---

[8] See *Britain's Top 2,000 Private Companies 1980* (Jordan & Sons Ltd, 1980).

small. In consequence, though nearly all companies in the United Kingdom are unquoted, their contribution to total output and employment will be proportionately very much less, as will be their share of any given industry or market in which they operate. However, as will be seen more clearly later, the contribution of unquoted companies remains extremely important overall on any accepted measure; they play a significant part in virtually all sectors of the economy and are in particular the predominant type of company in some of the fastest-expanding sectors of the economy.

Small firms have of course been the subject of a major Committee of Inquiry (the Bolton Report) (see Chapter 3) and numerous other studies. There are however several reasons for distinguishing carefully between the characteristics associated with small companies, and those associated with unquoted ones. In the first place, there exist many unquoted companies which in terms of sales, capital and employment are very large by any standard. Second, combining comparable data on quoted and unquoted companies of different sizes in principle permits us to distinguish the separate effects of size and status (i.e. quoted or unquoted) with interesting differences between the two appearing. Third, recent interest in trying to establish a market for the shares of small companies suggests that it is important to understand the consequences of such arrangements, independent of size effects.

Despite these distinctions it is important to see the work that follows in the context of the debate on small firms. In the last year or two there has been a growing belief in the superior efficiency and dynamism of small firms and in their role as major providers of new employment. This has now found expression in government policy initiatives to promote the founding and development of small firms.[9] Given that under present arrangements all such companies will be unquoted, appraisal of the opportunities and constraints faced by unquoted companies will be of direct relevance. It is, in addition, over ten years since the Bolton Report on small firms was published; a decade which has seen much greater fluctuation in economic activity than in the preceding twenty-five years and much greater pressure for adaptation and change. These have been caused, amongst other things, by pressures resulting from a ten-fold increase in oil prices, the advent of North Sea Oil and a high exchange rate, substantial sectoral shifts in output and growing competition from newly industrialised countries. Effective financing and management of business, upon which survival and growth in such an environment

---

[9] See Finance Act (1980; 1981). The relevant measures include the Business Start-up Scheme, the Venture Capital Scheme and the Loan Guarantee Scheme.

crucially depend, are not likely to be independent of the institutional and economic relationship between a company and its shareholders. While therefore much of our work will be concerned with larger unquoted companies, and in particular those large enough for a quotation to be feasible, the results also have significance for the debate on the role of small firms in the economy.

(c) *The financial system in the United Kingdom*

That growth of the UK economy has been inadequate over a long period of time, and probably back into the last century, is now generally well known and documented. A low level of investment has probably been the cause most often cited, though evidence establishing it clearly as a cause rather than a consequence is rarely presented. To the extent that a boost to investment would promote faster growth, the adequacy of sources of finance for investment has been a popular subject of inquiry, the most recent major example being the deliberations of the Wilson Committee of Inquiry into the workings of the financial system in the United Kingdom.[10] It is therefore of great significance that unquoted companies by definition are cut off from one major source of funds. Whether this tends to inhibit their efficiency or growth, and if so, to what extent alternative sources can be found to compensate, is important not only to an assessment of the unquoted company sector but also to the debate over the adequacy of the supply of investment funds to industry.

(d) *Capital taxation*

Unquoted companies face a particularly severe problem as a result of the system of capital taxation now in force in the United Kingdom. Since the Finance Act of 1975, gifts made during an individual's lifetime (on a cumulative basis per donor) and property in his estate on death are subject to capital transfer tax, the rate of which rises progressively from 5 to 75 per cent. In addition lifetime gifts are regarded as realisation of assets and therefore subject to capital gains tax as well. Therefore, whether the holder of shares in an unquoted company attempts to pass them on during his life or leaves them in his estate on death, he or his estate is liable to capital taxation despite the absence of any actual realisation of the assets. For the holder of quoted shares an appropriate proportion can be sold to meet the liability. For the holder of unquoted

<hr/>

[10] Wilson Committee to Review the Functioning of Financial Institutions, Cmnd 7937 (1980).

shares no such ready market exists, particularly if the shares represent a minority holding. In many cases therefore there is great pressure to sell the company as a whole as the only means of meeting the combined tax liability. In general this will involve acquisition by another company. Many quoted companies therefore face the prospect of independent survival for only one generation; the sector as a whole is at a severe disadvantage *vis-à-vis* the quoted one and to some extent the successful companies within it face absorption by the quoted sector, or by overseas owned and based companies.

In the past this problem has been much less severe. Prior to 1975 early transfer of assets escaped a tax liability and avoided Estate Duty on death. The impact of the new system can be delayed by avoiding transfers during life. But as the number of unquoted company shareholders leaving unquoted shares in their estate on death grows, so the present structure of capital taxation in the United Kingdom will increasingly undermine the position of unquoted companies as going concerns. Whether this is a cause for concern naturally depends in part on the value of the unquoted sector to the UK economy.

(e) *The current position in industrial economic analysis*

Another reason for inadequacy of investigation has been the isolation of different disciplines involved in the study of industry over a long period of time. Until recently economists focused exclusively on companies' price, output and investment decisions, with little reference to financing of companies and none at all to management. These latter topics were studied both normatively and descriptively in isolation, using different methods. It is only in the last twenty years or so that these different strands have begun to be integrated properly.[11] The pattern of ownership, the institutional setting of a company's financial arrangements and the constraints and opportunities facing management teams have all been seen as inextricably linked with economic performance.

The major advance in this process was the publication in 1963 of *The Economic Theory of Managerial Capitalism* by Robin Marris.[12] Like most, if not all, seminal works, antecedents can be found,[13] and it has

[11] See D. A. Hay and D. J. Morris, *Industrial Economics: Theory and Evidence* (Oxford University Press, 1979) ch. 1 for a more extensive discussion of these historical trends.

[12] R. Marris, *The Economic Theory of Managerial Capitalism* (Macmillan, 1963).

[13] The work of Penrose, Downie and Baumol is of particular importance. See E. Penrose, *Theory of the Growth of the Firm* (Oxford, 1959); J. Downie, *The Competitive Process* (London, 1958); W. Baumol, 'On the Theory of the Expansion of the Firm', *American Economic Review*, vol. 52, no. 5, December 1962, pp. 1078–87.

been subject to much revision and development, not least by Marris himself. But the 1963 publication marks the first systematic integration of financial and managerial aspects of company behaviour with the explanation of growth, profitability and other performance characteristics of firms, and the presentation of a tractable framework for analysing such issues. Central to Marris's own thesis was the view that large companies, while owned by shareholders, were controlled and directed by salaried managers. The managers' salaries, status and power were tied much more to the size of company than to profitability. Hence provided that profitability exceeded some minimum acceptable level, Marris viewed the objectives of company managers as predominantly being growth maximisation, rather than profit maximisation as almost invariably assumed by economists hitherto.

Several points need to be emphasised in the present context. First, the Marris-type firm was a large, diversified public company of a readily recognisable sort. Indeed the large disparity between giant industrial companies increasingly dominating production, and the essentially passive single-product firms of most economics text-books was a major spur to the development of Marris's approach. At least by implication small companies were still presumed to adhere much more closely to the traditional text-book norm.

Within the Marris framework it is the existence of a managerial group different from, and perhaps only loosely constrained by, a dispersed group of shareholders, which differentiates the Marris firm from alternative types of company. Though the size of a company is important, it is not this characteristic *per se* which is the source of differentiation but the relation between manager and shareholder. In so far as any simple means of distinguishing the two classes of firms are to be used, Marris-type companies are quoted, the others unquoted. Indeed tests of Marris's hypotheses have specifically tried to compare the performance of companies controlled by salaried managers with ones of similar size controlled by their owners. This simple classification, however, when used for the purpose of testing economic theories should not be accepted without criticism; heavily concentrated holdings of shares in quoted companies would effectively remove most managerial discretion; trading in the shares of unquoted companies does exist sometimes beyond the control of owner-managers; and more detailed investigation of unquoted companies reveals other more subtle but equally important distinctions not so far mentioned (see Chapter 5). However despite all this, the distinction between owner-controlled and managerially-controlled companies and the concepts of 'managerial discretion' and 'shareholder enforcement' have all come to occupy key positions in the literature of industrial economics.

Second, although Marris envisaged his model applying to large public companies with growth objectives, it was in practice much more general. It permitted integrated analysis of production and sales, finance and management even if the assumption of profit maximisation were to be retained. The pursuit of growth may well be a prime motivation amongst managers in small as well as large companies. Increasingly therefore the Marris model can be seen as a general framework for analysing all types of company, the key distinctions between different types being the extent of managerial discretion to act free of shareholder constraints and the sources and availability of finance. The relation between managers, owners and financiers has thus become a principal feature in explanation of company performance. The status of a company as quoted or unquoted is undoubtedly the key factor in this relation.

This emphasis has been fostered by a parallel development also partly stemming from the work of Marris. As he pointed out, companies are increasingly diversified, with many of their most important choices revolving not around individual price and output decisions but around the selection of new products and markets. Research, as well as the development of new ideas into new products, market penetration and associated investment are therefore key elements in the competitive process. Performance in any one market is less crucial in a diversified firm and this can weaken the immediate consequences to a company of it being relatively inefficient. For both reasons the decisions of providers of finance between competing companies have increasingly been viewed as of equal importance to those of customers deciding between competing suppliers, in the enforcement of efficiency through market forces. To the extent that a stock market acts as an efficient allocator of resources through the process of takeover, as well as in new issues, this switch of emphasis from product markets to financial markets is all the stronger. Here again the extent to which a company's shares can readily be bought and sold is at the heart of the issues involved.

A very recent but particularly interesting development of Marris's work is that of Odagiri.[14] He argues that the ability of Japanese firms to pursue growth, sometimes at the expense of short-term profits, has been high because of the absence of a highly developed stock market to enforce discipline. This he believes has been a key element in generating

[14] H. Odagiri, *The Theory of Growth in a Corporate Economy: An Inquiry into Management Preferences, R & D and Economic Growth* (Cambridge University Press, 1980).

faster growth of the Japanese economy as a whole. Quoted companies in the United Kingdom may frequently experience great pressure to preserve short-term profits, even at the cost of foregoing longer-term benefits, in order to maintain shareholder confidence. If this argument has merit, then comparisons of quoted and unquoted companies are of particular importance.

2.4 OUTLINE OF THE BOOK

In summary, little is known about the contribution of unquoted companies as a group to the UK economy. Yet their defining characteristic is now of major concern both in academic work in the field of industrial economics and for the issue of efficiency in the industrial and financial sectors. Advantages and disadvantages peculiar to unquoted companies, particularly those arising from taxation, are probably not widely understood, yet are potentially major factors in determining the overall health of the economy. Increased availability of data now offers a good opportunity to explore these matters.

Against this background the programme of work described below is as follows. The next chapter reviews existing literature and summarises the more important indications of the significance of the unquoted sector. Chapters 4–7 then constitute the major new evidence. Chapter 4 estimates the contribution of the unquoted sector to the UK economy as a whole. Chapter 5 reviews the evidence coming out of a detailed investigation, including interviews, of a sample of unquoted companies carried out in 1980. It considers the ownership, management and financing of unquoted companies in some detail and looks at the impact of taxation. It seeks to identify those factors which most clearly differentiate the behaviour of quoted from that of unquoted companies. Chapter 6 examines comparisons of performance between the quoted and unquoted sectors. First, it does this in aggregate. It then takes the largest samples of individual company data available to us for both the quoted and unquoted sectors, compares them industry by industry and attempts to measure the statistical significance of the differences discovered. While this reveals much that is interesting, the analysis is all at a fairly aggregate level. To correct this, smaller matched samples of quoted and unquoted companies were established as a basis for more detailed investigation and the results of this work are also presented. The chapter also investigates the evidence for the light which it throws on the business objectives pursued by the two groups of companies. Chapter 7 then reports the results of detailed comparative analysis of the financial behaviour of quoted and unquoted companies. Balance-sheet and flow of funds are compared; and the issues of financial constraints and efficiency in the use of finance are discussed. All differences between the two groups are subject to tests of statistical significance.

3 A Review of Previous Research into the Unquoted Sector in the United Kingdom

3.1 INTRODUCTION

The purpose of this chapter is to draw on some of the previous research on the unquoted sector in the United Kingdom to provide a background for the subsequent analysis of the book. There are two strands in this literature. The first concerns itself particularly with *small* firms. The most comprehensive work in this area was done by the Bolton Committee of Inquiry on Small Firms.[1] While much of this literature is very interesting, it is important to reiterate at the outset that it is somewhat tangential to our main interests. It is certainly true that all small companies are likely to be unquoted, but not all unquoted companies are small. Since our focus is on the problems faced by *all* unquoted business, the small-firm literature is too restricted in scope. This is not merely an academic point. 'Small firms' are identified as a particular problem for policy, and a certain amount of legislative preference already exists (e.g. the lower rate of corporation tax on taxable profits less than a certain figure, or the exemption from VAT for small traders). The logic of applying these benefits to a rather ill-defined small-business sector only makes sense if it can be shown that the problems are related exclusively to size. This is far from being self-evident. The second strand of literature is of more interest to us. It basically aims to compare the performance, and business and legal environment of different kinds of firms. It therefore provides a more useful starting-point for our own analysis which follows. This literature, however, is limited. There is, of course, a very extensive literature on

[1] Bolton Committee of Inquiry on Small Firms, Cmnd 4811 (1971).

firms generally in industrial economics which it would be pointless to try to summarise here.[2] However, it is notable that much of the empirical work that has been done in UK firms in recent years has been restricted to the quoted sector.[3] There is nothing particularly remarkable in this: information about quoted companies has been more readily available than that about unquoted. But it does mean there is possibly a substantial bias in the literature, since the results need not be representative of all types of company. (Exactly the same possible bias exists in the American literature on the economics of firms.)

3.2 SMALL FIRMS

The Bolton Committee's formal terms of reference defined the scope of their inquiry as firms with less than 200 employees. There is some suggestion in the report that the Committee found this definition rather unhelpful. Thus the report draws attention to various qualitative characteristics that they deemed to be of the greatest significance. These were that the firm had a relatively small share in its market, that it was run by its owner, and that it was independent (not part of some larger enterprise, even in association at arm's length). In an effort to allow for these factors, at least to some extent, the *quantitative* limits were set at 200 employees in manufacturing, an annual turnover of £50000 p.a. (1970 prices) in retailing and twenty-five employees in construction.

A postal questionnaire to 3500 firms revealed some of the characteristics of these small firms. Approximately 40 per cent were incorporated (the rest were either partnerships or sole traders). Of these about nine-tenths were 'close companies', with a controlling interest held by one or two persons. The average age of the owner-manager was 54 years. This is paralleled by a surprisingly high average age of firms themselves: in manufacturing, 22 years. Few of the owner-managers had any higher educational or professional qualifications. A study of their motivations gave very large weight to a desire for independence, and an unwillingness to accept help or advice from 'outsiders'. Their financial

---

[2] See D. A. Hay and D. J. Morris, *Industrial Economics: Theory and Evidence* (Oxford University Press, 1979).

[3] For example: A. Singh and G. Whittington, 'Growth, Profitability and Valuation', Department of Applied Economics Occasional Paper no. 7 (Cambridge University Press 1968); L. Hannah and J. Kay, *Concentration in Modern Industry* (Macmillan, 1977); S. J. Prais, *The Evolution of Giant Firms in Britain* (Cambridge University Press, 1976); G. Meeks, *Disappointing Marriage: A Study of the Gains from Merger* (Cambridge University Press, 1977).

structure suggested a low proportion of finance from external sources, and a large number had never borrowed at all. There was a notable difference between fast- and slow-growing firms. The former had borrowed substantially to finance their expansion, with bank finance being the main source. But the direction of causation is not clear: fast growth may have enabled them to borrow, rather than borrowing itself being an engine of growth. Overall the small firms had fewer fixed assets, and were more liquid than larger firms, which suggests financial conservatism. Small firms apparently enjoyed a good industrial relations record, despite evidence that they paid less.

The Committee reported on the economic performance of small firms. Net output per person employed was up to 18 per cent lower in small firms, probably reflecting lower capital intensity, but the return on capital was markedly higher, whether measured as a return on net assets, total assets or equity. This higher return was offset by a greater variability, and hence presumably more risk. The report saw a particular role for small firms which goes beyond their immediate performance. This is their competitive challenge to monopolistic large producers. It concluded that even if a small firm is not apparently doing very well, it may be performing an immensely useful role in helping to keep larger companies efficient. Naturally this is impossible to measure. Small firms were also thought to be more flexible than large ones in adapting to new needs in the market, though in terms of formal R and D, their employment of qualified scientists and engineers and their 'output' of innovations was found to be proportionately much less than that of larger firms. However 'innovation' is notoriously difficult to measure objectively. A further role of small firms identified by the report was their function as specialist suppliers to large firms. The theoretical point has been made by Stigler.[4] Efficiency in a sector as a whole may be best served by a vertical disintegration of production. Thus a number of large producers may support a penumbra of small firms each supplying a single specialist input or product. If each of the large producers had to do this for itself, within its own operations, it would not have the advantage of either scale or skill specialisation which is achieved by the small firm supplying to several producers.

The report estimated the total contribution of small firms to the UK economy as 19 per cent of gross national product, GNP (or nearly one-quarter of GNP produced in the private sector). However it also drew

---

[4] G. J. Stigler, 'The Division of Labour is Limited by the Extent of the Market', *Journal of Political Economy*, vol. 59, 1951, pp. 185–93.

attention to the contraction of the small-firm sector in the period 1935–68. In manufacturing, the employment share of small firms had fallen from 44 to 9 per cent, and the output share from 41 to 25 per cent. Between 1924 and 1963, the number of small firms in manufacturing had fallen by 73000. A similar pattern had occurred in all other sectors except retailing and road transport. In retailing, the numbers of firms had fallen, but their share in output and employment had not reduced. This pattern of decline in the small-firm sector has been paralleled in other developed economies, except for North America. However, in a ranking of thirteen industrial countries by the proportion of manufacturing employment in small establishments in the mid-1960s, the United Kingdom had the lowest percentage of all.[5] The United States had a noticeably higher birth rate of new companies, though UK companies appeared on average to last longer.

The Committee gave its judgement that the decline in the UK small-business sector had levelled off by the end of the 1960s. This was also suggested to the Wilson Committee[6] (see Table 3.1).

TABLE 3.1   Small Enterprises in UK Manufacturing

Year	Numbers (1000s)	Share (%) of total employment	Share (%) of net output
1963	65.7	21.3	18.0
1968	66.1	20.8	18.1
1970	70.9	21.3	18.5
1973	74.1	20.7	17.1

Source: Interim Report *The Financing of Small Firms*, of the Wilson Committee to Review the Functioning of Financial Institutions, (see table 2.1, p. 45; table 2.2, p. 45; table 2.3, p. 46).

In manufacturing, the share of small firms in employment (on the original Bolton definition) was barely different between 1968 and 1973 and the actual number of such firms had risen significantly. The share in output was however slightly lower.

In the construction industry, the number of small firms had contracted, but no faster than the industry as a whole. In retailing, the rate of decline identified by the Bolton Committee has continued, and the share of the small firm sector has also fallen. Evidence from the later

[5] Bolton Committee of Inquiry on Small Firms, ch. 6.
[6] Wilson Committee to Review the Functioning of Financial Institutions, Interim Report, *The Financing of Small Firms*, Cmnd 7503 (1979) appendix 2.

1970s is not reliable, and the decline in all economic activity at the beginning of the 1980s, as a result of depression, makes it difficult to discuss long-term trends.

Having outlined the trends in the small-firm sector, the Bolton Committee then turned to the reasons for these trends. Some of the adverse factors they traced to technological and economic factors. They pointed to the scale advantage of large firms in the areas of optimum plant size, R and D facilities, managerial services and marketing. Declining transport costs and the reduction in tariffs meant that local markets in which small firms had thrived were no longer protected from national or international competition. Despite all these factors, the Committee emphasised the continuing need for a healthy small-firm sector to maintain competition, to provide specialist services and goods to large firms and to provide a 'breeding ground' for new products and new entrepreneurial talent. (More recently policy attention has switched to small firms as a source of employment. An MIT study[7] published in 1979 showed that 88 per cent of new jobs in the United States between 1969 and 1976 were created by small businesses, and 66 per cent by firms employing less than twenty people. The possible implications for UK policy are obvious.)

The Committee also identified adverse factors arising from the growth of the State. The first was that the State had restricted the domain of operation of the small firm. Second, State procurement contracts tend to go to large producers. Third, legislation often places a disproportionate burden on small firms, in terms of form-filling and unproductive administration of legislation. Further, the taxation of wealth could be a major disincentive to small-firm owners, and potential entrepreneurs.

Finally, the Committee returned to the long-debated issue of whether small firms are constrained by lack of suitable sources of finance. This was first suggested by the Macmillan Committee in 1931.[8] The 'Macmillan gap' referred to the lack of provision for small and medium-sized businesses seeking external finance of up to £200000 (equivalent to more than £2 million in 1980). The gap was between the personal resources of the founder, and the minimum required for a flotation of an issue on the Stock Exchange. The gap was filled to some extent by the formation of the Industrial and Commercial Finance Corporation (ICFC) in 1945, and by other specialist development capital companies.

---

[7] Massachusetts Institute of Technology report, cited in *The Economist*, 29 September 1979, p. 104.

[8] Macmillan Committee on Finance and Industry, Cmnd 3897 (June 1931).

But the adequacy of these institutions, particularly for smaller businesses, was in some doubt.

Having identified the problems of the small-firm sector in Part I of their report, the Bolton Committee turned in Part II to analysis and policy recommendations. The scope of this analysis was very wide, including such diverse elements as the problems of independent craftsmen, the effect of EEC entry and the effect of development controls. But three areas claimed most attention from the Committee: finance, taxation and legislation. We look at these in turn, referring to subsequent publications in these areas where appropriate. It should be appreciated that we are summarising the information contained in these publications. Some of the conclusions and recommendations arising from these works have already been acted upon and the current situation may therefore differ substantially from the review here. This is particularly true in the area of taxation. For this reason we will only briefly summarise the material in that area.

In addition to the Bolton Committee investigation[9] the financing of small businesses has been looked at recently by the Wilson Committee.[10] The main features of the balance-sheets, remarked on by both reports, are the reliance on bank finance and trade credit, the absence of long-term loans, except from directors of the firm, and the reliance on retained earnings to finance investment. The main question at issue is whether this pattern reflects the preferences of these businesses, or whether they are constrained on the supply side by the lack of alternatives. The method adopted by both research reports was to review the whole supply side with a view to identifying 'gaps'. The Wilson Committee supplemented this with interview surveys seeking evidence of dissatisfaction on the part of the firms with the sources of finance available to them. We summarise the supply side first.

The main sources of all categories of finance for small businesses are the clearing banks. The two points most at issue are availability, and the terms on which finance is offered. The Bolton Committee argued that the small-firm sector was particularly affected by credit restrictions, e.g. 'ceilings' on lending by the banks. When these were more severe bigger firms tended to pre-empt a large share of the available credit, partly because small firms are particularly prevalent in industries which are not usually given priority by the government or Bank of England, e.g.

---

[9] Bolton Committee of Inquiry on Small Firms, Research Report no. 4, *Financing Facilities for Small Firms* (Economists Advisory Group) (London, 1971).

[10] Wilson Committee to Review the Functioning of Financial Institutions, Interim Report, *The Financing of Small Firms*.

retailing and construction. Credit restrictions also led to a general toughening of banks' assessment of risks, with a particular impact on small firms. Finally the trade credit position of small firms tended to worsen when restrictions were being operated: large firms would demand prompt payment of accounts, but delay paying their own bills.

Both reports suggest that the credit terms available for small firms may be quite onerous. Rates of interest were as much as 2 per cent above those of larger businesses. The level of security required is often quite high, with typical security ratios of net assets to borrowing in the range 2:1 to 4:1. Personal guarantees were also required on some occasions. Alternatively, the bank would require the firm to be in credit for at least part of the year. The banks justified their cautious policy by the observation that small firms' borrowing involves very considerable administrative costs. The lack of financial sophistication of small firms makes the task of the bank manager much harder in getting together the information required to vet a loan request. Where the borrower has no assets to pledge against the loan as security, the manager has to make a general assessment of the creditworthiness of the borrower, and the viability of his project. Further, the banks argued that the high degree of competition between them in attracting business customers meant that no single bank could afford to be too harsh on such borrowers.

Hire purchase and plant equipment leasing ranked second to bank finance as a source of borrowing in the Bolton Committee analysis. The finance is provided by finance houses on given terms. However there were a number of problems reported. First, the finance is specific to an actual transaction, i.e. the purchase of a piece of equipment, and thus lacks flexibility. Second, despite a down payment system to protect the lender, creditworthiness was still an important criterion. Small firms were often excluded because they were new, making for greater uncertainty about their future cash flow. Third, under the close company rules for corporate taxation, a company which hired or leased its equipment found it harder to make out a case for substantial retention of profits within the business.

Medium- and long-term finance is available from a number of financial institutions. Clearing banks and their subsidiaries, merchant banks and ICFC were prepared to offer loans of up to 10 years' duration. Insurance companies and pension funds would provide mortgage finance for buildings. But only a very small part of this finance went to small firms as defined by Bolton. The reason is that high investigation costs and recurrent administrative costs made most of these institutions reluctant to lend below a minimum level of transaction. Not surprisingly, such finance tends to be available only for well-established firms.

The main source of equity finance for small companies is the entrepreneur himself (or his immediate family) and the retention of profit in the enterprise. However, it is *prima facie* unlikely that these will always be adequate. What then are the prospects for a small business to obtain outside equity participation? A new issue leading to Stock Exchange quotation is subject to minimum limits which excludes all small firms. However the real barrier is somewhat higher than these limits and is determined by the initial costs. Thus in 1970, the Bolton Committee reported, an issue of £¼ million would incur costs of 6–7 per cent of the sum raised. The proportion fell to 3.2 per cent for an issue of £1 million. The Wilson Committee suggested an 'economic minimum' of around £5 million in 1978, equivalent to pre-tax profits of about £1 million. It was precisely this difficulty that ICFC was intended to meet, and the Bolton Committee thought that this institution had effectively filled the 'Macmillan gap'. However the Wilson Committee felt that some alternative to ICFC should be available. They reported in some detail on the development of the over-the-counter (OTC) market in unlisted securities, under rule 163 of the Stock Exchange. It was reported that £160 million of new capital had been raised in the period 1972–8 by twenty broking firms. The main disadvantage of this system is that the discount on issues of unlisted equity capital may amount to 20 per cent, compared to an equivalent listed security.

A significant need for finance identified by the Wilson Committee is venture capital, particularly for risky projects associated with new technology. The National Research Development Corporation (NRDC) and Technical Development Capital Ltd (TDC) are key institutions in this area. NRDC are involved in the task of encouraging invention. Their participation is particularly flexible, with loans being repaid by a royalty on sales, which does not in any way threaten the independence of the innovator. If the project is a very large part of the firm's operations, NRDC will take an equity stake, but they avoid managerial involvement. TDC is a subsidiary of ICFC. It operates 'down line' from NRDC, providing finance for launching products or processes when the R and D stage is complete. It is prepared to lend quite small sums, and more recently has taken a closer interest in the management of the companies in which it is involved. However the Wilson Committee reported that the overall scale of their operation was small, largely because they are not known well enough.

The Bolton Committee concluded in 1971 that there were no 'gaps' in the market on the supply side, but small firms did suffer adverse effects in three respects. First, they are less well informed about sources of finance, and less well advised. Second, lenders have less knowledge about the affairs of small firms. Third, average transactions costs vary inversely with the size of firm, so small firms suffer from higher overall capital costs. The Wilson Committee broadly concurred, pointing out that the higher costs to small borrowers frequently reflected the higher costs incurred by lenders in terms of risk, administration and investigation of loans. Their main recommendations involved a more flexible approach by existing institutions as far as small firms were concerned. But they also argued for measures to make it easier for such firms to obtain equity finance. This is the only recommendation which has immediate relevance to our concern with quoted and unquoted companies.

The Bolton Committee reported at some length on the taxation problems of small companies. Since many of the problems are discussed in Chapter 4, only general points are recorded here. The Committee identified three disincentive effects of taxation. The first was to inhibit the starting of a business. However they noted the evidence that the incentive to set up a company arises as much from the desire for independence as from the pursuit of wealth. The second related to the development of existing businesses, the main disincentive identified being Estate Duty. The third was the taxation of profits in an inflationary situation. The effect of inflation, in the absence of inflation-adjusted accounts, is to overstate real profits. Where these are the basis for taxation, 'too much' tax will be paid, and hence less can be retained in the business for future growth. On the basis of their analysis the Bolton Committee made a number of suggestions for reform. Some, like the abolition of the shortfall provision for those companies, and the provisions to allow Estate Duty to be paid in instalments, have subsequently been put into effect.

A third area of concern to small companies was identified by the Bolton Committee as the provision of information. This has two aspects. One is the quantity of information required, especially by government departments. The administrative burden on the entrepreneur was agreed to be substantial, and the Committee urged as much simplification of the requirements as was compatible with the needs of government for information about their activities. The other aspect is the disclosure provisions of the 1967 Companies Act. The two objections, apart from the argument that it represents an invasion of privacy, are that the availability of the accounts could reveal the situation of a small firm to its competitors, and that the costs of disclosure are high. The latter was not accepted by the Committee as a reasonable point, since every company needs to produce audited accounts, and the effort involved in filing these in Companies House is not large. Making information available to competitors is more of a problem, especially where a company is highly dependent on a few customers, but the Committee felt that such public information was essential to protect the public, especially creditors or potential creditors.

3.3 COMPARISONS OF SMALL AND LARGE COMPANIES

There have been four studies of the financing and performance of firms since the early 1950s. We consider the scope of these enquiries, before reporting their results under three broad headings – balance-sheet comparisons, sources and uses of funds, and profitability. The first study was that of Bates.[11] The data came from a survey of small firms conducted at the Institute of Statistics at Oxford in the late 1950s, which covered a sample of 335 private firms with fewer than 100 employees and net assets less than £¼ million between 1954 and 1956. This information was compared with information on larger unquoted companies published in *Economic Trends*[12] which relates to 1962. The second study was published subsequently in *Economic Trends*.[13] A stratified sample of 1689 exempt private companies was analysed for the years 1961 and 1962, on the basis of information submitted to the Inland Revenue. (Such firms were not required to publish their accounts until 1967.) This sample was compared with information derived from published accounts of public quoted and unquoted firms. The third study was published by the Economists Advisory Group in 1975, reporting the results of a research study directed by Bannock.[14] The object of the study was to assess the profitability of the larger private company in Britain. Their criterion was a total revenue exceeding £200 000 in 1971. After excluding a number of companies where information was

[11] J. Bates, *The Financing of Small Business* (Sweet & Maxwell, 1964); 'The Profits of Small Manufacturing Firms', in P. E. Hart, *Studies in Profit, Business Saving and Investment in the UK* (Allen & Unwin, 1965); J. Bates and S. J. Henderson, 'Determinants of Corporate Saving in Small Private Companies in Britain', *JRSS* Series A, pt 2, 1967; J. Bates, 'The Activities of Large and Small Companies', *Business Ratios*, Summer 1967, pp. 3–14.

[12] 'Non-quoted Companies and their Finance', *Economic Trends*, February 1965.

[13] 'Patterns of Company Finance', *Economic Trends*, November 1967.

[14] Economists Advisory Group (G. Bannock), *The Larger Private Company in Britain* (Wilton House, 1975).

inadequate, a basic sample of 27 500 remained. However more than 12 000 were subsidiaries of other firms in the sample. Consolidation gave 15 000 financial units, of which nearly 12 000 were private companies. The public companies were distinguished as quoted and unquoted UK companies and unquoted foreign companies. The final study was carried out for the Wilson Committee.[15] Almost 300 firms were included in the sample, divided into two groups: small, with capital employed less than £250 000 in 1975, and medium-small, with capital employed greater than this (up to a maximum of about £4 million). The results were compared with published information for large listed and unlisted companies.

Analyses of balance-sheets in these studies (together with that of the Bolton Committee) are summarised in Table 3.2. Abstracting from the trends which affect all categories of companies, a number of differences can be observed. Unfortunately the distinction between large and small, and between quoted and unquoted is blurred; only for 1962 can we make both comparisons. However a number of common features emerge from consideration of all years. On the asset side, fixed assets are more important for quoted companies than for small/unquoted ones. Stocks have the same weight in balance-sheets, but small firms are owed significantly more in trade credit. They also tend to be significantly more liquid in the form of cash and short-term deposits. On the liability side, the quoted companies have a larger proportion of long-term liabilities, the major difference being accounted for by long-term loans. Shareholders funds do not show great differences so long as loans from the directors of small companies are treated on the same basis as equity. Small firms are more dependent on bank overdraft and other short-term finance. They also borrow more in the form of trade credit.

Analysis of sources and uses of funds generally supports the interpretation of balance-sheets given above, though the pattern may vary substantially from year to year depending on business conditions. One important issue is the appropriation of gross income to interest and dividends, taxation, depreciation and other provisions, and to retentions in reserves. The main distinctions come in the first and last items. Quoted companies pay out more in interest (on long-term loans) and dividends, and retain less in the business. In 1975, large quoted companies paid out as dividends 43 per cent of their profits after depreciation and tax. The comparable figure for their smaller unquoted rivals was 16 per cent. This kind of differential is also apparent in the data for 1962. The corollary of this is that quoted companies are more

[15] Wilson Committee to Review the Functioning of Financial Institutions, Interim Report.

TABLE 3.2 Balance-Sheets of Different Types and Sizes of Companies, 1956, 1962, 1968 and 1975*

Balance-sheet heading	1956† Small	1956† Quoted	1962‡ Exempt private small	1962‡ Exempt private large	1962‡ Large unquoted UK	1962‡ Large quoted	1968§ Small	1968§ Quoted	1975‖ Medium-small	1975‖ Large
Total fixed assets	32.2	39.3	32.6	33.1	40.2	49.1	34.1	46.3	32.8	39.7
Current assets:										
Stocks	32.1	30.2	24.1	25.0	24.0	25.1	24.9	24.4	30.2	27.5
Trade and other debtors	25.8	19.0	32.4	29.3	26.3	19.2	27.0	23.0	32.7	27.8
Liquid assets	9.9	11.5	10.9	12.6	9.4	6.6	14.1	6.2	4.2	5.0
	100.0	100.0	100.0	100.0	100.0	100.0	100.0	100.0	100.0	100.0
Current liabilities:										
Bank overdraft	6.5	2.8	10.9	8.2	6.2	4.7	8.6	6.2	15.0	12.6
Trade credit, etc.	25.8	21.4	33.7	26.7	28.9	21.0	0.0	23.0	33.7	28.5
	32.3	24.2	44.6	35.0	35.0	25.6	38.6	29.2	48.7	41.1
Capital and reserves:										
Loans	2.2	10.0	2.5	2.1	6.7	9.1	5.1	12.5	7.3	10.3
Tax reserves		2.8	2.8	3.9	2.8	2.9		2.8	7.6	7.4
Minorities				0.8	1.8	2.1		2.4	0.2	2.1
Preference shares			2.6	3.4	2.8	4.9	1.5	2.8	0.7	0.7
Equity and reserves	65.5	65.8	47.4	54.9	50.8	55.3	54.9	50.2	35.4	38.4
Capital employed	67.7	75.8	55.4	65.0	65.0	74.4	61.5	70.7	51.3	58.9

* All figures are percentages of total assets.

Sources:
† Bates, 'The Activities of Large and Small Companies'. Small: companies with less than 100 employees.
‡ Economic Trends, November 1967, table E. Exempt private small: assessed profits (for tax purposes) between £4000 and £20 000 p.a. Exempt private large: assessed profits > £50 000 p.a.
§ Bolton Committee of Inquiry on Small Firms, Cmnd 4811 (1971) p. 13, table 2 XIII. Small: in manufacturing, firms with less than 200 employees; in retailing, firms with turnover < £50 000 p.a.
‖ Wilson Committee to Review the Functioning of Financial Institutions, Interim Report, The Financing of Small Firms, appendix 4, table 4.1. Medium-small: capital employed of £250 000 or more in 1975. Large: Business Monitor M3 sample of quoted and large unquoted companies.

reliant on new issues of debt and equity. Small companies are correspondingly more dependent on bank credit and trade credit.

Clearly it is important to know whether these differences have a significant effect on the efficiency and growth of the different classes of company. Prior to these however we need to know the causes of the disparities. The preceding comments suggest four types of cause:

1. The differences largely or entirely depend on whether there is access to the market for equity finance.
2. The differences reflect specific problems faced by smaller firms, such as higher transactions cost, worse information, higher risk assessment, etc.
3. The differences reflect the preferences of the controllers of the companies concerned.
4. Differences in the tax regimes.

There is therefore considerable scope for further analysis. However a still more fundamental question is whether the differences identified in aggregate really exist. Two serious problems have not been fully faced in previous work. The first is that the balance-sheet ratios may well reflect sectoral differences. Disaggregation at the level of manufacturing and non-manufacturing is insufficient to dispel doubts on this score. Second, there is no proper statistical analysis of the differences. For example, some differences in *averages* may well have arisen by chance, and not signify statistically significant differences. It is particularly the case that measured ratios for smaller companies show much greater variability than those of quoted companies. This should make us pause before we accept comparisons made on the basis of average values alone.

Comparisons of rates of return on capital in the quoted sector and the unquoted/small-firm sector have also been made by various reports. Thus an article in *Economic Trends*[16] gave estimates of average rates of return (net income as a percentage of net assets) for various categories of companies in 1961–2. It found that private exempt companies had rates of return larger than those of non-exempt unquoted and quoted companies. But there was little difference between the last two categories. The Bolton Committee[17] reported a similar disparity between their sample of small firms and quoted firms in 1968. The Wilson Committee[18] found that this disparity was persisting in 1973–5,

---

[16] *Economic Trends*, November 1967, table 1.
[17] Bolton Committee of Inquiry on Small Firms, p. 45, table 4.IV.
[18] Wilson Committee to Review the Functioning of Financial Institutions, Interim Report, *The Financing of Small Firms*, p. 60, table 4.6.

though the differences were quite small, and they noted that the averages concealed a very wide dispersion of profit rates. However the most substantive study is that done by the Economists Advisory Group. Their sample was large enough to permit disaggregation into industrial Orders, and to distinguish private, public unquoted, quoted and foreign-owned firms. Unfortunately the asset data collected proved to be unreliable, so the results refer only to profit margins, for the period 1968–71. The study finds that private companies had higher returns on turnover than quoted companies in eight out of seventeen manufacturing industries in 1971, and that their margins had improved in ten out of seventeen in the period 1968–71. However this really tells us very little about efficiency. A smaller profit margin may reflect a lower capital intensity of operations, with a smaller share of profits in total value-added. Furthermore, no tests are presented to demonstrate the statistical validity of the differences discovered.

3.4 CONCLUSIONS

This summary of the existing literature on the unquoted sector in the United Kingdom suggests a number of areas for research. First, we need to look much more clearly at the apparent differences between unquoted and quoted sectors. This will involve disaggregating the information to discuss differences in sectoral composition. It will also involve careful analysis of the question of whether the critical differences are a matter of company status or company size. Since it is the quoted/unquoted distinction which is of most interest in this work, it suggests the comparison of samples of quoted and unquoted companies matched for size as far as possible. It also suggests that we should attempt to discern systematic relationships between important financial and performance variables and size. Second, having established what differences actually exist, we need to consider whether they have real effects on the efficiency and growth of the economy. (That is not to restrict the evaluation of the unquoted sector to economic effects alone. However it seems sensible to keep our enquiry within such bounds.) Third, we need to *explain* those differences. Suppose we identify some difference between quoted and unquoted. Suppose further that we can associate this with some real impact on the efficiency of the economy, such that it becomes of interest to policy-makers. Then we need to understand how the differences have come about, so that the policy changes may be apt and have the intended consequences. That is why it is so important to examine the behaviour of firms with respect to the objectives of the owners and managers, and in the light of constraints on the firm arising from the legal, fiscal and financial environment.

4 The Contribution of the Unquoted Sector to the UK Economy

4.1 INTRODUCTION

This chapter makes quantitative estimates of the share of the unquoted company in such national aggregates as gross national and domestic income, employment and gross domestic fixed capital formation. The availability of data has constrained us to make 1975 the benchmark year for the work. Wherever possible, the analysis has been compared with results obtained for other years, but the core of the work is centred on 1975.

4.2 GENERAL STATISTICAL PROBLEMS

Any attempt to assess the contribution of unquoted companies to the UK economy must get to grips with two questions. The first is the most useful measure of contribution. The second is the availability of appropriate statistics. In our case, what we can achieve is severely circumscribed by the latter, so we will discuss that first.

The major difficulty in measurement is that the distinction between quoted and unquoted companies in the private sector does not feature at all in the criteria for distinguishing different types of firm in official statistical sources. These sources usually enable one to establish the size of the private sector, distinguished from public corporations, and central government and local authorities. The National Income and Expenditure Accounts have gone further since 1975 in distinguishing industrial and commercial companies, and financial companies, within the private sector. Employment data is broken down into private employment and private self-employment, but that is as far as official sources go, and even then, as we shall see, the breakdowns leave much to be desired. This means that we must approach the estimation of the contribution of unquoted firms by an indirect route. This requires us in the first place to estimate the contribution of quoted companies, in so far as we can. These estimates are then deducted from the totals for the private sector to arrive at figures for the unquoted sector.

Our source for information on quoted companies is the computer file of UK quoted companies' accounts, derived from the analysis of quoted company accounts carried out in the Department of Industry, and maintained in the Department of Applied Economics at Cambridge by Dr G. Meeks. This data will be referred to as the 'Meeks data' in this work. Unfortunately the data bank is very far from complete in its coverage of quoted sector companies. First, while it includes companies engaged primarily in manufacturing, distributive trades and some other services (notably construction, transport and miscellaneous services), financial services are completely excluded. Second, the list includes only those companies which in 1973 had net assets of £5 million or more *or* gross income of £½ million or more. Third, it excludes all companies whose activities are wholly or primarily outside the United Kingdom. The first point is dealt with here by confining our attention to the industrial and commercial sector, and ignoring the financial sector. The second is coped with by sampling the quoted companies not included in the Meeks data. Specifically, in 1975, the base year for our study, the Meeks data base had 1044 companies with the variables required for our study. A scrutiny of the *Stock Exchange Year Book* for 1975 revealed a further 768 quoted companies not appearing in the Meeks data file (excluding those in the financial sector and those operating solely overseas). The method of sampling these companies, and the results obtained, are contained in an appendix to this chapter. It was encouraging to find that their contribution is quite small (e.g. less than 4 per cent of the sales of the quoted sector): hence it is unlikely that the lack of detailed information about these companies will bias the results reported below. The exclusion of companies operating mainly or wholly outside the United Kingdom, though quoted in London, raised some difficult problems for the assessment of the gross profit contribution, which we will discuss below in the appropriate section.

The contribution of a sector to the national economy is usually measured by its share in gross domestic product (GDP) or gross national product (GNP). The former refers to production within the geographical territory of the economy. The latter includes all production which generates income for residents, including their receipts from property or activity overseas. At the level of the firm, the equivalent measure to GDP is value-added by its activities in the United Kingdom. This is the sum of its payments to factors of production, i.e. wages and salaries to labour and gross profits earned as a return to capital. Gross national income would add to these the profits earned by wholly-owned subsidiaries overseas, and any other payments made by such subsidiaries for services (e.g. management, consultancy, etc.) rendered by UK residents to them. These GDP measures can be broken into the contributions of wage and salary income, and of gross profits. A further refinement would be to deduct capital consumption (depreciation) from the gross measures to obtain an estimate of contribution to *net* domestic product and *net* national product.

National income type measures may be supplemented with estimates of a sector's share in the use of factors of production, labour and capital. Employment is particularly important as an objective of government policy, so the employment potential of different sectors of the economy has attracted a great deal of attention. Estimates of capital stocks in different sectors are not available, unfortunately. Capital stocks at the level of the firm have to be measured in terms of book values of assets. These are normally valued at the historic cost of their acquisition, though there have been many discussions of ways of at least adjusting for the effects of inflation. However such adjustments are not common practice. National estimates of capital stock, on the other hand, are now fully adjusted for inflation, and for real depreciation based on estimated asset lives in different sectors. As the two are not on a comparable basis, we are not able to arrive at the share of the unquoted sector by an expedient of deducting those stocks accounted for by quoted firms. However this difficulty does not extend to the current level of gross domestic capital formation. Given the importance attached by governments to investment as a means of creating employment and generating long-run growth in the economy, this is a significant statistic for comparative purposes.

Our estimates are for the year 1975. This was the last year for which the complete Meeks data were available at the time the analysis was carried out. In an appendix to this chapter we compare our estimates with those made by Merrett and Lehr[1] for 1966. These were approximately updated for 1973, but the results have not been published. However the updating involved no new research as far as the methods of estimating were concerned, and so probably are not particularly reliable. Our method improves upon that of Merrett and Lehr by using

---

[1] A. J. Merrett and M. E. Lehr, *The Private Company Today* (Gower, 1971).

better estimates of the size of the quoted sector, and by making use of more detailed national income statistics, particularly those relating to overseas earnings.

4.3 THE CONTRIBUTION OF UNQUOTED COMPANIES TO NATIONAL AND DOMESTIC INCOME: GROSS PROFITS

The method of estimation is to obtain estimates of income from employment and gross profits arising in the unquoted and quoted sectors. These can then be aggregated to obtain a rather rough estimate of the division of GNP and GDP between the secors. Our main sources for the national figures are the CSO publication, *National Income and Expenditure, 1966–76*.[2]

To set the analysis in context we consider first the aggregate data relating to industrial and commercial companies, financial companies and public corporations.[3] Table 4.1 shows that 76 per cent of the gross trading profits component of GDP was produced in the private sector, and 24 per cent in the public corporations in 1975. The private-sector contribution conceals a netting-out of a negative contribution by financial corporations from gross trading profits of £11 455 million in the industrial and commercial sector. The negative contribution arises from the fact that the financial sector provides a number of value-adding services (e.g. banking) for which the charges do not cover costs. This sectoral deficit is offset by transfers representing interest on loans to other sectors. In 1975 these amounted to £2674 million from the industrial and commercial sectors alone.

The proportions of gross profits in the private sector attributable to quoted and unquoted companies can only be estimated approximately. Our method is to deduct the share of quoted companies from the total. Three problems arise. First the Meeks data excludes the financial sector. Hence we are not able to consider that here, and need to disaggregate the totals so as to exclude that sector.[4] Second, the accounting data underlying Meeks's data includes in gross trading profit that element arising from subsidiaries and branches abroad. Fortunately, some data on such earnings are available in *Business Monitor* M4 series, 1976,

---

[2] Central Statistical Office, *National Income and Expenditure 1966–76* (HMSO).

[3] CSO, *National Income and Expenditure*, tables 5.4 and 5.5.

[4] CSO, *National Income and Expenditure*, table 5.8.

TABLE 4.1 The UK Company Sector, 1975 (£ million)

Appropriation account of the company sector:	Industrial and commercial	Financial	Consolidation of industrial and commercial and financial	Public corporations
Income in UK:				
Gross trading profit	11455	−1778	9677	3067
Rent and non-trading	1353	7613	5673*	451
Income from abroad (net of tax)	1883	580	2463	40
	14691	6415	17813	3558
Allocation:				
Dividends, debt interest, etc.	2451	4552	4485*	} 1957
Interest (short)	2429		1654*	
	4880	4552	6139	1957
Charities	37	5	42	
Profits due abroad	447	175	622	
UK taxes on income	962	993	1955	5
Balance undistibuted (saving)	8365	690	9055	1596
	14691	6415	17813	3588
Other items:				
GDCF	6983	1652	8635	3949
Increase in value of stocks	2278	45	2323	916
Taxes paid abroad on income from abroad	3414	211	3625	

* Consolidation of industrial and commercial and financial sectors nets-out financial flows between the sectors: hence these figures are not the sum of the figures in the previous two columns.

Source: CSO, *National Income and Expenditure*, tables 5.4 and 5.5.

which gives details of overseas transactions affecting UK companies.[5] This gives the net returns (after depreciation and overseas tax) as £1583 million to direct investment. Our Table 4.1 shows income from abroad as £1883 million. So we deduce that this should be divided between trading profits (£1583 million) and non-trading income (£300 million). Table 4.1 also shows that tax paid abroad on this net income was £3414 million: this is apportioned as £2870 million attributable to trading income and £544 million to non-trading income. Finally *Business Monitor* M4 gives £824 million as depreciation attributable to income on direct investment overseas. This is all attributable to trading income. Hence our revised estimate of the gross trading profits of companies, both at home and abroad, is made up as follows:

		1975	*£ million*
Gross trading profits in UK			11455
Overseas income	Net profit from direct investment	1583	
	Tax paid abroad	2870	
	Depreciation deducted from overseas profits	824	
		5277	5277
			16732

Of this total trading profit, Table 4.1 shows that companies paid short-term interest of £2429 million, or 14.5 per cent of gross profits. The Meeks data for quoted companies only gives operating profit after deduction of short-term interest. Unfortunately we do not have information on the division of short-term interest payments between quoted and unquoted sectors. Hence we have to assume that they are proportionate to operating profits in both cases,[6] and gross up the Meeks profit figure by approximately 17 per cent. The results of making these adjustments are shown in Tables 4.2 and 4.3.

The last column of Table 4.3 gives the gross profit contribution of quoted companies to the profit component of gross national income arising from the activities of companies in the private sector, excluding the operations of financial companies. By subtraction we can thus arrive

[5] *Business Monitor* M4 series, 1976, table 1.1.

[6] This will introduce a bias if unquoted companies are more reliant on short-term borrowing. Chapter 7 in fact shows that this is the case, but we have no means of making the necessary adjustment. The effect on the calculation is, however, very small.

TABLE 4.2 Gross Profits by Sector: Industrial and Commercial Companies, 1975 (£ million)

	Gross profits in UK	Overseas				UK and overseas total
		Net profits	Depreciation	Tax	Total gross profits	
Mining	25	114	59	207	380	405
Manufacturing	5386	832	433	1508	2773	8159
Construction, distribution transport, other services	3744	371	193	673	1237	4981
Total	9155	1317	685	2388	4390	13545
Other	–	266	139	482	887	–

Source: Calculated from CSO, National Income and Expenditure, table 5.8, and Business Monitor M4 series, 1976, table 1.1.

TABLE 4.3 Gross Profits by Sector: Quoted Companies, 1975 (£ million)

	Meeks's data	Sample (allocated between sectors)	Total	Grossed up by 17% for short-term interest	Col. 4 as % of UK and overseas total (Table 4.2)
Mining	227	11	238	278	69
Manufacturing	5322	249	5571	6518	80
Services (Sectors 50–88)	1585	74	1659	1941	39
Total	7134	334	7468	8737	65

Source: Own calculations from the Meeks data base of quoted companies, and sample of other quoted companies not included in that data base.

at the contribution of unquoted companies. These are as follows: mining 31 per cent, manufacturing 20 per cent, services (construction, distribution, transport, other services) 61 per cent. The total for all these sectors is 35 per cent.

The contribution of quoted and unquoted companies' profits to the gross *domestic* product is harder to estimate. We might however make the assumption that all overseas income accrues to quoted companies. This is an overestimate in that we know that some of the larger unquoted companies do have sizeable overseas interests. It is an underestimate in that the Meeks data, and our sample, excluded quoted companies whose operations were primarily overseas, but presumably add to the flow of profits to UK companies arising from overseas direct investment. We do not know the size of these errors in estimation, so we have to proceed on the basic assumption that they are self-cancelling. The results of these adjustments are shown in Table 4.4.

We may now relate our estimates to the total contribution of gross corporate profits to GDP given in the national income accounts (£12 744 million in 1975, see Table 4.1). Some 24 per cent of this total is attributed to the public corporations. Our estimates in Table 4.4 suggest that quoted and unquoted companies in manufacturing and services contributed 35 and 37 per cent respectively. The portion unattributed reflects the omission of private sector, agriculture, mining and financial services.[7]

4.4 THE CONTRIBUTION OF UNQUOTED COMPANIES TO GROSS DOMESTIC INCOME: EMPLOYMENT INCOME

The estimation of domestic income arising from employment in quoted and unquoted sectors is simpler than the calculation of gross profit contribution, in that we may safely ignore overseas income. On the other hand, the national income statistics are less helpful as they do not distinguish between income from employment arising in the private and

---

[7] The pattern is particularly complicated by the negative gross *trading* profits of the financial companies (−£1778 million in 1975). These arise because customers are not charged the full cost of the financial services they use. Hence, *for the purposes of national income accounting*, the profit contribution of the financial sector is negative. From the point of view of the financial companies themselves, the pricing of services at less than cost is a means of attracting savings and lending business. The returns on this activity will then offset the losses on services, and from a conventional point of view ensure that financial companies are profitable. Returns on lending to industrial and commercial companies are *transfers* of profits earned in those sectors to the financial sector.

TABLE 4.4 GDP: Arising from Gross Profits

Sector	Gross profits in UK	Gross profits of quoted companies	Gross profits arising overseas	Estimated UK gross profits of quoted	Estimated UK gross profits of unquoted	Per cent of gross profits in UK arising from: Quoted	Unquoted
Manufacturing	5386	6518	2773	3745	1641	70	30
Services	3744	1941	1237	704	3040	19	81

Source: Calculations based on information in Tables 4.1, 4.2 and 4.3.

public sectors.[8] To make progress we have to allocate this income on the basis of employment.[9] Allocation on the basis of employment involves the assumption that the labour market is sufficiently flexible for employees on average to receive similar remuneration whatever sector, public or private, quoted or unquoted, they happen to work in. The results of this allocation are given in Table 4.5.

The data derived from Meeks and from the sample of quoted companies that do not appear in the Meeks data are much easier to use than in the case of gross profits. The figures specifically are restricted to remuneration paid in respect of the UK activities of the companies concerned: hence they correspond to a measure of gross domestic product arising from income from employment. However they do need to be adjusted, as the following comparison suggests. The Meeks data give an average remuneration per employee in manufacturing quoted companies as £2600 p.a. The comparable figure for all private-sector manufacturing, derived from national income and employment statistics for 1975 is £2930, or some 12.7 per cent greater. In services, the comparable figures are £2224 and £2840, a difference of 27.7 per cent. Such discrepancies cannot be explained in terms of differences in remuneration in the quoted and unquoted sectors. Rather they may be traced to the fact that the Meeks data for 1975 are drawn from companies having the end of their financial year at any time between April 1975 and March 1976. They do not therefore correspond precisely to the calendar year. Unfortunately, 1974–5 was a period of very great wage inflation in the UK economy: the wage index rose 26.5 per cent between the third quarter of 1974 and the third quarter of 1975. Thus companies reporting early in the year will have wage costs substantially lower in the financial year than in the calendar year. This could well account for the 12.7 per cent discrepancy in remuneration per employee in manufacturing, but not for the larger discrepancy in the service sector, which must also reflect differences in sectoral composition between quoted and unquoted sectors. We have attempted to compensate for inflation by adding 13 per cent to the reported wage costs of the quoted sector.

The results of these adjustments are given in Table 4.6. In manufacturing, the quoted companies' share of employment income is significantly lower than their share of gross profits. This reflects their

[8] CSO, *National Income and Expenditure*, table 3.1, GDP by Industry and Type of Income: Income from Employment.
[9] *Economic Trends*, no. 303, January 1979, pp. 131–6, table 1; *Department of Employment Gazette*, July 1976, pp. 727–33, table 3.

TABLE 4.5 GDP: Arising from Income and Employment, 1975 (£ million)

Sector	Private sector employed	Self employed	Public corporations	Central and local government	Total
Agriculture	513	352	–	13	879
Mining	215	5	1299	180	1519
Manufacturing	20947	356	825	479	22308
Construction	3010	1035	36	91	4560
Transport	1186	194	2482	–	3952
Distribution	5509	972	–	–	6481
Miscellaneous services	6583	1162	–	–	7745
Insurance, banking	2968	524	–	–	3492
Public sector	–	–	–	11238	11238
Gas, electricity water	–	–	1397	–	1397
Total	40931	4600	6039	12001	63571

Source: Calculations based on CSO *National Income and Expenditure*, table 3.1; *Economic Trends*, no. 303, January 1979, pp. 131–6, table 1; *Department of Employment Gazette*, July 1976, pp. 727–33, table 3.

TABLE 4.6 GDP: Income from Employment, Attributed to Quoted and Unquoted Companies 1975 (£ million)

Sector	Private-sector total from Table 4.5	Quoted companies reported wage costs	Quoted companies adjusted for wage inflation	Unquoted	Percentage Quoted	Unquoted
Manufacturing	20947	11246	12708	8239	61	39
Sectors 50–88	16288	3412	3856	12432	24	76

Source: Table 4.5, and own calculations based on Meeks's data base for quoted companies, plus small sample of other companies.

scale and capital intensity. Unquoted companies tend to be smaller, and more labour-intensive in their operations: so their share of labour income is naturally higher.

The total estimated contribution of unquoted companies to domestic income from employment was around £20 670 million in 1975. (This excludes that arising in the financial sector, £3950 million, at least part of which must arise in unquoted companies.) This represents about 30 per cent of all domestic income from employment, and just under half of the labour income arising in the private sector, including income from self-employment.

4.5 THE CONTRIBUTION OF UNQUOTED COMPANIES TO NATIONAL AND DOMESTIC INCOME

In this section we aggregate the estimates of gross national and domestic income from profits and labour income to arrive at the overall contribution of quoted and unquoted companies to the UK economy (not forgetting of course that financial institutions in the private sector have not been considered at all). For gross domestic income the relevant data are taken from Tables 4.4 and 4.6. For gross national income the information comes from Tables 4.2, 4.3 and 4.6. The totals are given in Table 4.7.

Two features are worthy of comment. First, the contribution of unquoted companies in the manufacturing sector is very substantial. We have already seen that this reflects the contribution of labour income. (The very large share of unquoted companies in the services sector has already been noted.) Second, the total contribution of quoted companies in manufacturing and services combined is less than that of unquoted companies whether one considers gross domestic or gross national income. This is all the more notable given that we have a 'bias' in our method which increases the share of quoted companies, by attributing all overseas income to them, and by adjusting their labour income for inflation.

Total GDP in 1975 was about £93 000 million. Hence unquoted companies in manufacturing and services (as defined in this analysis) accounted for some 27 per cent. This compares to 22 per cent for the quoted sector. Both of these figures would be increased by inclusion of the financial sector which is almost wholly in the private sector. Once again the substantial contribution of unquoted firms to the economy is emphasised.

TABLE 4.7 Contribution of Quoted and Unquoted Companies to GDP and GNP 1975

	Gross domestic income (£ million)		Shares (%)		Gross national income (£ million)		Shares (%)	
	Q*	UQ†	Q	UQ	Q	UQ	Q	UQ
Manufacturing	16453	9880	62	38	19226	9880	66	34
Services	4560	15472	23	77	5797	15472	27	73

* Quoted; † Unquoted.

Source: Tables 4.4 and 4.6.

4.6 EMPLOYMENT IN THE QUOTED AND UNQUOTED SECTORS

Our analysis of the sources of national and domestic income in the private sector has already suggested that the employment contribution of unquoted companies is likely to be substantial. Given the importance of employment policy at a national level, the ability of unquoted companies to create employment is of considerable interest. Our method of calculating their employment share follows the previous procedure. First we estimate employment in the private sector, according to broad branches of industry.[10] Then we subtract the employment in quoted companies as given by the Meeks data, supplemented by our sample of further quoted companies.

To set the analysis in context, we first consider the national distribution of employment by sector and industry group. Table 4.8 shows that private-sector employment accounted for 64 per cent of the total employment of nearly 25 million at mid-1975. A further 8 per cent was self-employment in the private sector, and 8 per cent in the public corporations, leaving 20 per cent in public authorities. For comparative purposes we need a breakdown of the 'other services' category, which includes distributive trades, miscellaneous services, insurance and banking, professional and scientific, etc. We then construct for comparison with our quoted company data a composite services sector including construction, distribution, transport and communications and miscellaneous services, but excluding financial services. We also have to make the assumption that 15 per cent of the employment in distribution and miscellaneous services arises in the self-employed sector.

The estimates are presented in Table 4.9. We should note that these estimates have involved far fewer heroic assumptions in arriving at the breakdown between quoted and unquoted companies. We shall therefore accord them a greater degree of confidence than we were able to place in our estimates of contribution to national and domestic income. Two features are noteworthy. First, unquoted companies make a substantial contribution to employment in manufacturing. Second, the unquoted sector as a whole (ignoring the financial sector) accounts for more than a quarter of all UK employment (as shown in Table 4.8).

[10] Our main source is *Economic Trends* no. 303, January 1979, pp. 131–6. Unfortunately this source does not give a sufficiently detailed analysis of the service sector for our purposes, so we have supplemented it with data from the *Department of Employment Gazette*, July 1976, pp. 727–33.

70

TABLE 4.8 Employment by Sector and Industry at Mid-year 1975 (thousands)

Industry/sector	Private-sector employees	Self-employed	Public corporation	Central and local government	Total
Agriculture	387	267	–	10	664
Mining	50	1	302	–	353
Manufacturing	7149	121	284	57	7611
Construction	1122	386	13	179	1700
Gas, electricity and water	3	–	347	3	353
Transport and Communication	479	78	1003	36	1596
Other services	6588	1033	84	4614	12319
Total	15778	1886	2033	4899	24596

Source: Economic Trends, no. 303, January 1979, pp. 131–6.

TABLE 4.9   Employment by Quoted and Unquoted Companies, 1975
(thousands)

	Total private-sector employment	Quoted	Unquoted	Employment share (%) Quoted	Unquoted
Manufacturing	7149	4428	2721	62	38
Services	5736	1572	4164	28	72
Total	12885	6000	6885	47	53

Sources: Table 4.8, and own calculations from the Meeks data base on quoted companies and from small sample of other quoted companies.

Adding the financial sector, agriculture, and professional and scientific services, the total is likely to be of the order of 30 per cent. This is therefore of the same order of magnitude as the employment share of quoted companies.

We would have liked to have complemented this analysis of employment with data referring to capital use in the quoted and unquoted sectors. Unfortunately the data to do this are simply not available.

4.7 GROSS DOMESTIC CAPITAL FORMATION IN THE QUOTED AND UNQUOTED COMPANY SECTORS

The level of gross domestic capital formation in quoted and unquoted companies cannot be derived accurately. Official statistics do not make any distinction between investment in private and public sectors within a particular industry, e.g. within the transport and communications industry. Some progress can be made for manufacturing alone, if we assume that the company sector accounts for about 94 per cent of activity (estimated on an employment basis). Then a rough estimate is that the same proportion of all investment in manufacturing takes place in private-sector companies. The relevant figures are given in Table 4.10.

These suggest that roughly half of private-sector investment in UK manufacturing in 1975 was undertaken by unquoted companies. This is certainly an overestimate, as we have attributed all overseas investment to quoted companies, whereas some at least is certainly undertaken by unquoted companies. The figure is surprising in that the previous section suggested that unquoted companies accounted for less than 40 per cent

TABLE 4.10   Manufacturing Investment

GDCF in manufacturing, 1975	£ million
Quoted companies: Meeks's data	2604
: sample	121
Less overseas investment	(1082)
Quoted in UK	1643
Unquoted in UK	1644
All private-sector companies in UK	3287

of employment, and one might expect them to be less capital-intensive than their quoted counterparts. 1975 was (like 1976) a poor year for investment in UK industry, reflecting a substantial fall from a peak in 1974. So the estimate for 1975 may reflect a sharper cut-back by quoted companies compared to a more stable investment pattern in the unquoted sector (see Chapter 5).[11]

Finally we can calculate the share of quoted and unquoted companies in the savings of the corporate sector of the economy. This represents that part of gross profits that is neither distributed as dividends or interest nor paid out in tax. The saving of industrial and commercial companies in 1975 was £8365 million.[12] To this must be added £700 million arising from depreciation of overseas assets, giving a total of £9065 million.

Table 4.11 suggests that unquoted companies accounted for about half the corporate savings of industrial and commercial companies in 1975 and about 40 per cent of total corporate savings. This latter proportion is overestimated in so far as the quoted sample excludes quoted property companies; it is underestimated by the omission of unquoted financial companies. Once again, we conclude that the unquoted sector contribution is substantial.

[11] An alternative method of doing the calculations is to look at all investment, at home and overseas, by industrial and commercial companies. (*Sources*: CSO, *National Income and Expenditure*, table 10.3; *Business Monitor* M4 1976.) In 1975 domestic capital formation was £6983 million and overseas capital formation was £1505 million, making a total of £8488 million. Our best estimate of quoted company investment in the same year was £3583, or 42 per cent of the total. But this is seriously underestimated by this method, since it excludes the investment of quoted property companies.

[12] CSO, *Natural Income and Expenditure*, table 5.4.

TABLE 4.11 Corporate Saving

Corporate saving, 1975	£ million
Industrial and commercial:	
Quoted	4552
Unquoted	4513
Total	9065
Financial companies	690
Public corporations	1596
Total	11351

4.8 CONCLUSIONS

The conclusion of this analysis is that on any criterion the contribution of the unquoted sector to the UK economy is very substantial. In the private sector it contributes at last half of all domestic income from profits and employment. The unquoted sector makes a larger contribution to employment income than to income from profit. It is also more concentrated in the service sector where it accounts for 75 per cent of private-sector income. But this is not to say that its contribution in manufacturing is insignificant: on the contrary it accounts for more than a third of private-sector income.

In terms of factor use, we find that unquoted companies provided more than half of private-sector employment in 1975 and that they were responsible for about half the gross domestic capital formation in private-sector manufacturing in the same year.

These proportions serve to emphasise our contention that the unquoted company sector constitutes a major sector in its own right, and one which is worthy of particular study and consideration.

APPENDIX 4.1 ESTIMATING THE CONTRIBUTION OF QUOTED COMPANIES EXCLUDED FROM THE MEEKS DATA BASE

From 1975 onwards, the quoted company data base used in this study (the Meeks data) excluded those companies which in 1973 had net assets of less than £5 million and gross income of less than £$\frac{1}{2}$ million in the year. While one might expect those companies to make a small contribution to the quoted sector as a whole, much depends on their numbers and their size distribution. Certainly it is not safe to dismiss them from consideration until it can be shown what their contribution is. In this appendix we explain our method for making an estimate of this contribution, and present our estimates.

A comparison of the 1975 *Stock Exchange Year Book* with the list of companies included in the Meeks data revealed 768 companies not in the Meeks data base. This excludes those companies which operate in the financial sector, and those whose operations are largely or exclusively overseas. As a complete data check on all those companies was impracticable, a sampling method was used. First, the companies were ranked in terms of fixed asset size (the variable most easily obtainable from the *Stock Exchange Year Book*). Then a cumulative distribution was plotted. This showed that the smallest third of the companies accounted for about one-eighth of reported assets, the middle third for about one-sixth, and the largest third for the rest. A stratified random sample of twenty-four companies was then taken. Three companies each were sampled from the first two-thirds, and eighteen from the largest third, representing their approximate weight in the asset distribution. On the basis of the samples (labelled S1, S2 and S3 in Table 4A.1), an estimate was made of the contribution of all 768 companies.

The variance of the estimates is given by

$$\frac{(256)^2}{3}\sigma_1^2 + \frac{(256)^2}{3}\sigma_2^2 + \frac{(256)^2}{18}\sigma_3^2$$

where σ_1, σ_2 and σ_3 are the true variances of the variable in each sector. These can only be estimated from the actual samples themselves.

The results of this sampling method are given in Table 4A.1 as the standard deviation of the estimate. It is evident that some of the estimates are more reliable than others. Thus we might make the confidence limit for each estimate to be plus or minus two standard deviations. On this criterion, the correct value for operating profit would be ± 36 per cent of the reported total. At the other extreme the average number of employees is accurate to within 10 per cent, and gross value added to within 6 per cent of the total given.

The totals can be compared with the totals derived from the Meeks data base. As expected, the contribution of the 768 companies is small. The largest, 6.1 per cent, is in the terms of employment, the smallest, 2.3 per cent, is fixed assets, reflecting the higher labour intensity of these smaller quoted companies. They contributed 5 per cent of gross value-added, and accounted for 3.8 per cent of sales.

The conclusion to be drawn is that these companies are too important to be ignored completely when estimating the size of the UK quoted sector, but that a sampling procedure of the kind adopted here gives a satisfactory method for assessing their contribution.

APPENDIX 4.2 COMPARISON WITH ANALYSIS IN THE PRIVATE COMPANY TODAY[A.1]

Chapter 2 of *The Private Company Today* makes various estimates of the contribution of unquoted companies to the UK economy along the lines of the

[A.1] Merrett and Lehr, *The Private Company Today* (Gower, 1971).

TABLE 4A.1 Estimate of Contribution of Quoted Companies Excluded from the Meeks Date Base*

	S1	S2	S3	Total	Standard deviation of estimate	Meeks data total
Operating profit	78.9	131.0	123.9	333.8	60.1	7214.5
Number of employees	83257	121720	148537	353514	18700	5757573
Investment	9.9	53.4	55.9	119.2	12.3	3582.5
Retentions	49.4	60.1	56.2	165.7	21.4	4442.0
Employees' remuneration	153.0	197.3	444.9	765.2	23.5	14427.3
Tangible fixed assets	88.0	164.4	315.6	568.1	56.7	24758.6
Gross value-added	231.9	328.3	538.7	1099.0	36.2	21641.8
Sales	930.8	719.9	1949.4	3600.1	358.0	94303.7

* All in units £ million, except for employment.

Source: Own calculation from sample.

first part of this chapter. Merrett and Lehr had less tractable statistical sources to deal with, so they were not able to make the same estimates of contribution to GDP and employment. However certain analyses are comparable, and the main results are listed here.

(1) *GDP arising from profits.* Merrett and Lehr, table 2.6, (p. 14), shows private companies (i.e. unquoted) in manufacturing and distribution, operating in the United Kingdom, as generating 29 per cent of total gross trading profits in those sectors in 1966. This is not directly comparable with our estimates in Table 4.4 (p. 63), since the 'other services' category is excluded in Merrett and Lehr. Since other services constitute about 45 per cent of the private-sector GDP in aggregate services sector comprising construction, transport, distribution and other services, the exclusion is not trivial. We have therefore grossed up the Merrett and Lehr estimates for gross profits by 45 per cent, and assumed that all gross profits in other services should be attributed to the unquoted sector. The results are given in Table 4A.2. It is evident that the share of unquoted companies in gross profits rose in both manufacturing and services in the period 1966–75.

(2) *Employment.* Merrett and Lehr, table 2.3 (p. 9), gives a breakdown of private-sector employment into private and public companies in 1966. Our estimates are given in Table 4.9 (p. 71). Again, precise comparisons are not possible, but the estimates in Table 4A.3 are not likely to mislead. Once again, we have adjusted the Merrett and Lehr estimates to include 'other services'. The assumption is again made that all other services employment should be attributed to the unquoted sector. The conclusion is that the share of quoted and unquoted sectors in employment in manufacturing and services (as defined here) did not change significantly in 1966–75.

TABLE 4A.2   Percentage Shares of Quoted and Unquoted Companies in Gross Profits

Sector	1966		1975	
	Quoted	Unquoted	Quoted	Unquoted
Manufacturing	85	15	70	30
Services	28	72	19	81

Sources: Merrett and Lehr, *The Private Company Today* table 2.6 (adjusted for other services); Table 4.4.

TABLE 4A.3   Percentage Shares of Quoted and Unquoted Companies in Employment

Sector	1966		1975	
	Quoted	Unquoted	Quoted	Unquoted
Manufacturing	62	38	62	38
Services	29	71	28	72

Sources: Merrett and Lehr, *The Private Company Today* table 2.3 (adjusted for other services); Table 4.9.

5 The Behaviour of Unquoted Companies

5.1 INTRODUCTION: SOURCES OF INFORMATION

The previous chapters attempted to identify the contribution to the United Kingdom economy of the unquoted sector as a whole. In contrast this chapter focuses on the behaviour of individual unquoted companies and tries to bring out at company level those issues which most influence their actions. As far as possible it goes behind published accounts to examine the specific factors which make for differences of performance as compared with quoted companies, and provides a basis for more detailed statistical comparisons in the next two chapters.

As will be seen in Chapter 6, one main basis for analysis of unquoted companies at the level of the firm is a detailed data base of the accounts of fifty-four unquoted companies, three from each of eighteen sectors, and a comparable data base of 162 quoted companies, nine from each of the same eighteen sectors. Prior to the statistical comparison of the companies in these data bases, nineteen of the fifty-four unquoted companies were investigated in more depth, and it is this work on which much of this chapter is based.[1] The sample of nineteen covers fifteen of the eighteen sectors. They represent ninteen of the fifty-four who were prepared to help by providing more information than is statutorily available. As such they are potentially a biased, because self-selected, sample. However, their average balance-sheet, profitability and other items are reproduced in Table 5.1 together with equivalent figures for the remaining thirty-five of the fifty-four unquoted companies. It should be noted that, like the fifty-four (see Chapter 6, p. 165) the sub-sample of nineteen companies are all amongst the largest 1000 unquoted companies in the United Kingdom. In only three respects were the companies interviewed atypical of the whole sample:

[1] In addition two more unquoted companies not in the list of fifty-four were subsequently interviewed in order to help clarify certain matters that were still not fully resolved.

1. Their use of long-term liabilities as a source of funds was particularly low.
2. They maintained proportionately lower creditor and debtor positions.
3. They were slightly less profitable.

TABLE 5.1 Comparison of Interview Sample and Non-interview Sample of Unquoted Companies

| | Percentage of capital employed | |
	Interview Sample	Other unquoted companies in 'small sample'
Liabilities:		
Ordinary shares	22.0	17.5
Preference shares	3.1	1.9
Reserves	62.3	62.0
Long term liabilities	3.5	8.5
Deferred taxation	9.2	9.9
Assets:		
Fixed assets	53.2	57.7
Trade investments	1.8	5.4
Stocks and w.i.p.	64.8	67.9
Debtors	69.9	87.6
Securities and cash	10.2	11.8
Short term loans	20.0	24.3
Creditors	68.2	95.1
Dividends payable	1.8	1.5
Tax payable	8.5	8.6
Gross operating profit rate*	25.7	29.5
Profit net of depreciation	20.7	23.5
Profit net of depreciation and long-term interest	19.9	21.2
Profit net of depreciation, interest and tax	10.4	11.4

* Net of short-term interest.

As we shall see later, the first of these accentuates a difference between quoted and unquoted companies; the latter two diminish these differences. In no case however were there reasons to think that this systematically undermined the value of the views expressed in the interviews.

After detailed examination of the accounts, each of the nineteen companies was visited by either one or both of the authors. In each case, at least one, frequently two or three and sometimes up to five members of the company were interviewed, generally for two or three hours, about certain issues which are central to the comparison of quoted and unquoted companies. In all but one case the most senior interviewee was a director of the company; in the large majority of cases he was either chairman or managing director (chief executive) and usually was also a major, if not the principal shareholder. Table 5.2 identifies the position of the most senior man interviewed for the nineteen companies.

In no company did any one person by himself have a controlling shareholding. In two companies, one man plus his immediate relatives (wife, children) did have a controlling shareholding.

As business organisations the nineteen companies are a very heterogenous group. In 1976 they varied in size of capital employed from approximately £600 000 to £120 million and in return on capital from below zero to over 50 per cent. In terms of age, sector and competitive position they are again dispersed across a wide spectrum, but in terms of

TABLE 5.2   Identity of Principal Interviewees

Management position	Ownership position
Company Secretary	Minimal shareholding
Finance director	Small shareholding
Managing director	Principal shareholder
Managing director	Principal shareholder
Chairman	Major shareholding*
Chairman and managing director	Major shareholding
Managing director	Major shareholding
Chairman and managing director	Major shareholding
Chairman	Principal shareholder
Finance director	Minimal shareholding
Chairman	Major shareholding
Chairman	Major shareholding
Chairman and managing director	Principal shareholder
Finance director	Small shareholding
Chairman	Major shareholder
Finance director	No shareholding
Chairman and managing director	Principal shareholder
Chairman	Major shareholder
Finance director	Minimal shareholder

* A 'major' shareholding is either (a) over 10 per cent of total, or (b) in conjunction with shares held by spouse or in trust for children, over 10 per cent of total.

those characteristics which most distinguish them from their quoted counterparts they represent a much more and indeed surprisingly homogenous group. In broad terms these characteristics may be classified under four main headings: (a) structures of ownership and control, (b) finance, (c) taxation, (d) motivation and performance. In the next four sections of this chapter each of these areas is addressed. Under each heading the main objective is to describe the typical features of the unquoted companies investigated, as a basis for comparison with quoted companies and for modelling the behaviour of the unquoted company, which will be dealt with in Chapters 6 and 7.

5.2 OWNERSHIP AND CONTROL

(a) *The pattern of ownership*

As the sample of fifty-four companies from which the nineteen interviewed were selected was itself taken from the list of the largest 1000 unquoted companies published by Jordan & Sons Ltd, it is not surprising to find that the great majority of the nineteen companies were quite old. Although one converted from a partnership in 1942 and one from being a sole trader in 1945, all except three were originally founded in one form or another before the first world war, and the majority in the thirty years immediately preceding it. The three exceptions were both companies started after the second world war. One of the nineteen had been a public company until the 1920s but the shares were then progressively bought up by three directors from two families.

Apart from financial and property investments, all except three were essentially undiversified, and one of the three exceptions had greatly reduced the diversity of its operations very recently after a period of very poor performance and severe losses. This however simply reflects the attempt made in the investigation at company level to select, on the basis of industrial classification, undiversified companies for which comparison with quoted companies in the same sector would be most meaningful. The remaining two exceptions both had clearly identifiable main lines of business (hence their single-industry classification) but each had at least three other significant areas of operation and were in effect 'mini-conglomerates'. Several companies had integrated vertically backwards or forwards, but not to the extent of causing major change in the nature of their business.

In describing the pattern of ownership and control of the sample of companies, one distinctive characteristic is very evident. With four very partial exceptions mentioned below, all the unquoted companies visited were essentially what may be termed 'family businesses'. That is, the ownership of the shares was heavily or totally concentrated in the hands of one family or several descendant branches of one family, *and* furthermore, members of the family played a significant role in the day-to-day management of the company. Of the sixteen pre-1914 companies [2] two were now second-generation family firms, the majority (nine) were third-generation and five were fourth to sixth-generation family firms. Of the three post-1945 companies, all were in effect still first- (i.e. founders') generation. In one, the founder was chairman and managing director though his son was increasingly taking over responsibility. In the second, three unrelated founders had started the company as an offshoot of an existing company and were still very much involved with the company. In the third, the founder had been chairman until 1978 but then in a major change consequent upon sharply deteriorating trading conditions, had become a non-executive part-time director. Directly or indirectly however he still controlled over 80 per cent of the company's shares.

As mentioned above, four firms were not entirely family businesses. One first-generation company was still mainly owned by the three unrelated people who founded it. In one, the founder still had, with close relations, a controlling interest, but day-to-day management had to a considerable extent moved away from the family. The founder's son was too young to be a manager and was far from certain to have either the expertise or inclination to pursue such a career. Currently the company was managed by a part-time professional chairman and two full-time professional directors, one of whom was related to the founder.

In the third exception, members of one family still had a considerable presence both as directors and owners, but over 50 per cent of the shares were now held by a charitable trust. In the fourth, the company had been a family business until the death of the founder in 1965. Eighty per cent of the shares were then put into two trusts, one for the employees, the other a charitable trust to help deserving educational causes in the industry. At that point the company ceased to be a family business by the ownership criterion, but even here a distant relation from abroad, of the same name and with appropriate training, had been brought in five years before the death of the founder and was now chairman and managing director.

[2] This is to be understood as including those companies which once operated with a different legal status.

It is therefore only to a very limited extent that the companies investigated were other than essentially family-owned and family-controlled businesses. While it was always to be expected that a considerable number of unquoted companies would be family businesses, the fact that virtually all the sample companies were such, despite as a group being amongst the largest unquoted companies in the United Kingdom, and for the most part third- or more generation companies, illustrates the strong motivation of families to retain and maintain their role in the businesses which their ancestors created. The precise extent to which this role is maintained and its implication for control, finance and company orientation are matters referred to in more detail later.

In view of the family nature of the companies it is much less surprising that all except one are 'close' companies, the exception only being so because of very unusual ownership structure. It will be recalled from Chapter 2 that a company is close if it is either: under the control of five or fewer participators,[3] *or* under the control of its directors, *or* the ultimate destination of 50 per cent or more of the company's income, assuming full distribution, would be five or fewer participators, or participators who are directors. For the purpose of this definition, a participator's associates (i.e. a near relative, a partner, a fellow beneficiary under settlement or a trustee of a settlement in which the participator or relation is a settler) are included with the participator.

There is of course no reason why a family business as defined above should necessarily be a close company. If, for example, twelve cousins each hold $8\frac{1}{2}$ per cent of a company's shares and four of them constitute the board, then the company is not a close company but is nonetheless completely family-owned and family-managed. In practice however family shareholdings in the sample companies were more concentrated than this, and more importantly were generally much less dispersed throughout a family as far as major shareholdings were concerned (see below). The result was that all were close companies, the only partial exception being the one distinctive company already mentioned above, where 80 per cent of the shares were controlled by two participators, but as these were an educational charity and a trust on behalf of employees, for tax purposes the company was deemed not to be closely held. The other eighteen were therefore all subject to the special provisions which apply to close companies (see Section 5.4).

---

[3] The precise definition of terms used in company legislation is very complex but in general terms a participator is anyone holding shares, voting rights or an option to these, a loan creditor, or someone entitled to receive distributions, premiums or other benefits from the income or assets of the company.

In recent years increasing emphasis has been placed on the extent to which ownership and management control do or do not overlap as a determinant of a company's goals and behaviour.[4] The fact that a company is a family business, as defined, does not automatically entail a strong overlap between the two functions, much less an identity between them. In order to determine the extent to which the effective management of a company is in the hands of its owners it is necessary to examine a number of related issues, in particular the dispersion of shareholding, the holdings of those on the board and the constraints, if any, placed on managerial discretion by shareholders not on the board. Only after consideration of these issues is it possible to make inferences about firms' objectives and the level of enforcement costs,[5] i.e. the cost or difficulty which shareholders face in attempting to impose their own objectives if they differ from the managers who take the decisions which determine the firm's performance. Before looking at the structure of shareholding in detail it will be useful to make a few preliminary comments about the various types of shareholding encountered. Twelve main forms may be distinguished:[6]

  (i) Held by member of family on board in own name.
 (ii) Held by member of family not on board in own name.
(iii) Held in trust for children of family member on board.
 (iv) Held in trust for children of family member not on board.
  (v) Held in trust for close but not active family member.
 (vi) Held in trust for member of family on board.
(vii) Held in trust for employees.
(viii) Held in charitable trust.
 (ix) Held by non-family member of board.
  (x) Held by non-family non-member of board.
 (xi) Held by another company.
(xii) Held by financial institution.

The holding of shares in unquoted companies by trusts established for that purpose is a widespread and significant part of the overall pattern of shareholding. A trust may be one of the following types.

(1) *Beneficial.* The intended beneficiary has an interest in possession,

[4] See, for example, R. Marris, *The Economic Theory of Managerial Capitalism* (Macmillan, 1963); H. Radice, 'Control Type, Profitability and Growth in Large Firms', *Economic Journal*, vol. 81, September 1971, pp. 547–62. See also Chapter 2 (pp. 34–7).

[5] See G. Yarrow, 'On the Predictions of the Managerial Theory of the Firm', *Journal of Industrial Economics*. vol. 24, no. 4, June 1976, pp. 267–79.

[6] This ignores two cases where shares were held by nominees rather than in trust to reduce the legal number of share owners and thereby permit close company status to be retained.

that is, a right to the benefit. In general terms the beneficiary is treated for tax purposes as if he owned the property outright, except where a 'reversionary' interest or right to benefit only in the future is concerned.

(2) *Discretionary*. Here the trustees have discretion to make benefits available or not as they think appropriate. Intended beneficiaries therefore do not have an interest in possession or right to such benefits as are available. Because of this it is not possible to regard the property involved as belonging to an individual or group and so taxation of discretionary trusts is more complex, entailing initial or 'entry' charges, when the trust is set up, periodic charges during the life of the trust and an 'exit' charge when property is finally removed from the trust.[7]

(3) *Accumulation and maintenance*. This concerns settlements for the benefit of minors. Under certain conditions a trust may be established for children or grandchildren and, provided that the property is used for the benefit of the children concerned, any excess being accumulated, the periodic charges applicable to a discretionary trust are not payable, nor is the normal exit charge. The main objective of this is to remove a double capital taxation charge when property is transferred *de facto* only once, e.g. from father to son, but *de jure* twice, through the trust established during the child's minority.

(4) *Employee trusts*. If trust property can be applied only for the benefit of employees or their relatives or dependents, or for related charities, then under certain conditions the entry, periodic and exit charges are all non-payable.

(5) *Charitable*. Trusts established for charitable purposes avoid the three types of charge payable by a discretionary trust.

Other types of trust exist but these five cover all forms encountered in the sample companies. Some of the shares of fourteen of the nineteen companies were held by one or more trusts, generally of the discretionary or accumulation and maintenance form, with beneficial holdings the next most common. Three had employees' trust shareholders, but in only one case was this a significant shareholding. Only this company and one other had significant charitable trust shareholdings, in the latter case it being a controlling shareholding.

The existence of sizeable trust shareholdings complicates the process of identifying the number, concentration and degree of effective control

[7] The entry charge is calculated on the normal capital transfer tax basis. Periodic charges are made every ten years at 30 per cent of the normal rate. The exit charge is calculated on the normal basis but periodic charges previously paid are allowable against the exit charge. At present there are transitional arrangements pending the full introduction of this scheme.

of shareholders. It is not clear whether a trust should be treated as one shareholding or as representing as many holdings as there are beneficiaries. In addition they create a division between the ultimate beneficiary on the one hand and the immediate controller of the shareholdings and associated votes placed in the trust on the other. In practice the issue can be simplified in various ways.

It emerged from the interviews that certain guidelines were generally applicable in tracing the pattern of ownership through to ultimate control. Whenever beneficial trusts were significant the beneficiaries were family members, generally major shareholders in their own right and in all cases either on the board or closely related (parent, spouse or child) to a family member of the board. In addition the trustees were normally close friends or relatives or someone bearing a professional and direct relation to the company, e.g. company secretary or solicitor. In all but the most extreme circumstances it appeared right to conclude, and this was agreed by those concerned, that such shareholdings for voting purposes should be treated as part of the holding of the major family shareholder to whom the trust directly or indirectly, via immediate family, related.

Accumulation and maintenance trusts for children generally had trustees of the same general character, and again, in all but the most extreme circumstances would be regarded for voting purposes as going with the shareholding of the parents. Discretionary trusts, though in all cases having family members as beneficiaries, were more heterogenous. Some were for the benefit of individuals, generally a surviving spouse, others for the benefit of major branches of a family with a substantial number of potential beneficiaries. Given however that our major concern is with the extent to which the management group can exercise effective ownership control, rather more precise conclusions can be inferred.

In order for the shares held in a discretionary trust to represent an effective threat to control by the management group, several conditions may be regarded as simultaneously necessary. First, the designated potential beneficiaries must be other than immediate family. Second, the trustees must be other than members of the board, and third, of course, the board's direct or indirect shareholding must be less than 50 per cent. While in a mathematical sense this list is neither a necessary nor sufficient set of conditions to create such a threat, in practice it is the minimum set of conditions necessary. Of the sample companies only four met these minimum conditions, but in only one case were there any serious worries on the part of the existing management that its control might be threatened by a majority grouping of shares not under its effective control. In the other three cases (and to some extent even in the one exceptional case) there were in practice formidable safeguards as follows:

1. In each case the 'other' shareholders were family members albeit not immediate family. (For the four companies concerned the proportion of shares under the control of one family were, respectively, approximately 70 per cent, two over 90 per cent and one at 100 per cent.)
2. In the three companies where no threat was evident, a small number of family board members held shares running between 30 and 45 per cent of the total, but the 'other' shareholders were widely dispersed amongst other members of the family and/or amongst trusts of which they were beneficiaries. This pattern of shareholding made the prospect of a controlling shareholding being co-ordinated or built up against those of the board members remote.
3. Although it was not possible to ascertain the position in all cases, a number of the sample companies have articles which require the board's permission for a transfer of shares. The board is therefore in a position to halt any attempt to increase co-ordination by concentrating the smaller shareholdings.
4. With one exception, more distant family shareholders had no interest in the running of the company other than that of any shareholder concerned with the source of one form of his or her income. In other words, they were generally not in a position to offer an alternative managerial team or expertise. Therefore conflict of interest was normally confined to questions of dividend stream and realisation of capital rather than issues of operating policy or corporate strategy. Given the heavy if not complete dependence of company prospects on the existing management team, the mathematical possibility of a majority vote against the family board members was generally irrelevant and indeed normally regarded as no more than a hypothetical outcome.

This view is given weight by observation of the one exception. Here there was concern that the goodwill of more distant relations was not total and would have to be worked for if the company was to remain a family business. In this one case both management control and dispersed family ownership were in the process of moving down a generation. With the position of chairman and managing director moving (in stages) from father to son, and 75 per cent of the shares gradually moving from sisters of the former to cousins of the latter, the potential for a co-ordinated sale of a controlling interest by the cousins was recognised. It should however be added first that the proportion of shares held by board members was, at 25 per cent, the lowest of the sample companies, and second that it was one of the very few to have actively considered and twice almost achieved a quotation.

Overall, therefore, it appears reasonable to regard such discretionary trusts as single holdings, the trustees of which may bring matters of concern to the board: for example, share transfers, dividend levels, etc., but in very few cases will they represent any threat to the independence of the family members on the board. The few cases of employee and charitable trusts may be treated similarly.

The approach to trusts described above appears to reflect the realities of effective control and is the first factor to help simplify the process of interpreting the pattern of shareholding. The second simplifying factor is that, given this treatment of trusts across the sample companies, two very recognisable and not, in practice, very dissimilar patterns of share ownership emerged. Identification of the causes of these patterns, the purpose behind them and their effects made the analysis much more straightforward than the listing of twelve different types of shareholding on p. 83 might at first suggest.

The first pattern, which may be termed 'concentrated' is one in which, having 'allocated' beneficial and accumulation and maintenance trusts as described above, the overwhelming majority of all company shares are 'held' by a small number of family members. Seven companies fit into this category. In all cases, five or fewer major shareholders effectively control at least 80 per cent of the shares[8] with all or most generally being executive directors of the company. In three cases either one or two people effectively control 100 per cent of the shares.[9] Normally in these cases the ownership of the company is almost totally and directly represented on the board.[10]

The second pattern of shareholding may be termed 'quasi-concentrated'. Here a small number of major shareholders (up to eight) again have a substantial (though not always controlling) shareholding,

---

[8] In fact in six of the seven cases, three major shareholders control at least 80 per cent of the shares.

[9] Ignoring minimal allocations for special purposes.

[10] This concentration of ownership, though of course related to the issue of whether a company is closely held, is definitely not identical with that which confers close company status, because of potential differences between the statutory process of 'allocation' of shareholding and that pursued above.

but a much larger number of predominantly family shareholders, generally ranging from about twelve to over 250, control most of the remainder either directly or indirectly. Ten of the sample companies come into this category, the only partial exceptions being one company where two distinct branches of the same family were involved, and two other companies where in each case there are two unrelated families involved. In both cases one was a dominant and controlling family, and in neither case does friction appear to have been generated at any stage between the two family interests.

Thus seventeen of the nineteen companies were concentrated or quasi-concentrated. The eighteenth company was an exception, being a first-generation company with ownership still in the hands of the unrelated founders. Even here though, 50 per cent of the shares were in the hands of two people. For the remaining company, the pattern was not identifiable.

Given this overall picture it is now possible to derive some preliminary conclusions about the relationship between ownership and control in the sample companies. First, under the concentrated or quasi-concentrated pattern, the proportion of shares controlled by one family is normally very high. The (unweighted) averages for the two groups are fairly similar at 94 and 85 per cent respectively. The overall unweighted average is 88.5 per cent. Except for one somewhat anomalous case where the chairman and managing director was one of two trustees controlling both an employees' trust and a charitable trust, which between them had 80 per cent of the shares, no family had less than 60 per cent and only two had less than 80 per cent.

Second, the minimum number of individuals necessary to provide an effective controlling interest was generally very low, as shown in Table 5.3.

Third, and perhaps of greater significance, is the proportion of shares effectively controlled by family members of the board. This averages 69 per cent but the individual figures fall into four clear groups. Where identifiable there are (i) four companies without majority family control, (ii) five with slightly over 50 per cent, (iii) five with around 80 per cent, and (iv) two with 100 per cent. As already noted in only one case was concern expressed about the future position of family control on the board.

It is now possible to come to more precise conclusions about the nature of these family businesses and the extent of ownership representation on boards. Overall a very striking pattern emerges, with generally three or fewer family members, who are typically board members,

TABLE 5.3 Concentration of Shareholding*

Minimum number necessary for effective control	Number of firms in category
1	2
2	6
3	4
4	1
5–10	2
10+	1
	16

* Excluding the two non-family owned companies for which the pattern was not identified, and the one 'anomaly' described in the text. In practice it is probably appropriate to add the latter in as requiring only one person for effective ownership control.

required to generate a controlling shareholding. The great majority of the remainder of the shares are also held by the same family directly or indirectly, though in more cases than not in a fairly dispersed form. In practice, provided there is agreement between the key members any alternative company strategy to that favoured by this group is unrealistic and does not arise.

This does not of course mean that others both within and outside the family do not have influence, or that decision-taking is highly central-ised. As we shall see, internal and external expertise are essential ingredients in the performance of many of the companies investigated and the degree of decentralisation is a separate matter which is determined, either by design or default, in the light of the nature of the business, management style and personality. But it does indicate a clear and easily recognised concentration of ultimate control, by virtue of both ownership and management expertise and continuity in the hands of a small number of family representatives. It implies a very high degree of responsibility of these key people for the longer-term direction, rate and efficiency of company development. It also implies that a substantial proportion, and in most cases clear majority, of the ownership of such unquoted companies is directly represented on the board by major shareholders.

By itself this fact does not in any sense resolve the issues of whether conflict exists between ownership and management control; before that can be properly addressed it is necessary to examine the position and objectives of minority shareholders both within and outside the family and also the position of non-family directors and senior managers on the board. But this substantial overlapping of ownership and control is a major difference in comparison with most quoted companies and will be an important element, if not always predictable in its consequences, in the development of comparisons between the behaviour of quoted and unquoted companies.

As an introduction to these further issues it will be useful first to identify minority shareholders. In so far as most are other family members, in particular those rather more distant from the family members on the board, they have already been identified above. But an average of 11.5 per cent were held by non-family shareholders. There is however virtually no typical or systematic pattern to these non-family minority shareholdings, and they are best dealt with by a simple listing, as in Table 5.4.

In terms of control, the lack of importance of these minority non-family holdings has already been stressed. Yet they have significance in other ways. Their most persistent effect is to intrude on what would otherwise generally be much simpler dividend decisions. This point is considered in Section 5.3 on financial policy. Second, in three cases a small proportion of the total shares of the company are held by non-family directors. Their objectives may conflict with those of the family, particularly if they rely on their shareholdings for a significant proportion of their income.[11] Third, the presence of ICFC (Industrial and Commercial Finance Corporation) and of other companies (in one case through acquisition by a major UK quoted industrial company, in the other a foreign company) almost certainly creates pressures on financial policy. This need not necessarily appear as a pressure for higher dividends, as this will depend amongst other things on the company's internal financing requirements. But they constitute another skilled and informed group outside the family influence with the legal right to express a view on corporate policy and financial strategy. In this way they represent a monitoring force, the effect of which may be much stronger than their minority shareholding position might suggest. In the case of Company Q recognition of this was made explicit when a representative of the minority shareholding was appointed to the board. This issue, which relates to managerial discretion, is returned to later.

[11] See W. Llewellyn, 'Management and Ownership in the Large Firm', *Journal of Finance*, 24 May 1969, pp. 299–322, and W. Llewellyn and B. Huntsman, 'Managerial Pay and Corporate Performance', *American Economic Review*, vol. 60, no. 4, September 1970, pp. 710–20 for elaboration of this point. The matter is considered further in Section 5.5.

TABLE 5.4 Non-family Minority Shareholdings (NFMS)

Company	NFMS	NFMS (%)	Company	NFMS	NFMS (%)
A	–	0	J	–	0
B	Not applicable	–	K	Ex-employees	<10
C	Other directors, ex-directors	<10	L	Other directors	<10
D	ICFC	20	M	–	0
E	–	Negligible	N	Another family	40
F	Not specified	31	O	Distant branch of family	18
G	–	0	P	Ex-directors	19
H	–	Negligible	Q	Another company	$12\frac{1}{2}$
I	Other directors, ex-directors	<10	R	–	0
			S	Another company	34

(b) *Management structure*

Having examined the issues of ownership and control primarily from the ownership side, it is now necessary to look at it more specifically from the management and management control aspect. Four main issues are involved, namely the organisational pattern of holding and subsidiary companies; the management structure at both levels; the degree of decentralisation of effective decision-taking; and the relation between managers who are family members and those who are not.

All of the sample companies had either subsidiary companies or a divisional structure which in managerial terms was equivalent. If a distinction is drawn between a main board which primarily comprises executive directors in day-to-day touch with the running of a business on the one hand, and a holding company board to which the rest of the company is legally responsible but which takes little or no active part in day-to-day operations on the other, then the subsidiary companies were responsible to a main board in ten cases, to a holding company in three cases and to a main board which was itself responsible to a holding company in three cases.[12] In one of these last three cases, the directors acted as a main board in relation to one line of business but as a holding company board for all other lines, and in the two other cases the directors acted as a holding company board for most business operations but were responsible on a day-to-day basis for managing investments made by the company into other sectors. The number of legally separate subsidiaries varied from one to over fifty, but ignoring non-operating subsidiaries and combining those run as one unit the average number was 4.3 and the maximum nine. In five cases the subsidiaries were predominantly related to each other vertically, in seven cases predominantly horizontally, in three cases the basis was geographical and in four cases both vertical and geographical. Only five companies had subsidiaries which were less than fully owned and only two took a management role in subsidiaries in which there was not a controlling interest. Despite the various differences mentioned, all the companies comprised a 'senior' board with one or more subsidiary boards either directly under it (fifteen cases) or at one stage removed (four cases). It is to the composition and role of these boards in the decision-taking process that we now turn.

---

[12] In one of these cases the holding company was unlimited and therefore subject to much less strict disclosure rules. In one case the subsidiary controlled only a separate aspect of the business. All other operations came directly under the main board.

Table 5.5 gives the basic data on the composition of the senior (main or holding company) boards.

It is of interest to note that the distribution of the number of non-family executive directors (NFED) on these boards is bi-modal. The number of companies falling into each class, defined by the number of NFEDs, is shown in Table 5.6.

While the sample is small statistically speaking, the figures may reflect two management styles. In one (Group A) the senior board is composed of family members plus one or two non-family professionals, for example a finance director. Detailed business operations are managed at subsidiary board level. In the other (Group B) decision-taking is more centralised at senior board level and so a number of other non-family professionals, e.g. sales director, export director, chief engineer, etc., come onto the board as well. While in many cases managing directors of relatively autonomous subsidiaries will sit on the senior board, these are nearly always family directors. In *both* cases use of non-family expertise is substantial.

Although voting at board meetings was very much the exception (see below) it is perhaps worth noting the relative numbers of family and non-family management in Table 5.7. In approximately half the sample companies, family members were numerically superior in the most senior active management positions. However as the third column of Table 5.7 indicates, these are almost entirely the companies with two or fewer non-family executive directors, which, it has been suggested, tend to be those companies with a somewhat higher degree of delegation of decision-taking to subsidiaries.

The structure of subsidiary boards is more varied and more complicated to summarise, because of the number of such bodies involved (a total of seventy-seven operating subsidiaries). However in six cases, the subsidiary board was very similar or identical with the senior board and in all but one of the remainder a fairly consistent pattern was maintained across the subsidiaries. The data are summarised in Table 5.8.

Again in very general terms, a subsidiary board typically has two family members and four non-family members. In only three cases were family directors in the majority at this level, but they were all Group A companies. All the companies interviewed except three reflected the unitary (U) form of organisation, but in view of their generally rather undiversified nature, this was to be expected. Of those reflecting a multi-divisional (M) structure, one was a mini-conglomerate and two were horizontally diversified within one sector.

So far we have described only the bare facts of organisational

TABLE 5.5 Composition of Senior Boards

Company	Total	Family		Non-family	
		Executive	Non-executive	Executive	Non-executive
A	8	2	2	4	—
B	6	1	1	4	—
C	6	3	—	2	1
D	4	3	—	1	—
E Holding	10	4	—	5	1
Main	10	4	—	5	1
F	8	6	—	2	—
G	11	7	—	4	—
H	7	3	3	1	—
I	7	2	—	5	—
J	10	2	1	5	2
K	3	2	—	1	—
L	5	2	3	—	—
M Holding	4	4	—	—	—
Main	7	2	—	5	—
N	6	2	2	4	—
O	5	2	1	1	—
P	5	—	1	2	2
Q	5	2	1	2	—
R Holding	7	5	—	2	—
Main	7	5	—	2	—
S*					
Average†	6.5	2.9	0.8	2.5	0.4

* Figures not available.
† Where both holding and main boards exist, only the more senior is included.

TABLE 5.6 Non-family Executive Directors (NFED)*

Number of NFED	Number of companies	
0	2 ⎫	
1	4 ⎬	Group A
2	4 ⎭	
3	0	
4	4 ⎫	
5	4 ⎬	Group B
6 +	0 ⎭	
	18	

* Excluding one non-family company.

TABLE 5.7 Relative Numbers of Family and Non-family Directors

	All board management	Executive board management	Group classification
Family majority	10 (9)*	10 (9)	9A† + 1B
Equal numbers	2 (2)	1 (1)	1A
Non-family majority	6 (7)	7 (8)	1A + 6B

* Figures in brackets show effect of including main board instead of holding company in the three cases where both existed.
† A and B refer to the groups defined in Table 5.6.

structure and management composition. This however is only the background to the more important but much less tangible issue of the location of power, responsibility and effective management control within the companies interviewed. Although strict classifications are impossible to make, the widely used distinction between strategic decisions and operating decisions was found to be useful and in most cases was readily recognised and thought applicable by those interviewed. However this distinction is in principle a functional one, primarily used to clarify decision-taking relationships in an organisation. Our concern was more with the distribution of power and effective control, and while participation in strategic decision-taking tends to be more associated with control than is the case with operational decisions, it appeared more appropriate to focus on three other characterisations of decisions.

We began by identifying six main activities of 'top' management. These are:

TABLE 5.8 Composition of Subsidiary Boards*

Company	Family members		Non-family members
A	2†	(2)	4
B	1	(1)	4
C	3		2
D	1 or 2		2–4
E	2		2–6
F	6		2
G	2		4–5
H	3	(3)	1
I	1 or 2		2–5
J	0 or 1		4–7
K	2		4–6
L	2		3
M	1		1–3
N	2		2–6
O	2		5
P	0		5–10
Q	2	(1)	4–8
R	1 or 3		4–8
S‡	–		–
Average	1.8		4.2

* Executive directors only.
Non-executive directors are added in brackets. Apart from two exceptions, there were only non-executive directors on a subsidiary board where the latter was identical to the senior board.
† Figures indicate the most usual number.
‡ Figures not available.

1. Formulation of long-term development strategy, e.g. markets, products, acquisitions.
2. Formulation of major policy, e.g. degree of decentralisation, corporate structure, financial policy.
3. Examination and approval of annual budgets.
4. Preparation and approval of longer-term (normally three to five years) plans.
5. Monitoring of performance on a short-term basis (usually monthly, but sometimes daily, sometimes quarterly). This might focus on work flow, production, stock levels, etc.
6. Approval of requests for capital finance above a certain limit.

By locating the group in each company responsible for most (and in the majority of cases, all) of these activities it was possible to identify where overall management control lay. These functions were generally in sharp contrast to the provision of information for budgeting purposes and responsibility for meeting targets within the monitoring process which usually went with day-to-day operating responsibility.[13] The latter were none the less frequently in the hands of very senior management, including some who exercised considerable influence both from within and outside the board.

On this basis it is possible to equate effective strategic management control in each company with its main board, or holding company board if no main board existed. Where both existed the main board in all cases exercised this control.

The primary location of operating decisions was as follows:

Senior and subsidiary boards similar or identical	7
Responsibility split between senior and subsidiary	5
Separate subsidiary boards responsible	6

Summarising the above analysis generates Table 5.9, which attempts to relate both ultimate control and operational decision-taking to the position of the family to which the companies belong.

TABLES 5.9 Location of Strategic Control and Operational Decision-taking

	Location of strategic management control	Location of operational decision-taking
Group with family majority	10	6
Group without family majority	6	10
Ambiguous	2	2

Thus in only just over one-half of these 'family' businesses did strategic management control clearly lie with a group of which the family was a majority. For operational decision-taking the proportion fell to one-third.

The distinction between ultimate control and operation decision-taking responsibility is however only one characteristic in the location of

---

[13] It might be argued that the dependence of the controlling group on information supplied by those outside it makes it vulnerable to control loss. We regarded this as less serious than might be supposed because of the size of the companies and the absence in most cases of either long lines of communication or typical bureaucratic dysfunctional behaviour such as biased information, empire building or inability to allocate responsibility clearly.

effective control. For in practice, as in virtually all organisations, smaller informal groups will emerge by virtue of their specific position within the hierarchy, natural ability or expertise, or, of particular significance in the present context, by virtue of ownership. It was in fact possible in sixteen of the nineteen companies interviewed to identify an 'effective controlling group', which was sometimes identical to the senior board but was generally narrower than it, and which exercised informally most or all of the strategic functions previously noted. This further concentration of control is summarised in Figure 5.1 which shows the number of companies which have different combinations of family and non-family members in their effective controlling groups.

Number of non-family members \ Number of family members	0	1	2	3	4
0			3		
1			1	2	
2		3	1	2	
3					
4		2	1		
5					

FIGURE 5.1 Identity of Effective Controlling Group

The figures in the grid indicate the number of companies with the composition of their effective controlling group as shown on the axes.

In addition however, in all except two cases, the family managers on the subsidiary boards were also on the senior board, whereas across sixteen companies fewer than half the non-family members of subsidiary boards also sat on the senior board. No company thought it realistic to expect that a board would attempt to take a decision against the views of a family representative of the senior board sitting on the subsidiary board.

(c) *The ownership/management overlap*

At this stage a third characteristic must be brought in. In most cases it is the same family individuals who are both part of the effective controlling group *and* members of subsidiary boards *and* major shareholders. Table 5.10 illustrates the extent of this overlap.

This may be summarised as follows. In only four of the fifteen cases did the family representatives amongst the effective management controlling group not have an effective ownership control.

In six cases the family representatives were in a minority amongst the effective management controlling group. In only two cases did these conditions overlap, and in neither case did the family's control appear to be threatened. It was threatened or had in effect ceased to exist in two cases (indicated by a dagger in Table 5.10). In one case this was the result of the near collapse of the company, and in the other because of the almost simultaneous handing on both of company shares and management control to a new generation. Although these are only two cases out of nineteen investigated, it was thought that these probably did in fact represent the two most likely ways in which the concentration of ownership and control described above might be dissipated. Finally, attention must be drawn to the one non-family firm, for even here three key people on the board had founded the company, held 60 per cent of the shares; and one of these, as managing director, was the only executive director.

Of the fifteen companies listed in Table 5.10, eleven are unambiguously 'owner-controlled', i.e. not just legally owned but effectively managed and directed by their owners. None were unambiguously 'management-controlled', i.e. effectively directed by non-shareholders, but in two the effective management groups did not to any great extent hold shares, nor were members of the group dependent on profitability, directly or indirectly for their income. In this sense they may be classified as 'management-controlled' companies. For the remaining two companies in Table 5.10 the position was ambiguous. It may be added that of the four companies omitted from Table 5.10 for lack of sufficient detailed information, three were none the less almost certainly owner-controlled, and one largely management-controlled. This two-way classification is of interest because it has been hypothesised in the past that the two types of company will exhibit very different types of business objectives. This question is examined in Section 5.5.

It is now possible to report on the remaining issue relevant to management control, namely the relation between family and non-family board members and the perceived extent, if any, of conflict of interest between them. In nine of the fourteen companies for which it was possible to pursue this matter there appeared to be no such conflict. This does not of course imply that differences of view between the two

TABLES 5.10 Overlap of Ownership and Effective Management Control

Company	Number of family members in controlling group	Number of non-family members in controlling group	Per cent of shares effectively held by family members in controlling group*	Per cent of shares effectively held by non-family members in controlling group
M	2	0	100	–
N	2	0	60	–
Q	2	0	70	13
D	3	1	52	–
R	3	1	80	–
O	2	1	81	2
C	3	2	54	–
H	2	2	40	Minimal
L†	1	2	25	–
I	2	2	10	Minimal
F	1	2	12	–
P†	1	2	81	–
A	2	4	100	–
K	1	4	54	Minimal
B	1	4	80	Minimal

* Some figures are approximate.
† Cases where interviews revealed some concern about continuing family control.

groups did not exist from time to time, but that as far as those concerned were aware, these disagreements represented normal professional differences of view unrelated to the distinction between family and non-family members. Very rarely, if ever, was consensus not obtained after full discussion. The basic causes of disagreement in the remaining five cases are listed below:

1. Non-family management view that family management was too conservative and too short-sighted. The former desired more major changes in the direction and rate of development of the company than the latter was prepared to accept.
2. Non-family management fear that the family wished to retain its controlling position in the management structure despite increasing evidence that the necessary expertise no longer existed within the family.
3. Non-family management view that the family retained too tight a centralised control, and that the two most senior positions were beyond the reach of them. There appeared to be some tendency for non-family managers eventually to leave because of this.
4. Potential tension because effective control was now in the hands of non-family members after the founder (and effectively controlling shareholder) had become non-executive following severe trading problems.
5. In the past, various parts of a business had been very much under the control of individual non-family 'barons' who had not always operated as the senior board would have wished. However, this situation had been changed through removal of individuals concerned, and no such conflict continued to exist.

It is noteworthy that except for possibly (1), in none of these cases did potential or actual disagreement reflect a conflict of interest between management and shareholders as such. Nor did they arise because family representatives are to some extent company 'bankers' as well as managers, while the non-family representatives generally are not. Rather these conflicts tend to reflect purely managerial differences which are, however, caused by virtue of the fact that one management group also has substantial ownership rights. If, as the majority of cases suggested, this managerial difficulty can be circumvented, there appears to be a strong probability of reasonable unity of interest among family and non-family members within the effectively controlling group.

Despite the relative lack of observed conflict, most of the companies were over the long term very much aware of the twin problems of management recruitment and retention of family control. With regard to the first of these, which is not of course a problem peculiar to family businesses, a substantial minority of the companies faced what may be termed the 'Penrose' problem. Penrose has been responsible for introducing a familiar management problem to the mainstream of industrial economic literature.[14] Recruitment of managers places an upper limit on the growth rate of a firm; faster growth would require more new managers, but after some point faster recruitment *slows* the growth of the firm, first because the average expertise of the management is reduced, and second because the training and integration of the new management detracts excessively from the operational work of the existing management.[15]

For smaller companies the problem may often be more acute. This is partly because it is more difficult to place management training on a regular and systematic basis. But perhaps more importantly, smaller companies will have few middle managers from which to select personnel with the exceptional abilities necessary to take on the top management responsibility of helping to run a company. A significant number of the sample companies drew attention to the problem of identifying and recruiting people with the necessary ability and expertise to fill the most senior management positions. Naturally all preferred to recruit to such posts internally if possible, but one-third of the companies had been forced to recruit directly from outside because no suitable internal candidate was available.

Superimposed on this, for unquoted companies still effectively under family control, is the problem of maintaining that control. That the great majority of them wish to retain control cannot be doubted, and this applies both to ownership control and management control. Most were anxious to be able to pass on both the shares of the company and the key management positions to the next generation in as far as this was feasible. Notably, very few had ever, or would ever, consider obtaining a quotation just because this would create the risk (and in some cases the likelihood) of eventual loss of control; see Section 5.2(d). This stance appears to reflect, first, the fundamental wish to pass both property and responsibility on to descendants; second, a determination to keep the company, which may be regarded as a major manifestation of the family's existence as a successful united entity, in continuing very close

---

[14] See E. Penrose, *Theory of the Growth of the Firm*, 2nd edn (Basil Blackwell, 1979).
[15] See D. A. Hay and D. J. Morris, *Industrial Economics: Theory and Evidence* (Oxford University Press 1979) pp. 299–304, for a summary of these points.

association with the family; and third, a belief that a family business with members of that family at its head enjoys considerable advantages in its relations with its customers, bankers and workforce. Less certainly, it perhaps reflects the belief that management cohesion and success are more likely to occur if the managers within the effectively controlling group are on a par with each other in terms of share ownership. The advantage of family management is that it can help to provide this balance without loss of family control. These issues are touched upon again later. Apart from taxation effects, which are examined in Section 5.4, the major obstacle to the passing on of ownership intact is the fragmentation of shareholdings that tends to occur from generation to generation. Various means to combat this have been sought, including the setting up of family trusts which permit dispersion of family beneficiaries but centralised trustee control, and the buying in of shares by major shareholders, be they individuals or trustees, whenever possible.

On the question of management succession within the family it was possible to identify four types of company.

First, there were four companies in which there was no serious concern to bring members of the next generation of the family into the management of the company. Second, there were five companies who had identified, and in some cases had already brought into the management structure, individuals of the next generation of the right age, regarded as having the requisite ability and interest in pursuing such a career. In the third group, there were seven companies who were keen to recruit such individuals from the family but currently could not find anybody meeting these qualifications. In three of these cases there was an age gap, with the eldest potential family representative being in his teens, and therefore at least ten to fifteen years away from being able to contemplate such a role. In two of the seven cases, individuals had been consulted but were not inclined to enter the family business. In the other four cases the existing management did not consider that the requisite talent was available, and had already, or eventually would, recruit from outside the family.

The fourth group consisted of three companies which explicitly were very anxious to maintain strong family representation in the management of the company but at the same time had reservations about the quality of management available to them. In two cases substantial changes in the organisational structure of the company had occurred or were strongly contemplated in order to circumvent this problem. One of these companies had put all its operations except one under operating boards; these were responsible to a holding company which also had direct responsibility for the remaining activity. This was seen as a means of having skilled non-family managers at operating board level but without losing completely the family nature of the business. The other of these two was contemplating splitting the business up into smaller units as a means of making the management task easier, it being recognised that unless this worked in permitting continued family management, then increasing autonomy of decisions and the breakdown of the family nature of the business was inevitable. The final company in the group had no clear plan of action to deal with the problem.

Overall there is a preference for recruiting future top management from within the family, but in the large majority of cases there is also a recognition that unless the requisite skills and ability are brought to the top management, the company and its shareholders will all suffer. Across the sample companies, less than one-third regarded themselves as comfortably able to meet both aims simultaneously.[16]

We conclude that although there is relatively little explicit conflict of interest between family shareholding managers and non-family managers, there is nevertheless in many cases a long-term problem of meeting the desire of the ownership-controlling group both to retain family control of the management of the company and to obtain the skills necessary to maintain a successful company. If the solution of this problem increasingly shifts the balance of the effective management-control group towards non-family members, then the observed lack of conflict, which at present stems from the presence of family members in both the management and ownership structure, may be put at jeopardy in the future. In this connection it is noteworthy that at least two companies currently bringing non-family members into key positions within the effectively controlling group were anxious to transfer sizeable shareholdings to them. This appears to be much less to do with remuneration linked to shareholdings, as in most cases this is small (see Section 5.3); rather it seems to be a recognition of the fact that tensions may arise if the distribution of shareholding and distribution of management responsibility amongst the effectively controlling group are out of line.

[16] It may be speculated that this is very much a post-Second World War problem. It is unlikely that the high degree of family management continuity evident over several previous generations would have occurred if such difficulties had been thought to exist. Management itself has increasingly come to be seen as a skilled profession requiring both ability and training, thereby reducing the scope for perpetuating family management. In addition the opportunities and career mobility facing the post-war generation has been much greater, again weakening the links between generations.

The overlap of ownership and control has come to be recognised as an important issue because it is inextricably linked with the concept of discretion over resource allocation. The essence of the so-called 'managerial' revolution in economics is that salaried managers in large public companies have very considerable discretion to follow courses of action which they desire, independent of the wishes of the owners. The main import of this section has been to suggest that a relatively small number of individuals are able as a group to exercise a decisive influence on the actions of the unquoted companies interviewed, that the concentration of effective ownership control within that group is also generally high, and that this concentration is rather more than a simple listing of the shareholdings of the company would indicate. This creates three types of distinction from the typical quoted company with highly dispersed shareholding:

1. By virtue of ownership control, the managers concerned will tend to have complete discretion over resources.
2. There is no reason to presume difference of interests between the key management and the key shareholders of unquoted firms, as there is in quoted firms.
3. Whereas conflicts of interest in quoted companies are likely to be between management and shareholders, divergences of interest in unquoted companies are likely to be first, between shareholders within the management and shareholders outside the management, and second, between managers with shareholdings and managers without them.

It is important to identify what limits there are to the discretion of the owner-managers, if neither other managers nor other shareholders are in a position to impose them. Potentially a major constraint on that discretion is the set of market conditions which the firm faces. To varying degrees, discussed in Section 5.5, the companies interviewed faced the usual constraints on their strategy, pricing, marketing, production and design decisions which arise from the existence of numerous competitors.

Yet the question of discretion remains important because many major decisions, though influenced by market conditions, are to an important degree tangential to them. In particular the degree of diversification, the rate of expansion, the allocation of funds to competing internal and external claims, and the overall risk–return trade-off regarded as acceptable, are all matters which can affect the performance and development of a company, whatever the state of competition faced in any specific market.

Two types of potential constraint are the annual accounts and a company's auditors. In a quoted company the main source of information to the shareholders concerning company performance are the annual, and in some cases, quarterly, accounts. The declaration of the auditors is the only assurance that the information provides, within the framework of standard accounting procedures, a true and accurate picture of the company's position. Formally at least, a major difference between quoted and unquoted companies lies in the much tougher disclosure and auditing required by the Stock Exchange for quoted companies. These procedures are not without some drawbacks, and examples exist of companies whose true position is quite other than that indicated in its audited accounts. However this should not lead one to ignore the very important constraint on managerial discretion that they represent, particularly as shareholding has become more concentrated in the hands of skilled and knowledgeable institutions such as merchant banks and pension funds. It is therefore instructive to examine the role and significance of the accounts and auditors with respect to unquoted companies.

Until 1967 private companies did not need to publish accounts. Since then only unlimited companies can avoid this obligation. All others are required to prepare accounts and make copies available to Companies House in London. A copy of the accounts of any company is available for public consultation at a small fee, and photocopies can be ordered if required.

The interim evidence suggested some practical effects of these requirements. First, since major and usually controlling shareholdings are directly represented on the board, the statutory accounts are very much less important than for quoted companies. The number of shareholders outside the management with a desire to obtain this information is much smaller. The majority of shareholders know much earlier, and in far greater detail, all the information that appears in the published accounts. Only four of the sample companies attached any great importance to their statutory accounts. The auditors, while acting to ensure that the accounts are accurate, were rarely if ever regarded as a constraint on the execution of business policy. The accounts and the auditors, while both having specific roles to play, could not be regarded as a major constraint on management discretion.

Yet it certainly is not the case that either the accounts or the auditors were disregarded. With respect to the accounts, eight companies recognised that their bankers would be concerned with the published accounts when considering their lending on either a short- or medium-term basis. Five companies knew that potential customers reviewed their accounts when contemplating contracts and in four cases potential suppliers also. Leasing companies, contract insurers, ICFC, institutional debenture and preferred shareholders and ECGD were all also mentioned as bodies who would take cognisance of the published accounts in the period in which they had financial dealings with the companies. In addition eight companies had institutional, family or other minority shareholders who would pay attention to the accounts, and would make their concerns felt if performance was inadequate. Finally a number of those interviewed indicated that the accounts, either in themselves or in comparison with competitors' accounts or sectoral performance, were a reflection on their own abilities as managers.

Similarly the role of the auditors is not without significance. In eight companies they acted as tax advisers and in five as financial advisers. Across the nineteen companies they had in addition advised on information systems, computers, sources of loan finance, investment analysis and banking matters. Overall ten of the nineteen regarded relations with their auditors as being close or very close. In three cases positions on the board had been offered to an auditor, the auditing function then passing on to another member of the auditing firm. Few of the companies thought this affected the actual audit, which typically was carried out by more junior members of the auditing firm. But in many cases it ensured valuable and professional advice, primarily on financial and tax matters. So while the stringency of the audit may be less severe with unquoted companies because of the absence of Stock Exchange rules, the auditors, by exercising a consultancy and advisory function still play an important role, though one which rarely will impinge on the authority and discretion of the owner-manager group. Finally in some cases the auditors were responsible for the very important function of share valuation. This however is considered in detail in Section 5.4.

(d) *Pressures on management and ownership structure over time*

To what extent is the picture developed above on the basis of nineteen companies representative of the unquoted sector as a whole? With regard to the central feature, namely the high degree of overlap between ownership control and effective management control, it seems reasonable to regard the situation described as fairly typical. Virtually all firms start off very small, owned by the one or two individuals founding the firm. Many will stay in this form indefinitely. Those that are successful, which grow and survive to subsequent generations will experience the pressures to fragmentation of ownership and control seen above. As this group of nineteen companies demonstrates, there are strong personal forces opposing fragmentation. At least until very recently it has generally been possible, even amongst companies which are both large in relation to most unquoted companies and fairly old, substantially to avoid fragmentation. In only four companies was the family character of the business disappearing or non-existent and in three cases this was primarily if not solely, due to the absence of descendants willing and competent to take over the management.

From discussions with the companies we would expect only four types of important deviation from the pattern described. In the first, shareholders over the generations have become much more widely dispersed, with relatively little concentration of holdings under any member of the family. Except perhaps via trustees, the predominantly family shareholders have very little influence over either appointments to, or the actions of, the board. Some members of the family still have careers in the company, but the family nature of the business has disappeared and the non-family managers are in many ways in a similar position to their counterparts in quoted companies, except that the constraints placed on them by major shareholders monitoring performance are different.

The second exception is companies which at some point have sold a substantial block of shares to a financial institution. Several companies mentioned this as the preferred solution if faced, as a result of a death or financial shortage, with the need to place some of the company's shares outside family control. Indeed, given the impossibility of establishing a trading market in the shares other than amongst a relatively small number of institutions, this might well be the only alternative.

The third exception would be companies the majority of whose shares had gone into charitable or employee trusts. In the two cases of this amongst the sample companies, it happens that some measure of family control was still present. However in one of these cases it was to some extent fortuitous, and there is no strong reason to think that family control can be retained given the situation that led to such placing of shares.

The sample companies illustrated tendencies towards all three of these situations albeit in no case had such a process become complete. It is therefore reasonable to presume that a number of larger and older unquoted companies will have developed one or other of these different characters. There are, however, mechanisms available in most cases to avoid these changes, and in addition, a strong desire in most cases to avoid them. For these reasons the picture developed earlier is likely to be fairly typical.

The final exception is a company formed by unrelated individuals to produce and market a product. Undoubtedly there will be a number of companies started in this manner. Only one of the sample companies fell into such a category. In this company there appeared to be no plan to hand the company on to the next generation. Instead the intention was at some point to obtain a quotation in order to put funds in the shareholders' hands. It is not possible to generalise from this as to the fate of such a company which attempted to stay unquoted. However it was suggested to us, on the basis of familiarity with other unquoted companies, that such a company, if it became sizeable, would be unlikely to retain this structure. On the management side, as the company slipped a generation, if not much sooner, there would be strong pressure towards a concentration of effective management control into only one or two families at most. Only in the rather unlikely event of there being three or more equally able new managers from different families and a matching number of evenly balanced senior management positions might this be avoided. On the ownership side, the normal irregularity of family trees would generally create imbalances in the degree of share dispersion, in the degree of association with the company and often therefore in the desire to hold on to inherited shares. The buying up of shares as available by those most concerned in the company, and the establishment of family trusts to centralise control of other shares under trustees closely associated with the company would then be familiar ways of retaining ownership control. In short, even in an unquoted company set up with diversified management and ownership, the forces towards concentration of effective ownership and management control are likely to be very strong, supporting the belief that the picture obtained from the sample companies is likely to be fairly typical.

Finally, one recent innovation should be mentioned. The Finance Act of 1981 included new regulations for the 'Business Start-up Scheme'. This in principle now permits 'outside' (i.e. unrelated) investors to invest up to £10000 per individual per year for five years free of income tax as a means of generating easier access to finance for small new companies. Up to 50 per cent of the equity of a company can be distributed in this way, and this would appear to offer strong prospects for building up unquoted but broadly owned companies, free from the pressure towards concentration of ownership described above. It is much too early to determine the impact of this development, but a number of difficulties are already evident. First, the investor must stay in for five years, must be quite separate from the company's owners and cannot work for the company. He cannot therefore offer any managerial expertise, effectively loses any influence over his investment, and so faces most of the problems that minority shareholders in unquoted companies face. Second, the sums involved are small and the class of eligible companies tightly drawn. It does not really address the fundamental problem of how to make equity investment attractive to an 'outsider' even though there will generally be no active market for his shares. Unless some scope to influence events is offered it is not clear that the scheme will have any significant impact.

(e) *Conclusions on ownership and control*

We conclude that in most unquoted companies there will be a very substantial overlap of ownership and management control in the hands of an effective controlling group, that this is likely to be the only major or widespread alternative to the pattern that exists in most quoted companies, and that the effective controlling group will normally have very considerable autonomy from shareholders outside the management and from managers without shareholdings. This suggests a high degree of independence of action within the constraints imposed by the product market and the suppliers of finance. The financial position of unquoted companies, and the objectives which the controlling group are likely to pursue are considered later, but one implication must be emphasised, namely the very high degree of flexibility that this pattern of ownership provides. Even in the larger unquoted company major decisions can be taken rapidly within the effective controlling group. Most of those interviewed felt that this was an important element in achieving a high degree of responsiveness to changing market and financial conditions.

5.3 FINANCIAL BEHAVIOUR

Financial structure is the second major area in which unquoted companies are likely to differ substantially from quoted ones. With regard both to sources of funds and uses of funds, unquoted companies face different constraints and opportunities from those of quoted companies. Initial examination of the accounts of the sample of companies interviewed revealed several main differences, which are examined in Chapter 7. Three were investigated in the interviews. They can be summarised by presenting some basic accounting statistics for quoted and unquoted companies derived from the samples used for statistical analysis in Chapters 6 and 7. These are given in Table 5.11.

The first major difference was the lower proportion of capital employed in unquoted companies financed by issue of ordinary or preference shares. Without a market in these shares, issues can generally only be made in a block to specific individuals, or occasionally to institutions, or to other companies, which will generally wish to be closely concerned with the running of the company. It is relatively rare for such a potential buyer to be both interested and able to take up a

TABLE 5.11   Summary Comparison of Accounts of Quoted and Unquoted Companies (Small Sample)

	Quoted	Unquoted
	Per cent of capital employed	
Issued capital (ordinary)	30.9	20.8
Issued capital (preference)	3.4	2.3
Reserves	50.3	61.8
Deferred taxation	5.2	9.0
Long-term liabilities	10.3	6.8
Fixed assets	65.2	54.9
Trade investments	5.3	4.6
Short-term assets	99.2	161.4
Stocks/w.i.p.	45.3	65.2
Debtors	46.3	84.8
Securities and cash	7.6	11.4
Short-term liabilities	77.5	119.3
Short-term loans	15.4	22.1
Creditors	40.8	86.6
Dividends payable	3.3	1.8
Tax payable	8.0	8.8
	Per cent of gross operating profit	
Depreciation	38.6	33.6
Interest (long-term)	6.9	4.6
Taxation	20.1	21.3
Dividends	11.1	6.8
Retentions	21.5	30.5
Minorities	1.8	1.1

share issue. The need for a new shareholder to be acceptable to the existing owners may further limit the field. The proportion of equity overall, that is including reserves, is however virtually the same. This reflects the higher level of retentions of unquoted companies which is both necessary, in view of the restrictions on issuing equity, and easier, in view of the higher returns on capital.

The second major difference concerns long-term debt finance. Table 5.11 and the interviews both clearly reveal that unquoted companies make much less use of long-term loans and/or debentures. Ten of the nineteen sample companies carried no long-term debt at all except, in two cases, in relation to holding of land and financial investment; a further three did so only as a funding of the permanent core of what had previously been rolling short-term debt with the banks. In addition one other company had largely completed a programme of buying in debentures and preference shares in order to remove its long-term debt commitments. These may be termed Group A companies. Thus only five companies (Group B) regularly relied on such finance and for one of these it was a relatively new phenomenon.

At first sight this is rather surprising. It might have been expected that in the absence of access to the stock market for long-term equity finance, there would be a tendency towards greater rather than less reliance on long-term debt in comparison to quoted companies. One major reason for the lower use of long-term debt is undoubtedly a strong preference among such companies for essentially conservative financial policies. Thirteen of the fourteen companies in Group A and one in Group B recognisably pursued conservative or very conservative financial policies where these terms were defined by reference to a norm as perceived by the companies themselves. (This included one company for whom a return to such a norm had been a major policy objective for the previous three years.) Four companies adhered to rather average financial structures and one explicitly recognised its financial position to be risky.

This conservatism, and the low or zero long-term debt position it encourages, are almost certainly best explained in terms of the unity of effective management control and ownership control. The fact that the management's own money is at stake, and the fact that because of the family nature of the business the management's own name and reputation are clearly and very publicly at stake, would seem the most plausible explanation for this finding. For the manager in a quoted company, the difference between long-term debt and equity finance may not be so great, it being a matter of professional skill to balance the mix of the two, to achieve an optimum in terms of cost, flexibility and deferability of payment. For the owner-manager of an unquoted company the difference may be very fundamental, with debt carrying external obligations and the risk of default implying heavy constraints on freedom of action and diminution of control. Equity finance carries none of these risks. Another reason may be the fact that whereas shareholders in quoted companies do have an option to sell their shares if they are unhappy with the company's performance, or alternatively may diversify risk through the holding of a portfolio, those in unquoted companies do not have the former option and have less scope for the latter. Repeatedly the view was expressed in the interviews that the running of the company was in effect a trusteeship on behalf of many individuals, demanding safe and prudent management.

In addition the distinctive nexus of management and ownership control is itself important. Three companies (one having borrowed from a US bank, one from ICFC and one contemplating borrowing from a US bank) commented that medium- or long-term borrowing from ICFC or US banks was an attractive proposition, but borrowing from UK banks much less so. This had little to do with the cost of funds offered, but arose because the UK banks involved were much more stringent about securing loans on the property of the company and about detailed monitoring of the companies' activities both before and during the period of the loan. This in part appears to stem from the fact that unquoted companies rarely can go back to shareholders for more funds if their financial position becomes weakened. Without such fall-back the risks of unsecured lending are increased. This may also help explain why gearing is relatively low. As only one of these companies was in Group A, it would not be right to make any simple inference that the UK banks were even more conservative than the companies, and in any event the number of companies involved is far too small. But the control nexus is vital, so that the provision of finance which puts constraints on the nexus will be much less acceptable than that which is less restrictive.

There is however another factor which throws a rather different light on the low gearing of unquoted companies, namely their greater use of short-term loans. Three companies, again reflecting conservative financial policies, carried virtually no short-term debt (though one of these was amongst the five Group B companies making regular use of long-term debt). Four companies had rules of thumb which restricted short-term debt to levels sufficient to cover either stocks, or debtors, or debtors minus creditors or some combination of them. The majority however in principle carried whatever short-term debt was thought necessary for the efficient running of the business at the time. Two had diversified their sources of short-term finance within the banking sector, primarily to safeguard against getting caught by general or sectoral restrictions imposed on the banks; one had been subject to very close monitoring after near collapse; but in general the sample companies experienced no difficulty in obtaining whatever overdraft or short-term loan facilities they felt they required. Indeed it is of particular note that although the interviews were conducted in a period when control of the money supply was both the major government economic target and also proving difficult to achieve, none of the companies interviewed had any fears about being unable to obtain all the short-term funds that they requested, often to cover extremely high and unplanned stock increases. Partly this reflects successful attempts by the banking sector to allocate their lending to maintain production and employment, at the expense of consumption, but it is also a manifestation of the very close relationship between most of the companies and their banks, and of the unrealism of believing that banks can seriously contemplate not meeting the reasonable financial requests of established corporate customers.[17]

The overall debt position of quoted and unquoted companies is not markedly different, but taking the period 1967–78 as a whole, unquoted companies carried a slightly higher proportion of debt. (The changes over time are examined in Chapter 7.) The lower long-term debt therefore appears to reflect only a difference in the term-structure of debt. To the extent that short- and long-term debt are used to finance different types of expenditure there may not always be easy substitutability between loans of different length. But, as noted, some companies' long-term debt was a re-funding of the core of short-term debt. Several companies, when asked about low long-term debt, replied that there was no advantage in increasing it, since they could obtain all the debt finance they required in more flexible form, and in some cases on better terms through existing short-term debt arrangements. The lower long-term debt position can be explained therefore by the desire for independence and flexibility in running unquoted companies, and the fact that this matches the form of lending which banks have traditionally preferred.

The third financial decision to study in relation to unquoted

---

[17] Based on the view that at least small companies do sometimes have difficulties in raising bank finance, a loan guarantee scheme has now been introduced. Eighty per cent of loans up to £75 000 for two to seven years can be guaranteed, with a total of £50 million available. This is therefore a small scheme (though it may be extended) and the costs include a 3 per cent premium to the Department of Industry, but it may prove attractive to very small companies.

companies is dividend policy. As this represents a decision by management as to the income to be received by the owners, it is potentially a source of major difference between those firms where the management is predominantly the owners and those where it is not. In this regard a very distinctive pattern emerged across the nineteen sample companies. Only four companies maintained dividends above a minimal level. In three of these cases there was a definite policy of paying between one-quarter and one-third of net profit in dividends. In the fourth the main determinant was a dividends-per-share target. Of the other fifteen companies, one had paid no dividends in recent years, three only a very minimal dividend, and eleven had paid dividends which were minimal in comparison to net profit, though on occasion they might represent a significant income for the recipient. In four of these eleven cases the dividend would have been smaller still but for the need to consider fairly minority shareholders, who had little or no effective voice in the running of the companies. In contrast, three companies felt less concerned about minority shareholders because the latter had inherited the shares rather than paid for them, and were therefore regarded as a less urgent claim on the company's resources. A number of reasons existed for this very distinctive behaviour.

(1) Six of the fifteen companies paying few dividends did so because of their financing needs. These needs were predominantly fixed investment but also included short-term liquidity for the financing of working capital. Three of the six appeared actually to have faced a financial shortage in relation to existing plans, while the other three viewed their position more as one in which there were ample opportunities for expansion if the necessary funds were retained out of earnings.

(2) Seven of the fifteen paid no more than minimal dividends because of the high degree of overlap between management and ownership and because of the higher taxation rates applicable to unearned income. If this is a significant factor, we would expect to find managerial remuneration per head at a rather higher level in such companies than in those of comparable size and profitability which are not owner-managed. Some check on this can therefore be obtained from the accounts by considering the figures available on managerial salaries. Specifically the ratio of directors' remuneration to profits was calculated for both classes of company and found to be higher for unquoted companies (11.35 per cent of gross operating profit as against 8.11 per cent for quoted companies). However correlating this ratio against company size it was found that all of the difference could be explained by variation in size. No tendency for unquoted companies to pay out more

of their profit in this way could be discerned independent of size. It is not therefore confirmed that higher dividends would result, by virtue of a switch away from directors' salaries, if unearned income tax rates were lower.

(3) Ten of the fifteen companies were concerned to keep their dividends low in order to keep their share valuation low.[18] As the next section shows in more detail, a major problem for unquoted companies is that of ensuring the survival of the company as a going concern when principal shareholders die. However this problem is tackled, shares have to be transferred at some point and in general this incurs capital gains tax and capital transfer tax. It is the liability for these which often represents the major threat to the company's existence. The lower the valuation of the shares transferred, the less this burden becomes, so the dividends are frequently kept as low as is possible. This is considered below. One company planning eventually to go public was attempting to increase dividends in order to achieve the highest valuation possible on quotation.

(4) A more minor reason for a low dividend stream mentioned by two companies was the period of dividend restraint, coupled with the absence of any strong reason to adjust the stream significantly after the ending of restraint. This perhaps should be seen however as a mechanism by which dividends had been kept low for one or more of the three main reasons above, rather than as a reason in itself.

The fact that dividends were generally very low immediately directs attention to the so-called 'shortfall' (or more recently 'apportionment') issue. As mentioned previously, eighteen of the nineteen companies interviewed were 'close' companies. In principle, where ownership and management overlap, there is thought to be a great incentive to retain funds earned by the company, whether or not required by the business. This reduces dividends, which are likely to be subject to a high marginal tax rate, and may help to minimise capital taxation on share disposal. Even if retention of funds increased capital values, reflecting the increased resources of the company, capital gains attract a lower tax rate liability. In fact, however, this argument understates the incentive to minimise dividends in a family business. With no sale of the shares envisaged, nor any market on which to place them, the valuation of the shares will in many cases be based solely on the dividend stream. High dividends therefore both attract high marginal rates of income tax and

[18] Note that seven companies gave more than one main reason for minimising dividends.

increase the share valuation for purposes of assessing capital gains and capital transfer tax. Given that in many cases shares are transferred without payment, therefore generating no funds with which to pay capital taxation, it is the desire to minimise the latter which is probably the most important.

Until the Finance Act of 1980 (and therefore throughout the period for which we have data), the Inland Revenue had the power to determine a close company's 'relevant income': the income which the company 'should' have distributed. If there was an excess of 'relevant income' over actual distribution (the 'shortfall') the Inland Revenue could apportion this among the shareholders in proportion to their respective interests in the company and tax them as having received such income.

The key element in this mechanism is the determination of the 'relevant income' of a close company. In principle it is defined for a trading company as that income which can safely be distributed to shareholders without prejudicing the company's business requirements, subject to a maximum of 50 per cent of trading income.[19] Naturally this is a matter for judgement and negotiation, based on the circumstances of the company at the time when the dividend decision is made. However both current requirements and resources needed for the maintenance and future development of the company can be taken into account. Liquidity considerations, financing of working capital, capital investment plans and commitments will all come under scrutiny in this evaluation. Of the eighteen sample companies treated as close companies in this respect, none had ever had an apportionment made. For thirteen of these there had never been any need for discussion with the Inland Revenue beyond the provision of the necessary information. For five the decision not to make an apportionment was taken only after some more detailed investigation, requiring the companies concerned to justify their dividend level.

Four main reasons exist for this absence of apportionment despite generally very low dividends.

(1) Although existing or new shareholders could put up new funds, in practice the lack of access to the stock market means that these unquoted companies had to obtain all new equity finance from retained earnings. In at least a third of the companies this constituted a major reason for minimising dividends, and for several more provided

---

[19] For a non-trading company, and for investment income of a trading company, the relevant income is in principle all of its distributable income, where the latter includes development gains but not chargeable gains.

reasonable grounds for thinking that higher distribution might jeopard-ise future expansion plans. It is true that the low level of long-term debt suggests that investment plans could have been financed by increased gearing even if apportionment had occurred.[20] In some cases low or zero use of long-term debt may have been an indirect means of avoiding higher dividend payments. But it is implausible to think that the Inland Revenue could tell a company what its financial policy and risk–return ratio should be, particularly if overall gearing, including short-term debt, is no lower than in other companies.

(2) A number of companies argued that an unquoted company legitimately needs a higher level of liquid reserves because it cannot raise substantial new funds quickly if good investment opportunities appear. Again it may be objected that with generally low levels of long-term debt, such finance could be found, but again this ignores the company's revealed choice concerning its debt position.

(3) Nearly all the companies had significant short-term debt out-standing. It is always open to a company to use earnings to reduce such borrowing in order to reduce future interest charges, or to provide scope for borrowing for other purposes in the future. Seven of the eighteen companies noted that the existence of such debt obligations provided a legitimate and accepted justification for not paying a higher dividend.

(4) The overriding factor is that the companies interviewed were all attempting to develop and expand in an increasingly difficult economic environment. With one possible exception they were not excessively liquid. None could plausibly be regarded as incorporated in order to turn highly taxed income into lower taxed capital gains, as might be the case in some small 'one-man' businesses.

In determining shortfall, judgement is involved, and business plans are of considerable relevance. There is therefore some scope for companies to distort the picture to their own advantage. Investment plans may become rather more 'definite' than they were, working capital needs may be forecast on a more conservative basis, and so on. In view of the evidence that a number of companies were concerned to minimise their owners' liability to high marginal tax rates, such activities must be presumed to happen in some cases. But the Inland Revenue has wide investigatory powers, and a wealth of experience in implementing the

---

[20] This may not, however, be true if overall (short- and long-term) gearing is at a constrained limit. Apportionment does not of course actually change the level of funds available to the company if shareholders finance the larger tax bill from elsewhere, but often they need to realise funds from the company in order to pay the higher taxation.

provisions. Repeated failure to fulfil investment plans or ever-increasing liquidity, for example, would attract attention.

The incentive to avoid a high pay-out is very great, and the incentive to maintain and develop a successful company is also strong. In these circumstances, bearing in mind the shortfall provisions and the Inland Revenue powers, close companies will be disposed towards considering new investment opportunities. While only two companies explicitly stated that the shortfall provision had been an important factor (and by implication a bad influence) in persuading them to make an investment expenditure, most were well aware of the type of additional investment expenditure they would make if funds were available from past earnings. Most companies were in a position to embark on further investment fairly readily if the requirements of working capital and liquidity were such that the planned low dividend could not otherwise be justified. Such investment would contribute to the expansion of the company, reduce income taxation and, provided that valuation was based on dividend stream and not assets, reduce capital taxation also. While only one of the companies was particularly liquid, very few felt any strong financial constraint. Three groups were identified with regard to the general question, on any existing or contemplated operations.[21] Four felt no particular constraint but would have investigated or carried out more expansion if more internal funds had been available. Five had experienced constraints in that they had to delay or drop projects which they deemed to be in the company's interest because adequate funds were not available.[22]

There is of course a difficult problem of interpreting answers on this issue. Many company managers, knowing their financial position, may not even contemplate additional projects. They therefore experience no shortage of funds, even though they would have expanded further if more funds had been available. However most of the first group, and paradoxically even two of the second group, believed that they could raise new debt finance quickly and easily if they so wished. This tends to support the view that investment was geared to the funds available, as part of the consequences of the shortfall provisions. The implications of this are examined in Chapter 7.

The sample companies were questioned as to whether they had contemplated or ever would contemplate 'going public', that is obtaining a quotation. This carries the advantage of easier access to equity

---

[21] Including one that had until recently been under very severe financial restraint as a result of substantial losses.

[22] No answer was obtained from one company.

finance and generally results in a very substantial increase in the value of the shares because of their marketability. However it also carries the responsibility of conforming to the detailed Stock Exchange rules on disclosure of information.

The exceptions to this are, first, the recent developments of a small 'across-the-counter' market, set up by M. J. H. Nightingale but now operated by Granville; second and more important, a subsidiary Stock Exchange listing of 'unquoted' companies, known as the unlisted securities market (USM), which is subject to rather less detailed disclosure requirements. The latter was set up after no fewer than forty companies had responded in seven months to a suggestion that rule 163 of the Stock Exchange rules, originally designed for very small organisations (football clubs, etc.), could be used as a means of getting a form of listing without incurring full responsibilities or full costs. It involved no entrance fee, reduced advertising and accounting costs and cut the overall cost of a listing by around 50 per cent. In addition a minimum of only 10 per cent of the shares, as against 25 per cent on the main listing, was required to be floated. Disclosure rules are in fact fairly strict and not so very different from those applying to the main listing. So far, placings have generally been made with institutions, and individual investors have not entered the market, but this may change as familiarity with the USM grows. The market may well become quite large eventually, not only because of the gap in financing of companies which it fills, but also because there appears to be little incentive for companies in the USM to graduate to the main listing unless shortage of finance forces it. The switch entails more cost, more disclosure and few advantages apart from prestige. The initial intention that such a switch would normally occur after companies had reached a certain size or profitability now seems unlikely to be fulfilled. The significance of this development in the present context is considered below. But these options were not available in the period of our investigation. Initial reactions were that they did not materially change the basic arguments for and against obtaining a quotation.

Of the sample companies only one had actively contemplated going public, twice embarking on the necessary procedure, but failing to find the right market conditions at the crucial time. The 'non-family' company in the sample was planning to go public eventually, two other companies had vaguely contemplated such a move, but the remaining fifteen all clearly rejected it. Nearly half regarded it as inevitably leading to ultimate loss of control. While in most cases this could in principle be avoided because of the effective concentration of shareholdings in family hands, in practice the companies were not so sanguine about the outcome, for two reasons.

First, for a few of the quasi-concentrated companies, ready marketability of shares would permit other companies or institutions to build up a large shareholding over time by buying out small family shareholders. Second, and much more significant, it would be open to a competitor or customer to take up a sizeable proportion of the shares issued. This was regarded as rather likely in many cases. In four cases the opinion was backed by the evidence of very substantial offers already having been made for the companies concerned. Such a shareholding, even if a minority one, would jeopardise trading with other established customers, or alternatively create an incentive for the latter also to take a shareholding. It was very unlikely therefore that quotation would be consistent with effective control beyond one generation, and for a considerably shorter period in a 'quasi-concentrated' shareholding. Many of the companies concerned recognised that they might nevertheless have to go public at some stage either to raise funds, or to put cash in the hands of existing shareholders, or most probably to finance the payment of capital taxation. Others recognised the problem created for minority shareholders by non-marketability and the advantage of putting marketable shares in the hands of managers. But for the great majority of these companies quotation was seen as an action to be avoided if at all possible, with the issue of non-voting preference shares regarded as a preferable means of getting cash into the hands of existing shareholders.

In conclusion, the financing of unquoted companies has certain distinctive characteristics. While overall gearing is very similar to that of comparable quoted companies, their term-structure is quite different with long-term debt used very much less. Dividends are generally kept very low, partly to permit adequate equity finance to be retained and partly because of the tax implications. Investment is fairly closely related to earnings, sometimes because a conservative borrowing policy and lack of access to the equity market create a shortage of funds, but also because of the taxation penalties attached to under-utilisation of earnings. As a result few felt that they ever actually experienced serious financial shortage, and even fewer would wish to obtain a market quotation for their shares.

As in the previous section it must again be asked to what extent these considerations are likely to be typical or representative of unquoted companies as a whole. In as far as the financial characteristics described follow from the ownership/control pattern, then given that the latter is typical so probably is the former also. However, it is arguable that much smaller unquoted companies, not always having the same flexibility over investment, either might have to pay larger dividends or, if there are still gaps in the financial market, might experience greater difficulty in obtaining necessary finance and therefore pay even fewer dividends. On the evidence available to us this cannot be fully resolved.

5.4 TAXATION

Potentially one of the major differences between quoted and unquoted companies relates to the effects of capital taxation. Capital gains tax and capital transfer tax are in principle taxes based on individuals rather than companies. Where the ownership of shares is transferred either during life or on death, the individual or his estate is liable. If, for example, an individual sells a shareholding in a quoted company, he is liable for capital gains tax. The company in which he held shares is not affected,[23] though the proceeds of disposal of the shares may be required to meet the tax liability.

However the situation is very different for an unquoted company. As no market exists for the shares (and in many cases there are restrictions on the disposal of them), it is very difficult for a shareholder to sell his shares if he so wishes. Several sample companies attempted to maintain an informal market amongst members of the family and in some cases non-family directors, often with regular valuation of the shares being made by the board for this purpose. There are however severe limits to the extent to which this can be achieved. A shareholder, particularly a large shareholder, would have difficulty in selling his holding except perhaps to an institution. (Two companies had at some stage sold shares to financial institutions that could not be placed amongst existing shareholders.) A minority holding in an unquoted company is not generally very attractive, given that effective control lies elsewhere and dividends tend to be low. There are high information costs to investors in that the company's record and prospects have to be examined for the purpose of one purchase of shares, whereas very little more investigation is required in the case of a quoted company for large-scale and regular dealings in the shares. There is every prospect of being 'locked into' the shares if conditions deteriorate because of the absence of a market on

[23] The disposal of a large shareholding in a quoted company could influence the share price and indirectly thereby the company's activities.

which to trade. There may therefore be no way of realising the asset at a future date, whereas there is rarely any such difficulty with a quoted company. Several sample companies were not in principle adverse to an institution taking a minority shareholding and being represented on the board, but it was recognised that this could cause difficulties over dividend policy or lead to subsequent sale of the minority holding to a customer or competitor. Most profitable unquoted companies could sell their shares if a controlling interest were involved, but most wished to preserve the existing nature of the business and did not view their shareholdings as realisable capital.

The consequence is that shares in the sample companies were not sold, but transferred to other family members in the same or next generation, or held until death. But transfer or inheritance do not generate any funds to meet the capital gains and capital transfer tax liability thus incurred. The problem of meeting these tax liabilities, and the consequences of not being able to meet them other than by selling the shares (despite the obstacles described above) constitute central problems for unquoted companies and have significant implications for economic efficiency.

Prior to 1965 there was no liability for capital gains tax, and Estate Duty on death could largely be avoided provided shares were passed on sufficiently early before death occurred. Since 1965 there has been a tax liability on the capital gain realised and this includes any notional but unrealised gain if shares are transferred.[24] Since 1975 capital transfer tax has replaced Estate Duty and covers transfers *inter vivos*. Apart from allowances, the transfer of shares *inter vivos* involves payment of both capital gains tax and capital transfer tax (or deferred liability to payment under more recent hold-over relief policies). Transfer at death creates a liability for capital transfer tax only.[25]

Funds to meet these liabilities can be found in one or more of three ways:

1. Out of the shareholder's own income or other wealth. For many however this will be impossible, as their shareholding may represent a

---

[24] An annual allowance, currently (1982) of £5000, is exempt, and there is relief on gifts between individuals which can result in delay in the incurring of a liability. From 6 April 1982, CGT assessments will include an allowance for inflation.

[25] Capital transfer tax is payable only after a threshold limit of the cumulative amount transferred is passed. At the present time (1982) this stands at £55000. In addition there is an annual allowance, raised to £3000 in the 1981 Finance Act. Rates of tax on lifetime transfers are, for small sums, at half the rate on transfers at death. Where both capital transfer tax and capital gains tax are payable some 'double taxation' relief has now been introduced.

very major proportion of their wealth and a large sum in relation to
their income.

2. Out of past dividends accumulated on the shares and retained in one
   form or another for this purpose. With most earnings being ploughed
   back, with relatively high marginal rates of taxation on unearned
   income, and with the combined marginal rate of capital taxation at 50
   per cent over £100 000 this too is normally not possible.

3. The obstacles to the first two methods may well be enough to prevent
   any substantial transfer of shares during the shareholder's life. The
   tax financing problem then occurs on death. If one small shareholder
   dies it may be possible for the estate to pay the tax from other income,
   or out of funds realised from sale of the shares to existing
   shareholders. If, however, a substantial minority shareholder dies
   then it may be impossible to pay the tax except by selling the shares
   outside the existing shareholders, thus creating a 'dualistic' shareholding pattern, be it of concentrated or quasi-concentrated form.

In some cases sale of shares may result in a viable shareholding pattern. In
particular EDIT (Estate Duty Investment Trust) exists specifically to
buy up shares if this situation arises, and thereby to permit the company
to carry on, albeit with a new and important minority shareholder, but
as described in Section 5.2, there are strong pressures against such a
pattern surviving. For larger successful companies the likely ultimate
result is quotation, particularly as other shareholders die, creating
further pressure for a market in the shares. For smaller successful
companies, and possibly for some larger ones too, the likely outcome is
absorption into another company, often itself quoted. This is partly
because quoted companies, being larger on average, are more able to
absorb acquisitions and partly because, having better access to equity
funds, they are more able to finance mergers.

If a majority shareholder dies, or if two minority shareholders who
together have a controlling interest die within a short period, then
similar problems exist but on a much larger scale. The value of the shares
will be much higher, not just because more shares are involved but
because, conferring control, each will be worth much more. This reduces
the likelihood both that the tax can be raised from the estate without sale
of the shares and that existing shareholders will be able to buy the shares
if they are put up for sale. In such cases quotation or absorption is likely,
ending the life of the firm as an unquoted company. The consequences of
this for economic efficiency are examined later.

Nearly all the sample companies were very much concerned with this issue. Only four were actively considering an eventual quotation. The one company with 80 percent of its shares in employee or educational trusts could easily ignore it. But it had had to sell off some subsidiaries to raise funds to pay capital taxation prior to the establishment of these trusts.

In the case of two companies it was not possible to obtain much information.[26] Of the remaining twelve companies, seven had adopted the practice of transferring shares to the next generation each year up to the exemption limit. Two of these seven companies, plus a further three, had a quasi-concentrated shareholding that enabled small minority shareholdings to be transferred fairly easily. However the exemption limit is such that only three companies viewed their arrangements as sufficient to ensure the survival of the company as an independent entity beyond one generation. At least seven faced major reorganisation of ownership or an end to their independent existence within the forseeable future as a result of capital taxation.

In six of the thirteen companies, principal shareholders had taken out insurance policies, the main purpose of which was to provide for capital taxation in the event of their death. While this appears an efficient way of meeting the tax liability consequent upon sudden and unexpected death, as the age of the shareholders concerned increases, so the premium increases and takes on the character of a personal saving scheme against the eventual tax liability. As such it offers a solution only if adequate funds are available from other income or wealth of the shareholder, in which circumstance the problem of meeting the tax liability is much reduced anyway.

A number of other methods for minimising the impact were also reported. Two companies had created a market for their shares with valuations determined by the board. Several could defer the problem by transferring shares to a spouse under the exemption provision, and in several cases shares for sale had been placed with other members of the family concerned. One alternative adopted by five companies at some time was to issue non-voting bonus preference shares to existing shareholders which could then be sold to institutions, with in some cases a quotation being obtained. This simultaneously had the effect of putting cash in the hands of shareholders, creating funds for payment of tax and reducing the value of the shares to be transferred because of the

---

[26] Such tax liabilities fall on individuals rather than the company, and in both cases the interview was with someone who, not being a major shareholder or member of the main shareholding family, did now know the necessary details.

new and prior charge on earnings which the preference shares represented. In effect the shareholders converted a claim on future income into an immediate capital sum. In principle this is an effective way of enabling shareholders to realise the wealth which their shareholding represents despite the absence of a market for the sale of their shares. This can be important both where minority shareholders have otherwise to accept a low dividend stream because of the high degree of ploughback adopted, and where there is a need to build up resources to meet capital taxation liability. The fact that the shares are preference shares is a safeguard for the institutional (or other) purchaser against cessation of dividends because the preference shares remain non-voting only while the associated dividends are paid.

There are none the less some problems with this solution. First, it gears up the company to meet the prior charge of preferred dividends. This can materially reduce the normally high degree of flexibility of the existing management previously discussed. This may or may not be serious, depending on the cause of low earnings when they occur, and the extent to which financial markets operate effectively to finance temporary losses. It also discourages risk-taking and this may have deleterious consequences for company performance. It will interfere substantially with the extent to which earnings can be ploughed back for investment.

Second, there are restrictions on the issue of such shares if preference shares have been issued previously. Without the agreement of existing preference shareholders, a new issue cannot be made unless the previous ones are redeemed and ten years has elapsed. This prevents 'dilution' of non-voting preference shares. As redeemable preference shares are treated as distribution under the 1978 Finance Act, the issue has to be of irredeemable preference shares to achieve the objectives outlined above, in which case a court order is required to redeem them. Second-preference shares, paid only after previously issued preference shares, represent a financial instrument for avoiding some of these problems, but complicate the company's capital structure and are much less attractive to potential buyers.

Third, except for a short period in 1977–8 when preference share dividends, like interest payments, were payable out of pre-tax corporate income, they are, like ordinary dividends, paid out of post-tax income. This makes them much less attractive. In addition capital gains tax has of course to be paid on the full value of the proceeds of the sale of the preference shares. For both reasons the advantages of this option are now greatly reduced.

An important element in determining whether a company is affected by the incidence of personal liability for capital taxation is the valuation placed on the shares when transferred *inter vivos* or inherited. Fifteen of the nineteen companies had been involved in share valuation as a result of one or other or both of these. The exceptions comprised, first, three companies who envisaged that eventually they would go public. For two of these companies the shareholdings were being retained with a view to obtaining the best price possible when they were eventually sold. The third was more uncertain of the long-term position, but had contemplated quotation given that no member of the family was likely to come into the company's management. The remaining exception, having settled its shares in employee and charitable trusts, was not much concerned with share valuation.

Thus every company in the sample which was concerned to remain an independent and predominantly family business had had to obtain share valuations for taxation purposes. For just over half, the process of valuation was carried out primarily by the company's auditors, rather than by the directors themselves. The valuation naturally had then to be approved by the Capital Taxation Office (CTO). Especially where a small shareholding was concerned, this was a relatively short and simple process. But a significant minority of companies found it to be a complex and lengthy process, running into several years of discussion in some cases. For at least three companies, substantial rearrangement of portfolios was delayed because of the absence of any accepted figure for the value of the shares involved.

This situation arose because of the subjective nature of the process, the desire of shareholders to achieve as low a valuation as possible, and the dependence of a proper valuation on detailed information about current and forecast performance of the company in question. In addition the problem is aggravated where shareholders are making fairly regular transfers of shares, there being no reason to presume that the proper valuation is constant over time.

There also appear to be cases where the process is lengthened further as a result of changes of personnel at the CTO with an incoming officer having a different view to that of his predecessor as to the best basis for assessment. There can of course be more than one view as to which characteristics of the company's current and prospective performance are relevant, and what relative weighting should be given to them. A fairly extensive list of factors were brought into the discussion at different times for different companies.

The fundamental basis for nearly all valuations carried out on shares of the sample companies was the current dividend stream. It was generally felt that assets per share would be the fundamental criterion adopted by the CTO if a controlling interest was concerned. As in no case had such a shareholding been transferred, it was not possible to judge whether this would be so. Whether this is likely to be reasonable or not depends on the process used to value the company's assets. If the assets are valued on historic cost basis this may give an unrealistically low valuation because of inflation. On the other hand, the shares of numerous quoted companies are frequently at a very substantial discount on the accounted asset-backing, so assets may well represent a very poor guide to the market value of a company's shares. Whether the acquisition of a majority holding of the shares of a quoted company would necessarily put the price above the asset-backing per share is open to argument. Without evidence on this point there can be no certainty that asset-backing is the appropriate basis for valuing a controlling shareholding.

All actual transfers carried out by shareholders of the sample companies were minority holdings, and the fundamental criterion was therefore the dividend stream on which the shares are a claim. In fact the procedure used in all major cases was the following:

1. To determine the average dividend yield on a sample list of quoted companies of similar type. In practice this meant selecting relatively undiversified quoted companies in the same sector.
2. To add a premium to this yield to allow for the fact that the shares under consideration are unquoted. The absence of a market results in much lower value for shares, primarily because information about them is less available and also because they are much less realisable. This difference between quoted and unquoted shares is most evident when companies, obtaining a quotation, experience a very significant increase in the value of their shares.

The premium added varies substantially. Amongst the sample companies, 20, 25, 30 and in one case 40 per cent had all been used. This need not reflect inconsistency of treatment, for two main reasons. First, a number of other factors were in some cases taken into account, but not in others. A company's auditors and the CTO may allow for certain specific company characteristics in the premium added, rather than use a uniform premium, and then explicitly allow for other factors. Second, circumstances may make the dividend stream more or less appropriate as the basis of valuation. This could in principle be allowed for by variations in the premium added.

3. The resulting yield figure is then applied to the prospective dividend stream. The latter is of course a matter of conjecture. In practice the past trend of dividends, both over the long and short term, is generally the major basis, but this can be modified in the light of company, sector or even national economic prospects.

With only the variations noted under (2) and (3), this approach represented the basis for share valuation. However, at least four other factors were involved in negotiations and, much less frequently, affected the final valuation:

(i) Restriction on share transfer in the company's articles of association was a basis for a further increase in the yield figure applied to the dividend stream. In view of the potentially very severe constraint on realisation of assets which this type of restriction represents, this adjustment seems appropriate.

(ii) Shareholdings below 5 per cent and in one case below 10 per cent were given a more nominal value than the above procedure would generate, reflecting the fact that such holdings would be difficult to realise. This seems less appropriate given that the shares none the less represent a claim on a dividend stream. If the latter were minimal, then the 'formula' would reflect this and generate an appropriate nominal value.

(iii) Shortage of cash or liquidity could represent a reason for proposing a lower valuation. In effect this is a reason for believing that the dividend level could not be maintained in the near future.

(iv) High dividend cover could be a basis for a higher valuation. If cover is an indicator of the scope for dividend growth this appears reasonable. But if cover is very high because of the high proportion of internal financing, then it may well not be a guide to dividend growth. It is possible to ascertain empirically for quoted companies whether dividend yield is reduced by high cover. Work done by some of the sample companies and by the CTO suggests that this does occur up to a point, but beyond that further increases in cover have virtually no effect. By comparing the cover of an unquoted company against the empirical relation for quoted ones it is possible in principle to derive the adjustment appropriate for high cover. The major drawback to this is that the internal financing needs of the two may be different.

This does not exhaust the list of factors that may be deemed relevant. For example a price–earnings ratio might be examined, though this appears very rarely to have been the case. Nor does it exhaust the way in which these criteria are used. One company for example had a *reduced* premium because of restrictions on the transfer of shares, presumably reflecting the greater control over company ownership provided by the restrictions. The list does none the less cover all the main elements alluded to, in addition to the basic procedure for evaluation previously described.

Given the emphasis on dividend stream, and generally very low level dividends paid, the result for minority shareholdings was to generate rather low share valuations, particularly in relation to asset-backing. This is a major factor in enabling companies to preserve their independent status because of the lower capital taxation liability which it generates. Independent of this consequence the procedure appears to be appropriate. It accurately reflects the distinction between the company's assets on the one hand and the realisable wealth of minority shareholders on the other. The latter represents only a claim on dividends and is rarely realisable at a value approaching its asset-backing. It is none the less insufficient to solve the problem facing a company when a substantial minority shareholder dies, because of the difficulty of meeting the resulting tax liability in the absence of an established market for the shares.

In conclusion, there are a number of methods for delaying or reducing the impact of capital taxation on the survival of unquoted companies as independent entities. However for many unquoted companies the basic problem remains of how to avoid the sale of the company on the death of principal shareholders.

Because taxation has only been levied on transfer of shares since 1975, it is still too soon to know what the effect of it will be. However it is possible to make some observations on likely developments. The smaller companies will probably for the most part be able to avoid the problem because it will generally be possible, given the allowances available, and given a staggered transfer of shares over time, to meet the tax liability without substantial sale of shares. The largest unquoted companies will probably have to sell a controlling interest to another company, or obtain a quotation, but for a large number of intermediate-sized unquoted companies the options are much less clear.

Four main possibilities appear to exist:

(1) Financial institutions such as insurance companies, pension funds and merchant banks may buy up sizeable minority holdings in un-quoted companies as they become available and hold them as invest-ments. The management, with or without an effective controlling interest, would continue to manage the company, with the financial

institution monitoring its investment. Any doubts at the outset about the continuity of the dividend could be met by issuing preference shares against the ordinary shares, and the generally low dividend stream would be reflected in the share price.

Several of the sample companies were by no means averse to such a development, and in some cases would have welcomed a representative of a shareholding institution on the board. It must be stressed however that the low marketability of the shares would generally imply long-term institutional shareholding. In the event of company performance appearing to deteriorate, the option available in quoted companies of disposing of the shares would be absent. The financial institution would either have to accept passively the poorer return, or to become actively engaged in the management of the company. As both of these are generally regarded as unattractive by financial institutions in the United Kingdom, this particular development is unlikely to be widespread, at least at the present time.

(2) A second possibility is that financial institutions might build up majority holdings. This could arise over time as substantial shareholders die and their estates need to sell shares to pay capital taxation. While such a development is entirely a conjecture it is not unlikely in the long term. It would represent a major change in the nature of company ownership in the United Kingdom. It has the advantage for the institution concerned that their asset is much more saleable, offering control of the company assets backing the shares. As is now well documented,[27] financial institutions have very greatly increased their proportion of the shares of quoted companies. Given the pressures on unquoted companies to sell shares to institutions, an expansion of their operations into the unquoted sector would be a natural progression. Eventually a developed market in private companies might well exist between financial institutions.

(3) A third possibility is that shareholdings become much more fragmented and eventually highly dispersed as capital taxation forces the sale of large shareholdings amongst many small buyers. Presumably other members of the family and other members of management would be the main initial purchasers. In practice this is unlikely to be more than a temporary state of affairs. For the majority of the sample firms, small minority shareholders wished to be able to realise their shares either for consumption or alternative investment purposes. In some cases it is possible to envisage a large number of small shareholders generating a

---

[27] See Hay and Morris *Industrial Economics*, pp. 247–8 for a summary of the evidence.

small market amongst themselves for the company's shares, and this had occurred in three cases. Presuming no restriction on share transfer, there could be moves by minor shareholders to sell off holdings to institutions or other companies, or an attempt at grouping to achieve a more marketable controlling interest. However the probability of the latter appears very small given the concentrated or even quasi-concentrated shareholding pattern of the sample companies.

(4) The final possibility would appear to be a growing process of concentration of industry as first minority holdings and later controlling interests were bought up by other companies. One-quarter of the sample companies had been actively bid for at some point, and many could have found a buyer for a controlling interest from amongst their competitors, suppliers or customers without difficulty. This had been avoided in the past because it has been possible to pass on companies intact, without too great a constraint from capital taxation. This is coming to an end. It may well take up to a generation for the impact to become complete, but the prospect of eventually facing a capital tax liability which cannot be met other than by breaking up or selling off the company is already a serious disincentive to the further growth of the larger companies interviewed.

Trusts play an important role in determining the pattern of ownership of many unquoted companies. Their impact on the tax liability of such companies or their shareholders is however very small. This is because the underlying intention behind current taxation of trust property is to achieve parity with the tax liability which would have arisen had the property been held absolutely, i.e. in the beneficiary's own name. This results in very complex tax rules and some differences of approach, in particular the periodic charges on discretionary trusts,[28] but the fundamental pressures described above, which arise for companies as a result of capital taxation of individuals, still apply.

5.5 MOTIVATION

A major development in the analysis of industrial economic behaviour has been the hypothesis that a company's performance will systematically vary with its ownership and control structure. While the classical theory of the firm implied maximisation of shareholder wealth, a

[28] A trust may exist for considerably longer than a generation. Without the periodic change, capital in a trust might not be subject to any taxation over that period, whereas capital held absolutely would be, either on making a lifetime transfer or on death.

company controlled by salaried managers would be more concerned to maximise its growth subject to a profit constraint, because managerial rewards such as salary, status, power and security are more likely to be correlated with size than with profitability. The extent of the divergence from shareholder wealth maximisation would depend on the costs to the shareholders of enforcing their own preferences. This in turn would depend on the concentration of shareholding, information-gathering costs for shareholders and costs associated with obtaining concerted action.

The reason to hypothesise an alternative 'managerial' model was the fact that to a great extent the controlling management did not receive the profits. It was natural to associate this with the distinction between owner-controlled and managerially-controlled firms. The former group, i.e. companies for whom the controlling decision-takers *were* those with the claim to the profits by virtue of their ownership of the equity, would behave along more classical shareholder-wealth-maximising lines. Specific testing of this however has been very ambiguous. Most notably in the United Kingdom, Radice found owner-controlled companies both more profitable *and* faster-growing than equivalent-sized managerially-controlled firms.[29] This strongly suggests either that they were more efficient or facing a faster growth of demand or both. (This is in fact very likely; a company which has retained ownership control while none the less growing to the size of the quoted 'managerial' companies in Radice's analysis is not a typical owner-controlled company but a very successful one.)

The interviews with the nineteen sample companies provided an opportunity to investigate this issue, to generate hypotheses about the objectives of such companies and about systematic differences between them and quoted companies. As was described in Section 5.2, a very high degree of overlap existed between effective family ownership control and management control. It was concluded that none of the nineteen companies could unambiguously be classified as managerially-controlled by non-shareholders; however in three cases the effective management group was not to any significant extent a shareholding group, nor were members of the management group dependent on profits for their income, and in two cases there was some uncertainty as to the appropriate classification; the remaining fourteen were clearly owner-controlled.

It is however incorrect to infer from this that the fourteen acted as

[29] Radice, 'Control Type, Profitability and Growth in Large Firms', *Economic Journal*, vol. 81, September 1971, pp. 547–62.

shareholder-wealth-maximising companies in the classical sense. Indeed, the evidence suggests that the classical approach may need some reinterpretation:

1. Only five of the companies paid significant dividends. For most of the owners, remuneration from profit via dividends was of little consequence.
2. In eleven cases at least, dividends were low partly or mainly to ensure a *low* share valuation, generally because of capital taxation.
3. No owner-manager had been involved in any significant sale of shares during his life in order to realise the capital. Six had been involved in the issue of preference shares to existing shareholders, but in all cases this was either a means of getting funds into the hands of minority, non-management shareholders or a way of raising funds to cover capital taxation liability.
4. In only two cases did bonuses related to profitability appear to be an important source of income.

Much of this may be rather deceptive in one respect. The desire to keep the estimated (or 'market') value of shares low where minority shareholdings are concerned does not imply that there is any corresponding desire to keep underlying asset values low. It is quite consistent with this that company behaviour would seek a long-run maximum value of assets, which would be reflected in the *asset*-based value of the shares. Because of taxation and the absence of a market, this value may never become explicit. Its maximisation could none the less be an implicit motivation. This would be more in keeping with a classical view of the firm. It is therefore important to add a fifth point:

5. Based on consideration of past policy and development, and on directors' own assessments, eleven of the nineteen companies were clearly oriented to the objective of growth subject to a profit constraint, against only three which concentrated on increasing profit. (For five companies, interviewees made no comment or did not distinguish clearly any priorities.) From eleven unambiguously owner-controlled companies for which there was some indication of priorities in objectives, eight were classifiable primarily as growth-oriented and only three as profit-oriented. Several companies commented that only the management of a *quoted* company had to concern itself mainly or exclusively with profits and share price, precisely because they were acting for the owners rather than for themselves. Unquoted companies, being free from the danger of being taken over, were regarded as being able to take a longer-term

view and to concentrate on building up the size of the company without the need to pursue more immediate profitability increases, provided the level of the latter was adequate. This suggests that the usual picture of owner-controlled firms as classical wealth-maximisers may well not be correct. One major reason is very clear from the interviews. Thirteen of the companies (68 per cent) particularly emphasised the desire to maintain control and pass on a sound, secure and independent business as their fundamental objective. Reference has been made to the long association of many of the families with their businesses, and the widespread desire to identify suitably talented people in the next generation to come into the business. Both are part of a fundamental association between the owner-managers and the long-term future of their business. So predominant is this objective that any model of the unquoted company must reflect it fully. This tends to undermine the usual presumption that owner-controlled companies are necessarily less growth-oriented than management-controlled ones. In fact the only major barrier to the pursuit of growth as a main objective is the impact on unquoted companies beyond a certain size of capital taxation.

There are three conclusions that can be drawn. First, despite conventional reasoning to the contrary it is far from clear that owner-controlled firms act to maximise shareholder wealth, and there are some strong indications that many do not. While a desire for security may interfere with the pursuit of both profit and growth, the disincentives to paying dividends resulting from both income and capital taxation may cause companies to invest more and pursue strategies of faster growth. Second, while there are signs of a rather cautious approach to financing, which would follow from the determination to hand on a successful company, few companies saw themselves as explicitly following conservative strategies. Indeed seven companies recognised that they faced a high degree of risk in the market-place, and a further five a moderate level. Only three saw little risk in their operations (five were unclassifiable). This may partly reflect size, partly nature of the business. But more important, they were prepared to take risks because the money at risk belonged to the decision-takers. Virtually all the companies felt that their overlap of ownership and management permitted them to respond quickly and flexibly to a new situation, without the need to consult others or the fear of criticism for risking other people's money. This was felt to be a major factor in determining performance in a risky environment. Indeed two companies felt they could act too fast on occasion. Flexibility might break down if there were no consensus amongst the two or three principals involved, particularly as it was not realistic to think of a 'manager' quitting if he very much disagreed with policy. But given a consensus, action could follow very rapidly indeed.

Third, it is necessary to examine the statistical pattern of growth and profitability for the two types of company to see whether inferences can be drawn about overall company objectives. The above comments illustrate that unquoted companies cannot easily be categorised on the basis of *a priori* reasoning. The interviews provide fruitful insights into the motivation of unquoted companies, but it remains to be tested (in the next chapter) whether significant differences can be observed.

5.6 CONCLUSIONS

Certain clear conclusions emerge from the series of interviews conducted with unquoted companies. First, most of such companies are essentially family companies, with a fairly high degree of concentration of ownership in the hands of a small number of key board members. This does not inhibit the existence of a decentralised organisational structure, nor extensive presence of managers who do not own shares. It does however permit great independence, flexibility and centralised direction if desired. Considerable pressures exist which make it unlikely that alternative operational forms will exist on a substantial scale.

Second, their financial structure is very different from that of quoted companies. This involves a greater use of retained earnings than new equity issues, a shorter term-structure of debt, and much lower dividends.

Third, capital taxation is of particular significance to unquoted companies. Changes in recent years represent a major constraint on the continued existence of large unquoted companies. This in turn may have a disincentive effect on those building up smaller companies. This is particularly emphasised by the evidence that the long-term survival of such companies as independent entities is the overriding motive of those who own and control them. It is to the statistical evidence on their behaviour that we now turn.

6 Comparisons of Performance and Objectives of Quoted and Unquoted Companies

6.1 INTRODUCTION

In this chapter we set out the characteristics of unquoted companies in relation to their quoted counterparts and assess the relative performance of the two types of company.

The ideal data would be figures for production, employment and finance for all individual quoted and unquoted companies. These however are not available, nor would it be easy to cope with the vast number of unquoted companies if they were available. Instead therefore we carry out three separate investigations, using different data sources and methods appropriate to each source. The first uses the only systematic and directly comparable sets of data available on quoted and unquoted companies separately, the *Business Monitor* M3 series. This however permits only aggregate performance comparisons. The second uses the Meeks data base for individual quoted companies and tabulated results for the largest 1000 unquoted companies published by Jordan & Sons Ltd. Performance ratios for individual companies can be calculated before comparisons are made and this may give a notably different picture from aggregate comparisons. These data also provide the largest coverage of companies generally available from which to derive performance comparisons. The disadvantage is that the data on unquoted companies are summary and selective, thereby limiting analysis. The third data source attempts to correct for this. It was constructed specifically for this research and is taken directly from the published accounts of a sample of unquoted companies over a fourteen-year period. It can therefore be matched against a sample drawn from the Meeks data for quoted companies, as the latter is also taken direct from company accounts. Together these three different but complementary approaches provide a reasonable basis for assessing the relative performance of the two classes of company.

The next section considers how comparisons of efficiency performance can best be made, and notes difficulties which may arise in the process. The subsequent three sections then make such comparisons as are possible, each using one of the three data sources.

6.2 MAKING EFFICIENCY COMPARISONS

The concept of efficiency in economics is concerned with the amount of output that can be produced with a given bundle of resources. To produce more is equated with greater efficiency. Output is normally defined not as the market value of output but rather value-added, the difference between the cost of what the firm buys in by way of materials and what it receives from selling its final product. It is the difference in value which represents the activity of the firm. It does not, of course, exclude efficiency in using materials. Presumably a firm which economises successfully in its use of materials either has lower costs of materials bought in or higher value of output; in either case, value-added will be greater.

More difficult to quantify is the size of the bundle of resources used in production. If every type of production required fixed proportions of capital and labour (e.g. so many operatives per standard machine) there would be no problem. But it is well known that input ratios can vary even within sectors. A firm may adopt a labour-intensive or a capital-intensive production technique, particularly at different scales of operation. There is no way in which a simple measure of total productivity can be estimated since there are no common units in which to measure both inputs. However we can get some indication of efficiency in a number of cases. Suppose we compare two firms, one of which uses a more labour-intensive technique than the other. Then we would expect, if they produced the same output, that the labour-intensive firm would have a lower value-added per man, and a higher value-added per assets, than the more capital-intensive firm. In this case we can tell nothing about efficiency from consideration of these measures. Suppose, however, that value-added per man is the same in two firms, but that one has a higher value-added per unit of assets. Then we are justified in concluding that the latter is more efficient. The conclusion would be even stronger if one firm recorded higher values of both value-added per man and value-added per assets.

It is worth noting that there are conceptual difficulties about all three quantities used in these calculations. Value-added is the difference between the cost of inputs and the value of sales, adjusted for stock changes. Now the cost of inputs may not be an accurate measure of their quantity. For example, large firms may obtain quantity discounts on their orders of inputs. Thus their value-added could be larger without any greater production efficiency. The value of sales raises other problems. Suppose one firm makes very little (in physical units) but sells in a very specialised market at a high price, whereas another makes a large quantity for sale at a rather lower price in a wider market. Then value-added will be a poor indicator of *quantity* of output. However, we may adopt the attitude that from society's point of view what counts is producing things which people want to buy. The market price is an indication of the worth to society of each unit of output. High-priced outputs represent more 'output' of what society wants than low-priced ones. It is essential to bear in mind, in what follows, that it is this concept of efficiency rather than a physical concept which is being used in the analysis.[1]

The main difficulty in comparing factors of production is that their quality may differ. Thus two firms with the same size labour force will have different effective labour input if one has a higher proportion of skilled personnel. One way of accounting for this would be to weight each worker by his wage as an indicator of his efficiency-worth to the firm. But that would only be accurate if one believed that all differentials represented efficiency differences accurately. Exactly the same problem, though with greater emphasis, applies to the measurement of capital. In physical terms this is an extremely heterogeneous collection, including buildings, machinery, tools, work-in-progress and stocks. For most of these there is no current price, so a current valuation is not feasible. Besides, many have measurable value only in the use to which they are currently being put, which is scarcely an objective measure of their worth to society in general. So our only alternative is to use the financial

---

[1] Estimates of efficiency could therefore be distorted by higher prices arising from a monopoly position. But this will only concern us if, in our comparisons, there are reasons to believe that groups of companies judged as more efficient systematically contain more monopoly power.

measure of net assets in the balance-sheet. The economic rationale for
this is that the firm's accumulation of assets represents its use of a part of
the savings, both past and present, of society as a whole. Those savings,
which are in the form of financial assets, are limited, and our concern is
that they should be put to the most productive uses. The form in which
they are used – plant, stocks, etc. – is less significant. But there are two
further problems with this approach. The first is that most balance-
sheets include assets at historic cost. In a time of inflation the total will
represent an accumulation over time with a very different worth being
attached depending on the period in which the asset was acquired. This
is a particular problem with regard to fixed assets with a very long life. So
far as comparisons between firms in the same industry are concerned we
may be able to ignore this problem if we can assume that the asset lives
are not markedly different between firms. The values for assets in the
balance-sheets will be equally biased in each case. However, if one firm
has grown faster recently than the others its assets will be relatively
overvalued. Similarly an old firm will have relatively undervalued assets
compared to a new one. All of this presupposes that the firm has not
revalued its assets in line with inflation. Here some bias may arise since
such a revaluation would be more relevant to a publicly quoted
company, which wished to keep its shareholders informed, than to a
private unquoted company where normally the owners would be well
aware of the physical assets owned by the firm.

The second problem with asset values concerns allowances for
depreciation, and the valuation of stocks. On the latter, the best we can
say is that firms adopt different conventions in this respect. This makes
comparisons of stocks between firms quite unreliable, and we therefore
must restrict our analysis to the long-term items in the balance-sheet.
Allowances for depreciation have more economic significance. They
represent the fact that as the capital stock is used in production so some
of it is being used up. Some of this represents wearing out, but much is
related to obsolescence due to technical progress, so the value of assets
should be adjusted down in each year to allow for this depreciation, and
the measure of value-added in that year should be reduced by the same
amount. The most difficult problem here is whether the depreciation
calculated by the firm for balance-sheet purposes represents the real
attrition of the firm's capital. Since the firm pays tax on its profits net of
depreciation it has an incentive to arrange its depreciation in its accounts
so as to minimise its tax bill. At one stage this was the subject of careful
regulation by the Inland Revenue, but in the period with which we are
concerned firms had much more freedom to arrange their affairs in this

respect. However, while there may be bias in the accounts of a single firm, we have no reason to impute any general bias that could affect our comparison between quoted and unquoted firms.

An alternative method of measuring efficiency is to look at the returns on assets. The rationale for this is as follows. We suppose that the returns to labour are determined by the functioning of the labour market. Any firm will pay the 'going rate' for a particular class of skilled labour. In this case the additional value-added of a more efficient firm will accrue to profits. This will register as a higher return on the assets of the firm calculated as the ratio of net profits to assets. We are concerned that the savings of society should be channelled into those activities where efficiency is highest, and a high rate of return may be taken as an indicator of high efficiency. However there are some severe limitations to this argument which must lead us to be cautious about interpreting profitability differences. The firm may be earning a high rate of return because it is able to set a monopolistic price which exceeds the costs of production. The costs of production here include a normal return to capital, i.e. interest, risk premium appropriate to the sector and depreciation. The excess return is indeed an indication that the output of this firm is highly valued by society, as measured by the demand curve. But the situation overall is not in society's interest since consumer satisfaction would be increased by increasing output and bringing price down, which is precisely what a monopolistic firm will not wish to do. It will be appreciated that the interpretation of this situation is quite different from that in which a firm is selling at a competitively determined price, and is able to earn a higher return by keeping its costs down.

A second limitation is illustrated by the case where a firm which is operating efficiently shares out some of its excess returns with its workers in the form of higher wages than the 'going rate'. A particular instance is where a small firm pays a high level of remuneration to its directors. The reasoning is that the firm may wish to reduce its reported profit in case it is required to pay out profits under the 'shortfall' provisions. Such dividend payments would be taxed as unearned income whereas payments to directors count as earned income. The third limitation is that rates of return may differ between firms because of risk. Consider the portfolio holder's choice between investing in a firm that is undertaking speculative investments and a large diversified firm with several stable and well-established products. *Ex ante*, the portfolio holder will look for a higher expected return from the first. *Ex post*, the returns could be much lower or much higher, depending on whether the projects pay off, but on *average* we would expect them to be higher.[2] The relevance of this argument to the comparison of quoted and unquoted companies is apparent. We can correct to some extent by making sure that the size disparity in firms is not too great and by making comparisons only within sectors. But even so, some doubt must remain unless we can explicitly allow for differences in risk.

A third method of comparing firms' efficiency is on the basis of growth rates. The basic idea was suggested by Stigler in his development of the 'survivor technique' for discerning economies of scale.[3] The inference drawn from a higher growth rate for a firm, relative to the industry average, is that it is more efficient. But that superior efficiency may take various forms. An obvious form is that the firm has lower costs and is able to increase its market share by charging a lower price than others. But Stigler uses the concept in a wider sense. A firm may grow faster, for example, because it produces a better product, or because it markets the product in a way which is more acceptable to consumers, or because it provides better after-sales service. Stigler argues that such a firm is more efficient in the sense that it is better at serving the market than its rivals. On the other hand, it may well have higher costs because it offers a better product, but lower costs per unit of service supplied to the customer. Ideally we would wish to adjust our efficiency comparisons for quality of product, but that is not likely to be feasible, so a comparison of growth rates may give some useful further information.

Our conclusion is that no single method of judging efficiency, as described above, is likely to be convincing on its own. Each has its own drawbacks, but by looking at all of them we may hope to gain a reasonable indication if real differences exist between quoted and unquoted firms.

Although we have collected together a substantial amount of data from various sources there are inevitably major limitations. The broad data are for relatively few years and the detailed data over many years for relatively few companies. All derive directly or indirectly from company accounts which represent only a very summary statement of a

[2] This is a simplification of a rather more complex argument. In the capital asset pricing model [see D. A. Hay and D. J. Morris, *Industrial Economics: Theory and Evidence* (Oxford University Press, 1979) pp. 474–82 for discussion and further references], the risk of a share is measured by its contribution to the risk of a whole portfolio of shares. Thus an investor can achieve a diversified portfolio either by buying shares in a single, highly diversified firm, or by purchasing an appropriate portfolio of shares in a number of undiversified firms. Just because a firm is small and not diversified will not necessarily imply that it will be regarded as more risky.

[3] G. Stigler, 'The Economies of Scale', *Journal of Law and Economics*, 1958, pp. 54–71. The technique is discussed in Hay and Morris, *Industrial Economics*, pp. 77–81.

company's activities. At best statistical work based on such data can be suggestive only, though it may be strongly so in some cases. We have therefore thought it important for the most part to avoid more sophisticated and elaborate econometric tests. It is often difficult to establish a reliable understanding of behaviour even where the data are directly related to underlying economic decision-taking, and this is much more true when, as in the present case, the data are only loosely connected to underlying decisions. In addition a number of general hypotheses may be quite consistent with the type of data we have available, and the usual approach of testing a specific hypothesis concerning economic behaviour may easily generate spurious confirmation. Such difficulties are compounded by the fact that much of our data lends itself only to cross-sectional testing (i.e. comparisons of behaviour *across* companies) rather than time-series work (i.e. examining individual companies' behaviour over time) and this raises additional problems of interpretation. In general therefore we have preferred to pursue some basic statistical tests, mainly aimed at identifying differences between samples of quoted and unquoted companies, and then to attempt to determine whether these apparent differences are likely to be explicable by chance or by other basic characteristics of the companies concerned. In view of the very limited information available on the relative performance, objectives and financing of unquoted companies as a group this appears a valuable and appropriate first step. The results we believe are sufficiently interesting to warrant further more elaborate examination in the future.

6.3 AGGREGATE COMPARISONS OF PERFORMANCE

Aggregate data based on the annual accounts of quoted and unquoted companies in the United Kingdom have been available since 1967 in *Business Monitor* M3 *Company Finance*, issues 3–11, and this is the first source of data used. It does not permit comparisons of efficiency in terms of value-added, but it does allow us to look at the relative sizes of quoted and unquoted companies and compare their profitability and growth.

The figures are derived from the accounts of independent companies with interests in manufacturing, distribution, construction, transport and communications. Companies whose main interests are in agriculture, mining, shipping, insurance, banking and finance, and those operating mainly or wholly overseas, are excluded. Similarly subsidiaries of companies operating mainly or wholly overseas are not included, irrespective of their location. The companies are divided into quoted and unquoted categories (from 1972 the distinction being made solely on the basis of whether the company is listed).

Unfortunately we were unable to use some of the information in M3; in particular we could not use the breakdown of figures by sectors from 1967 to 1971. The reason is that only since 1971 have the aggregated data made a distinction between overseas and UK-controlled companies for both quoted and unquoted companies. Comparative analysis suggests that within both the quoted and the unquoted sector (but especially the latter) there are substantial differences of performance and behaviour between foreign and UK-controlled companies.[4] Furthermore the weight of foreign companies in the sample is much greater for the unquoted than for the quoted sector (for 1976 foreign companies comprise two-thirds of the unquoted, but less than one-tenth of the quoted sample). Our analysis therefore has to be restricted to the period since 1971, and the comparison between UK-controlled quoted and unquoted companies is aggregated across all sectors, since comparison at sectoral level is vitiated by the presence of foreign companies in the sample. This means that we cannot be sure whether the differences we observe at the aggregate level reflect differences in sectoral composition of the two samples or genuine differences in behaviour between quoted and unquoted companies.

The size criteria for inclusion of firms in the M3 sample have changed several times. In the period since 1971, the major change took place in 1975. Prior to that the sample included companies which in 1968 had net assets of £2 million or more *or* gross income of more than £200 000. From 1975, the cut-off points were changed to £5 million net assets *or* gross income of £$\frac{1}{2}$ million. M3 does not indicate whether the sample is intended to be exhaustive of all the companies satisfying the criteria. Over the period the number of companies in the sample changes year by year (usually decreasing). This can be attributed to mergers, acquisition, nationalisation and liquidation. The quoted sample fell from 1195 to

---

[4] For example, in the unquoted sample, foreign companies rely less on overdraft and more on long-term debt than UK companies. On average, foreign companies make more use of trade and other creditors as a source of funds. They pay higher dividends than UK unquoted companies. Foreign companies also pay higher wages to their UK employees. A number of possible reasons for the differences can be suggested. The differences might reflect (i) the sectoral distribution of companies, (ii) different ages of the companies; if foreign companies are on average more recently established, the greater reliance on external funds, and less on reserves, is easily explicable, (iii) different tax regimes for foreign owners, especially in respect of dividend receipts and capital taxation. There is no way in which these different possibilities can be assessed with the M3.

958 between 1971 and 1976. The unquoted sample fell more (in percentage terms) from 331 to 207 over the same period.

Two general caveats about the data should be entered at this point. First, the data, being drawn from company accounts, are not confined to the UK activities of companies alone. Second, the information for a given calendar year corresponds to the accounts of companies whose accounting years end between April of that year and the end of March of the following year. Approximately 40 per cent of the quoted companies have accounting years ending in the fourth quarter of a calender year, and 30 per cent in the first quarter of the next year. The corresponding figures for unquoted companies are 60 and 20 per cent.

The data are presented, aggregated across all the companies in the sample, in the form of detailed balance-sheets, detailed income and appropriation accounts, and supplementary information (available in notes to the published accounts) on turnover, exports, employment and wage costs. They were used to calculate, for each of the years 1971–6, indicators of efficiency and growth, representative flow of funds and various balance-sheet ratios. We now turn to the findings in so far as they point to important differences between quoted and unquoted companies.

The most obvious difference between quoted and unquoted firms in the sample is their size. Measures of average size in 1971 and 1977 are given in Table 6.1.

The largest size disparity is in terms of fixed assets or net assets (quoted companies are about four and a half times larger than the average unquoted company in the sample). The disparity is smaller for sales and employment. Clearly the quoted firms are more capital-intensive as a group. Except for sales, the ratio of quoted to unquoted company size rose during the period, but not substantially. The size disparity of the samples must immediately raise the possibility that identified differences between them arise from size rather than their ownership status. That is something which we cannot explore with the M3 data, but which we will return to in subsequent analysis.

A particularly important measure of company performance is the return achieved on its use of capital. This can be variously measured, but possibly the most relevant is the ratio of profit to the reported net assets of the firm (net, that is, of accumulated depreciation). We must immediately recall the previous caveats about such a measure. In particular we will expect the computed return to exceed the 'real' return (profits in current values as a ratio of assets also at current values), but this should not invalidate the comparisons.

146

TABLE 6.1 Size Difference in Samples of Quoted and Unquoted Companies

All measures are sample averages	1971 Quoted	1971 Unquoted	Ratio	1977 Quoted	1977 Unquoted	Ratio
Fixed assets (£000s)	12921	2988	4.32	32606	6972	4.68
Net assets (£000s)	19086	4228	4.51	52618	11526	4.57
Sales (£000s)	37895	11311	3.35	128664	39423	3.26
Employment	4710	1417	3.32	5647	1486	3.80

Figures for the years 1971–7 are given in Table 6.2. Two features are immediately apparent. First, both for unquoted and quoted firms the measure is rising over the period. This almost certainly reflects the accounting bias described. There is other evidence[5] that the real return was tending to fall across the whole UK private sector in this period. Second, there can be no doubt that throughout this period unquoted companies consistently recorded a higher rate of return on net assets. The discrepancy is not large, but it certainly cannot be attributed to chance. In principle it is possible that systematic differences in the term-structure of liabilities as between quoted and unquoted companies could explain the higher rate of return; a higher proportion of short-term liabilities *ceteris paribus* reduces the measurement of net assets and raises the measured rate of return. In practice however it can be seen that such biases are unable to explain the differences found. (This is demonstrated in Appendix 7.1. using the results on financial structure in chapter 7.)

Given this, it is of interest to disaggregate the rate of return figures into component parts in order to investigate further. The two possibilities are that the difference arises in terms of profit margins per unit of sales, or that it comes from generating different sales from given net assets. The relevant formula is:

$$\frac{\text{Profit}}{\text{Net assets}} = \frac{\text{Profit}}{\text{Turnover}} \times \frac{\text{Turnover}}{\text{Net assets}}$$

The values of these ratios are also given in Table 6.2.

These further calculations show that the profit margin earned by quoted companies, measured by the ratio of profit to turnover, exceeds that of unquoted companies. However this is more than offset by the ability of unquoted firms to generate a higher level of turnover from given assets. Again both patterns are consistent over the years, and must be taken as evidence of substantive differences. It is tempting to attach significance to these differences in terms of efficiency. However there are too many alternative explanations to make simple deductions. As previously mentioned, they may simply reflect the different sectoral composition of two samples.

Higher profit margins can come about in a number of ways. An

[5] See 'Profitability and Company Finance', *Bank of England Quarterly Bulletin*, vol. 21, no. 2, June 1981, pp. 228–31; also earlier articles in the *Bank of England Quarterly Bulletin*: vol. 20, no. 2, June 1980; vol. 19, no. 4, December 1979; vol. 18, no. 4, December 1978; vol. 17, no. 2, June 1977; and vol. 16, no. 1, March 1976.

TABLE 6.2 Performance Ratios: Quoted and Unquoted Companies, 1971–7

Year	Ratio of profit to net assets		Ratio of profit to turnover		Ratio of turnover to net assets	
	Quoted	Unquoted	Quoted	Unquoted	Quoted	Unquoted
1971	18.5	20.2	9.3	7.5	2.0	2.7
1972	21.2	23.4	10.3	9.0	2.0	2.6
1973	23.1	26.0	11.2	9.7	2.1	2.7
1974	22.4	24.3	10.0	8.6	2.2	2.8
1975	21.3	26.1	9.3	7.7	2.3	3.4
1976	24.1	28.5	10.1	8.2	2.4	3.5
1977	23.6	27.7	9.7	8.1	2.4	3.4

obvious explanation is that quoted companies, being larger, have a greater degree of monopoly power in their markets, and thus have more control over prices and margins on their products. However a similar pattern of margins would be generated if both quoted and unquoted companies operated in competitive price environments, but quoted companies were able to keep costs down by operating at larger scale, and achieved operating or distribution scale economies. The ratio of turnover to assets similarly can be explained by reference to efficiency. The conclusion would be that unquoted companies make better use of their assets and generate a higher level of output from them, but this ignores the use of labour in production. Efficiency needs to be looked at in respect of total factor inputs, not just capital. Between the two samples, the ratio of employment to assets is likely to be higher for unquoted companies,[6] so different labour intensity may account for at least some of the discrepancy between the two groups in respect of the ratio of turnover to assets. Despite this caveat, it is useful also to note that the higher ratio achieved by unquoted companies holds for the ratio of turnover to fixed assets, and for the ratio of turnover to working capital. Unquoted companies register average values of 4.6 and 9.1 respectively for these two ratios. The corresponding values for quoted companies are 3.3 and 6.5.

A third area of comparison between quoted and unquoted companies is the annual growth that they achieve in net assets. Fortunately data are given in *Business Monitor* which allow such growth rates to be calculated on an annual basis, though not over longer periods. The results are given in Table 6.3.

The evidence shows that, if we abstract from cyclical fluctuations in growth affecting both sectors, unquoted firms consistently achieve a higher growth rate. Various explanations can be adduced for this outcome. It may reflect the different sectoral composition of the two samples. Unquoted companies may have a particularly high stake in fast-growing sectors. Alternatively, it may reflect size differences: it is often suggested that it is easier for a small firm to achieve a high growth rate than for a large one. For example, if a large firm already has a large share of a particular market, its growth is likely to be constrained by the growth of that market as a whole, as there may be no scope for increasing market share (or it may be prevented from so doing by

---

[6] We cannot be sure as the available employment data refer to UK employees only.

TABLE 6.3 Annual Growth Rates of Net Assets: Quoted and Unquoted Companies, 1971–7

Year	Growth rate of net assets	
	Quoted	Unquoted
1971	8.7	10.5
1972	14.3	17.5
1973	16.6	20.1
1974	12.3	15.8
1975	13.1	16.9
1976	15.9	18.1
1977	11.0	15.5

consideration of legislation against monopolistic power). The firm with a small market share, on the other hand, has scope for rapid growth arising from increasing that share. Against the argument may be set the fact that larger firms are more diversified, and are more able to take up growth opportunities in a wide spectrum of markets. In fact evidence to be cited later in this chapter suggests that there is no systematic relationship between size and growth. The third, and most plausible, explanation of the differences in growth rates is the objectives and commitment of the firms themselves. The desire to build up the firm, and considerations of taxation, may lead the owners of unquoted companies to retain more profits within the company for reinvestment. Managers of quoted companies may need to pay out more in dividends to shareholders, and they may not be able to raise compensating amounts by new issues. This issue is examined in more detail later.

Because of the limitation of the data source, the number of conclusions which can be drawn is small, but they are still important. The data suggest that unquoted companies are on average much smaller and probably more labour-intensive; their profit margins are lower but the ratio of turnover to capital employed is higher, resulting in a higher rate of return on capital. Although the ratio of the average size of quoted to unquoted companies is slightly larger for 1977 than for 1971 (as measured by net assets) this is because of changes in the composition of the lists of companies; on an annual basis unquoted companies consistently generate higher aggregate growth rates. Against this background we now proceed to more detailed analysis of data on individual companies.

6.4 DISAGGREGATED COMPARISONS: THE LARGE SAMPLE

This section describes the largest comparable data sets available to us on individual quoted and unquoted companies.

The data on quoted companies were derived from the Meeks data base described in Chapter 4. Seven hundred and eighty-three companies were selected on the basis that they had retained their identity in the period 1970–5, and that data were available for that period.[7] For some of the comparisons slightly fewer firms were used. This was usually because calculated ratios were implausible for these companies in a particular year, or because a particular item of information was not available for that firm in that year. At the time the analysis was carried out, information for 1976 was not complete in the file.

The data on unquoted companies were derived from figures on the United Kingdom's top 1000 private companies compiled by Jordan & Sons Ltd. This annual publication which started in the early 1970s lists financial data for 1000 of the United Kingdom's largest unquoted companies by value of turnover. By its very nature, the listing cannot claim to have identified *the* top thousand. However, it does provide a very comprehensive data set of a kind which is simply not available elsewhere. Using the most recent issues of the publication we were able to construct consistent data sets, with a reasonable number of companies represented, for the years 1973–7 inclusive. The numbers were: 1973, 373; 1974, 972; 1975, 1054; 1976, 1037; and 1977, 859. That data were available for more than 1000 firms in 1975 and 1976 reflects the movement of firms in and out of the list. It is unfortunate that the years with a reasonable number of firms in the data set do not overlap more with the availability of information for quoted companies. This means that our substantive comparisons are made on the basis of 1975, though 1973 comparisons are made where data on a sufficient number of firms in one sector are available.

Despite the detailed information available in these two sources, our attempt to make the efficiency comparisons suggested in the previous section met with a number of problems. These are described here, and should be borne in mind when the subsequent analysis is read.

(1) Value-added is the sum of the wages paid by the firm and of its

---

[7] The original intention was to analyse the performance of the same group of firms over the whole period. Hence the restriction to those which retained their identity. Unfortunately it did not prove possible to match this with a similar run of data for unquoted companies.

trading profits after depreciation. Complete wage data do not exist because companies are required to publish only the remuneration of their UK employees. This limitation is made explicit in the list published by Jordan's. We infer that the same problem exists for the Meeks data. Our only comfort is that unquoted companies are less likely to have substantial overseas operations, and that the quoted company sample is restricted to firms that operate wholly or mainly in the United Kingdom; but in so far as firms have overseas operations, the financial details of which are incorporated in the profit-and-loss account and balance-sheet of their UK parent company, there is a definite inadequacy in the information. This does not apply if the subsidiary is run as an independent company which only remits profits to the parent. The latter will then be identified as non-trading profits and can be accounted for.

(2) Pre-tax is defined in Jordan's publication as 'Profits from trading after all charges except taxation. Depreciation, remuneration of directors and audit fees have already been deducted'. The equivalent measure in Meeks's data is operating profit minus depreciation. In terms of the given definitions, these two should be directly comparable.[8]

(3) 'Net tangible assets' are derived from the liability side of the balance-sheet as the sum of ordinary share capital, preference share capital, reserves and long-term liabilities, *less* intangibles. This measure was used in preference to the fixed assets measure because the profit figures quoted in Jordan's list are derived after payment of interest on short-term liabilities. The two measures of assets will diverge to the extent to which fixed assets are financed by short-term borrowings. The measure of fixed assets, derived from the asset side of the balance-sheet, was used for making comparisons between the growth rates of firms.

(4) Employment data relate to the United Kingdom only, and are subject to the same bias as wage income described above.

(5) Sales data were comparable between the two sectors.

(6) The companies in the Meeks data are allocated to Standard Industrial Classification (SIC) sectors on the basis of their principal activity. Not surprisingly, this can lead to a fairly arbitrary allocation in the case of highly diversified companies. SIC listings are not given in Jordan's publication, but a brief description of each company's activity is included. There are fewer highly diversified unquoted companies, but none the less it was not always clear how individual companies should be classified. Some misclassification may have resulted.

---

[8] However, communication with Jordan's suggested that in their data non-trading income had been included with profits for at least some companies.

The method of making comparisons adopted in previous research has involved aggregate indicators of performance of quoted and unquoted firms. Some comparisons have been made for all companies, irrespective of industrial sector: others have distinguished different industrial sectors. The difficulty with such comparisons is that we do not know how significant are the differences that have been discussed. Could they have occurred purely by chance? To pursue this question we have adopted a rather different perspective. The objective is to make fuller use of the evidence relating to an individual firm. Suppose we are making a comparison of profit rates. Our hypothesis is that the profit rate of an individual firm is affected by whether it is unquoted or not, and by the sector in which it operates, but that is far from all. In any sector, whether a firm is quoted or unquoted, it may have good or bad management; it may have a good or bad trading year; its balance-sheet may reflect transitional adjustments arising from a merger or a major investment programme. Hence one expects within a sample of companies to find a wide variation in performance about a mean which is determined by company status (quoted or unquoted) and the sector within which they operate. Our method then is to take *all* the companies within a particular sector and derive the characteristics of the distribution of individual returns. Given that our sample includes the majority of large quoted companies, and the largest unquoted companies, we can be sure that our analysis will give an accurate picture of what that distribution is. The companies are then distinguished according to status, quoted or unquoted. The question is then whether observed differences can be attributed to the chance impact of these other factors on the companies, or whether they reflect a distinct bunching of returns within that overall distribution. The appropriate formal statistical test is one which gives the probability of an observed difference being due to chance.[9] Conventionally we accept that a difference exists if there is less than a 1 in 20 probability that it occurred due to chance; if the probability rises to 1 in 10 we take note, but are not convinced. If it is less than that we ignore the difference as insignificant. (These conditions are usually described as being significant at the 5 and 10 per cent levels. A 1 per cent level of significance means that there is only a 1 in 100 possibility that the observed difference was due to chance.)

An alternative to the hypothesis that company status makes a significant difference is that performance is related to size. Since quoted

---

[9] The strict conditions for the test are violated in so far as the profit rates of different firms are related, e.g. the success of one firm may be at the expense of others.

companies tend to be larger than unquoted, there is a possibility that differences may be attributed to status where they should be related to size. Unfortunately we have too few companies within each classification (quoted and unquoted) in overlapping size classes to be able to control effectively for size in making comparisons. Instead we have looked for systematic size effects in performance within our samples of quoted and unquoted firms. If such effects are present, and are substantial, then the comparisons need to be more cautiously interpreted.

Measures of efficiency based on value-added per employee and value-added per fixed assets in 1975 are given in Table 6.4. Certain sectors are omitted because of lack of sufficient firms in the unquoted data set: Sector 24, tobacco; 37, shipbuilding and marine engineering; and 10, mining and quarrying. Sector 88, miscellaneous services, is included, but we have reason to believe that the types of firms differ substantially between the two samples. The unquoted firms are predominantly garages: the quoted ones are a much more diverse group. Sample numbers in other sectors are given in Table 6.4. It is clear that the unquoted sample is relatively small in some sectors, especially vehicles (Sector 38); bricks, pottery, etc. (46); and timber, furniture etc. (47); but it is strongly represented in construction (50) and wholesale distribution (81).

The variation within each sector sample was examined by calculating the coefficient of variation, which is the ratio of the standard deviation (our measure of dispersion) to the mean. Overall, for value-added per employee there was no discernible difference between quoted and unquoted firms, but value-added per fixed assets was much more variable for unquoted firms within a sector. This may reflect measurement problems.

Turning to results, for the nineteen sectors in which comparison was feasible with our samples, the mean value-added per employee of unquoted companies was higher in twelve sectors. However in only three, food, mechanical engineering and paper, printing, etc. were the differences statistically significant. Of the seven adverse comparisons only two were statistically significant; one of these was miscellaneous services where the validity of the comparison is in doubt. Our expectation was that the quoted sector firms, being on average larger than their unquoted counterparts, might be more capital-intensive, in which case the mean value-added per employee should be higher, each employee being equipped with more capital. That it should not turn out to be so is somewhat surprising, especially when taken in conjunction

TABLE 6.4 Value added measures of efficiency: quoted versus unquoted, 1975

Industry	Sector no.	Number of firms Quoted	Number of firms Unquoted	Mean value-added per employee Quoted	Mean value-added per employee Unquoted	Mean value-added per employee Difference	Mean value-added per fixed assets Quoted	Mean value-added per fixed assets Unquoted	Mean value-added per fixed assets Difference
Food	21	23	39	3.289	3.554	0.265*	0.843	1.292	0.449**
Drink	23	38	25	4.021	3.638	−0.383	0.449	0.831	0.382**
Chemicals	26	34	21	5.025	4.285	−0.740	0.885	1.513	0.628**
Metal manufacture	31	25	13	3.377	3.755	0.378	1.298	2.083	0.785**
Mechanical Eng.	33	89	42	3.563	4.308	0.745**	1.952	2.705	0.753**
Electrical Eng.	36	39	20	3.442	3.285	−0.157	2.222	3.461	1.239**
Vehicles	38	25	5	3.117	3.382	0.265	1.669	3.033	1.364**
Metal goods n.e.s.	39	47	16	3.481	3.712	0.231	1.338	2.478	1.140**
Textiles	41	53	31	2.656	2.875	0.219	1.389	2.119	0.810**
Clothing, footwear	44	24	13	2.253	2.055	−0.198	2.331	3.636	1.305**
Bricks, etc.	46	35	9	3.916	3.660	−0.256	0.990	2.498	1.508**
Timber, furniture	47	17	8	3.669	3.967	0.298	1.914	1.896	−0.018
Paper, printing	48	52	53	3.496	3.944	0.448**	1.335	1.625	0.290
Other manufacturing	49	30	13	3.301	3.315	0.014	1.362	2.507	1.145**
Construction	50	55	107	3.912	3.963	0.051	1.967	3.339	1.372**
Transport, comm.	70	8	23	3.499	4.933	1.434	0.852	2.122	1.270
Wholesale distribution	81	51	134	3.912	4.212	0.300	1.542	1.906	0.364
Retail distribution	82	61	60	2.986	2.486	−0.500**	1.052	1.355	0.303*
Misc. services	88	54	123	3.032	2.592	−0.440**	0.926	1.640	0.714**

* Statistically significant difference at 10% level.
** Statistically significant difference at at least 5% level.

with our comparisons of mean value-added per fixed assets, for these latter comparisons show that the unquoted sectors have a higher productivity in eighteen out of nineteen sectors. In fifteen of these cases the difference is statistically significant. Taking the measures together we find two sectors, retail distribution and miscellaneous services, where unquoted firms have lower value-added per employee, but higher value-added per fixed assets. In these cases we can make no comment on total productivity of factor use as between quoted and unquoted firms. Of the remaining sectors there are three, timber, furniture, etc., wholesale distribution and transport and communication, where no significant differences are evident on either measure. For all the other sectors there are statistically significant differences which favour unquoted companies.

To check the consistency of these results, comparisons were made for 1973 for the ten sectors in which there were sufficient data on unquoted companies. Comparisons of value-added per employee gave adverse differences in six out of the ten sectors, but only two (construction and retail distribution) were significant. In the other four sectors, unquoted companies had higher average indices, but this was only significant in mechanical engineering (Sector 33) as it was in 1975. Company value-added per fixed assets gave favourable differences to unquoted companies in nine out of ten cases, and three were statistically significant. We conclude that the 1975 results are not a freak observation.[10]

Our second method of efficiency comparison is to calculate the rate of return on net tangible assets, i.e. that part of the liability side of the balance-sheet which reflects the commitment of savings long term to the firm. The results are tabulated for 1975 in Table 6.5. Excluding the mining sector, the tobacco industry, the shipbuilding sector and the leather industry from both quoted and unquoted samples, because there were too few firms, and rejecting those companies from which the data were not available in that year, we ended with samples of 745 firms in the

---

[10] Before we conclude that the unquoted sector is more efficient, we need to consider the alternative explanations. Problems with the data have been discussed previously. However, we should perhaps look again at the exclusion of overseas wages and employment in calculating the ratios. The effect of these omissions will be to bias down the ratios of value-added to fixed assets for companies with important overseas operations, and to bias up the value-added per employee ratios for the same companies. Presuming that the profits share of income is rather smaller than the wage share, the former bias will be larger than the latter However, for this to explain the results of Table 6.4 one would have to postulate either that the unquoted sector had a very large part of its operations abroad, or that the share of profits in value-added is implausibly low. Also, in so far as one uses this to account for the large reported differences in average value-added per fixed assets, one is faced with the difficulty that the same effect does not show up as differences in value-added per employee, which should favour the quoted sector.

TABLE 6.5 Rate of Return on Net Tangible Assets: Comparison of Quoted and Unquoted Firms, 1975

Industry	Sector no.	Number of firms		Rate of return on net tangible assets		
		Quoted	Unquoted	Quoted	Unquoted	Difference
Food	21	23	55	0.176	0.208	0.032
Drink	23	38	29	0.164	0.173	0.009
Chemicals	26	32	23	0.184	0.220	0.036
Metal manufacture	31	24	17	0.127	0.173	0.046
Mechanical engineering	33	87	49	0.194	0.212	0.018
Electrical engineering	36	38	22	0.230	0.109	−0.121*
Vehicles	38	23	5	0.016	0.111	0.095
Metal goods n.e.s.	39	47	19	0.200	0.187	−0.013
Textiles	41	51	35	0.117	0.132	0.015
Clothing, footwear, etc.	44	24	13	0.214	0.144	−0.070
Bricks, pottery, etc.	46	35	9	0.179	0.197	0.018
Timber, furniture, etc.	47	17	8	0.146	0.198	0.052
Paper, printing, etc.	48	51	57	0.135	0.176	0.042
Other manufacturing	49	30	13	0.197	0.166	−0.031
Construction	50	53	117	0.215	0.204	−0.011
Transport, communication, etc.	70	8	42	0.190	0.264	0.074
Wholesale distribution	81	51	319	0.194	0.352	0.158*
Retail distribution	82	60	63	0.223	0.169	−0.054*
Miscellaneous services	88	53	123	0.052	0.113	0.061

n.e.s. = not elsewhere specified.
* Statistically significant difference at 5 per cent level.

quoted sector and 1018 in the unquoted. The distribution of the samples between industries is of some interest in its own right, as they represent approximately the distribution of the major companies in the quoted and unquoted sectors. Thus nearly 70 per cent of the quoted firms, but only 35 per cent of the unquoted, are in manufacturing. Construction (Sector 50) and wholesale distribution (81) figure prominently in the unquoted sector. Within manufacturing there are relatively few un-quoted companies in vehicles (38); bricks, pottery, etc. (46); and timber, furniture, etc. (47). The large number of quoted firms in mechanical engineering (33) is notable.

Table 6.5 shows that the unquoted companies registered a higher return on net tangible assets in 1975 in thirteen out of nineteen sectors. However only one of these was statistically significant. The comparison was adverse in six industries and in two cases the difference was statistically significant. The unquoted sector had the largest margin over the quoted sector in wholesale distribution, vehicles and transport, etc. For 1973, the unquoted sample dropped to 370 companies for which information was available, and comparisons could only be made in eleven sectors. Out of these, five were favourable to the unquoted sector, though only one was statistically significant. In the other six, unquoted firms had a lower return, the differences being significant in mechanical engineering and textiles.

Our conclusion must be that although the data do show some major differences in returns between unquoted and quoted companies, in the majority of cases we are not able to reject the hypothesis that the observed differences were due to chance. This can only be resolved by making comparisons over a number of years. What could be a chance difference in one year cannot be so easily ignored if it persists over a number of years. However, our results here are not inconsistent with the aggregate analysis of the *Business Monitor* series above. The conclusions were that the differences between the sectors which were notable in the late 1960s were narrowing in the first half of the 1970s. Whether this is a long-term feature can only be decided with information for a longer period of time (see Section 6.5).

The third method of efficiency comparison is to calculate growth rates between 1973 and 1975. Growth is measured in terms of employment, fixed assets and sales. The recorded growth rates for the last two are inflated by the rapid change in prices over the two years, but so long as it may be presumed that this affected the two sectors equally it should not interfere with comparisons between quoted and unquoted firms. Once again we were severely constrained in what we could do by the availability of information for the unquoted sector. We were able to calculate growth rates for fixed assets and sales for more than 280 companies, but for employment, data were only available for 186 firms. Furthermore, the information tended to be concentrated on a few sectors where unquoted firms are more important. In manufacturing, comparisons were possible for only six or seven out of the sixteen sectors. In the rest the number of unquoted companies was less than five and valid comparisons could not be made. Once again, the method adopted was to test for significant differences between the means of the two samples within each sector. The hypothesis is that the growth rate of a firm in any given period is a 'random' variable. This is not to say that the firm has no control over its own experience. Rather, in looking at a group of firms in a given period, while they are likely to have certain features in common – the growth of the market, the level of labour costs, the supply conditions for materials – they will also have their own particular features specific to the firm, e.g. varying quality of management, particular products, unforeseen difficulties such as strikes, etc. The incidence of these features is specific to any one firm but is random to a group of firms. Hence we expect the group to have an identifiable common element in their growth (the mean growth rate), and individual firms to do better or worse depending on their specific experience. Our samples of quoted and unquoted firms will have different means. Our concern is whether these differences are systematic or could have occurred by chance. The results of such an analysis are set out in Table 6.6.

The most striking feature of the employment situation in the period 1973–5 is the shedding of labour by quoted companies. In every sector except mechanical engineering and paper, printing, etc., quoted firms on average reduced their labour force. By comparison, in sectors for which there are firms in the unquoted sample, the average recorded change in employment is positive in fourteen sectors and negative in only six. Unfortunately, the experience of firms both in the quoted sector and the unquoted sector was very variable, and in only one sector does the difference reach statistically significant levels. The one sector is textiles, where, in a period of substantial contraction in employment by the quoted firms, unquoted firms achieved on average a modest rise in employment. At the very least the evidence supports the view that the smaller unquoted firms were generally effective in providing new employment opportunities at a time when larger firms were shedding labour.

One possible explanation of the employment pattern is that the

TABLE 6.6   Growth of quoted (Q) and unquoted (UQ) companies, by sector, 1973–5

Sector No.	Sector	Growth rates of employment 1973–5				
		Q		UQ		Difference of means
		Mean	N	Mean	N	
10	Mining	−0.163	9	−0.089	3	
21	Food	−0.461	22	0.064	16	0.525
23	Drink	−0.203	37	0.027	2	
26	Chemicals	−0.053	34	−0.029	5	0.024
31	Metal manufacturing	−0.486	25	0.136	2	
33	Mechanical engineering	0.005	89	0.056	10	0.051
36	Electrical engineering	−0.043	39	−0.124	6	−0.081
37	Shipbuilding	−0.061	4	–	–	
38	Vehicles	−0.101	25	−0.481	2	
39	Metal goods n.e.s.	−0.065	47	0.007	4	
41	Textiles	−0.104	53	0.060	9	0.164**
43	Leather	−0.046	6	–	–	
44	Clothing, footwear	−0.027	24	0.213	3	
46	Bricks, etc.	−0.089	35	0.069	2	
47	Timber, furniture	−0.119	17	−0.007	3	
48	Paper, printing	0.012	52	0.006	10	−0.006
49	Other manufacturing	−0.050	30	−0.149	4	
50	Construction	−0.397	53	0.044	25	0.441
70	Transport, communication	−0.053	8	0.053	6	0.106
81	Wholesale distribution	−0.007	51	0.014	38	0.021
82	Retail distribution	−0.024	61	0.022	14	0.046
88	Misc. services	−0.446	52	0.012	22	0.458

N is number of firms for which data were available.
** difference in means significant at 1 % level.
* difference in means significant at 5 % level.
† implausible values suppressed: possibly due to errors in data source.
Differences in means is calculated only if information available for at least 5 unquoted companies.

| Growth rates of fixed assets 1973–5 | | | | | Growth rates of sales 1973–5 | | | | |
| Q | | UQ | | Difference of means | Q | | UQ | | Difference of Means |
Mean	N	Mean	N		Mean	N	Mean	N	
0.194	9	0.177	3		−0.006	9	0.267	3	
0.165	22	0.419	27	0.254**	0.307	23	0.335	27	0.028
0.251	37	0.021	2		0.309	37	0.347	2	
0.202	34	0.612	8	0.410**	0.302	34	0.590	8	0.288**
0.175	25	+	4		0.266	25	0.377	4	
0.202	89	0.368	13	0.166**	0.252	89	0.787	13	0.535**
0.214	39	0.034	7	−0.180**	0.269	39	0.321	7	0.052
0.135	4	−	−		0.154	4	−	−	
0.188	25	−0.123	2		0.226	25	−0.103	2	
0.229	47	+	5		0.260	47	0.281	5	0.021
0.099	53	0.109	11	0.010	0.156	53	0.345	11	0.189**
0.268	6	0.053	2		0.180	6	0.021	2	
0.074	24	0.179	3		0.237	24	0.367	3	
0.178	35	0.668	2		0.260	35	0.544	2	
0.135	17	0.213	3		0.074	17	0.320	3	
0.229	52	0.442	10	0.213**	0.299	52	0.354	10	0.035
0.188	30	0.301	4		0.296	30	0.265	4	
0.196	53	0.449	26	0.253**	0.273	53	0.546	26	0.273**
0.180	8	0.408	9	0.228**	0.227	8	0.589	9	0.362**
0.164	51	0.916	95	0.752**	0.238	50	0.403	94	0.165*
0.177	61	0.614	15	0.437**	0.275	61	0.521	15	0.246**
0.182	52	0.384	32	0.202**	0.138	54	0.316	32	0.178*

quoted firms were shedding labour because they were being more efficient. For example, a period of rising labour costs could induce them to invest more and increase their capital–labour ratio. Unquoted firms would be absorbing labour because they were not investing at the same rate. However, the evidence on capital accumulation and growth of sales does not support this view. In the eleven sectors for which comparisons could be made, the average growth rate of fixed assets in the unquoted companies exceeded that of quoted firms in ten cases. Nine of these were highly significant statistically and represented a very substantial difference in growth experience. The sole exception was electrical engineering. The picture which emerges is that the unquoted firms were both investing more and taking on more labour than their quoted counterparts in this period. By contrast the quoted firms were investing at a lower rate and shedding labour. Not surprisingly, the expansion of the unquoted firms is reflected in the growth rates of sales. On this measure comparisons could be made in twelve sectors. In every case the unquoted firms had grown faster: in eight sectors, the differences were statistically significant.

Putting all the information together there is abundant evidence to suggest that in the period 1973–5 the unquoted sector was altogether more dynamic than the quoted sector. It was selling more, investing more and on average taking on more labour. This is consistent with the view of unquoted companies as a 'seed-bed' for fast-growing firms and products. The evidence is particularly strong for non-traded goods – construction, transport, distribution and services – which are the areas where unquoted companies have always been preponderant. However, there is also support for this view in the manufacturing sector, where unquoted companies did well in food, chemicals, mechanical engineering and textiles. Again these are sectors where unquoted firms are well represented.

6.5 THE EFFECT OF COMPANY SIZE ON PERFORMANCE

One of the important remaining issues is whether the differences detected between quoted and unquoted samples can be attributed solely to size differences between the firms in the two sectors. To explore this possibility we examined the relationship between firm size and efficiency indicators within both quoted and unquoted sectors. If a systematic size effect was found we then checked to see whether this could account for observed differences in the sectors. In general, we found that it could not, and the report of this analysis will therefore be brief. Previous work has been restricted to quoted firms alone;[11] so the extension of the analysis to the unquoted sector is particularly interesting.

Value-added per fixed assets was found to be negatively correlated with size, measured either by sales or net assets, in both quoted and unquoted sectors, in seventeen out of the nineteen industries. The exceptions were drink and vehicles. At least half the correlations were significant at the 5 per cent level. The relationship tended to be stronger for net assets than for sales and the regression coefficients were larger. The coefficients were also larger for the unquoted firms, suggesting that size effects may be more marked within that sector than in the quoted sector. This would be compatible with a non-linear relationship with size over all the companies in both quoted and unquoted sectors, with value-added per fixed assets falling sharply at first with increased size, but the effect becoming much less marked for the largest size group of firms.[12]

Value-added per employee showed no systematic relation to size of firm across all industries. However, both in the quoted and unquoted sectors, significantly positive associations were found for chemicals (Sector 26); mechanical engineering (33); and paper, printing, etc. (48). Once again the effect, as indicated by the size of the regression coefficients, was much larger for unquoted than for quoted firms, suggesting a non-linear relationship, i.e. value-added per employee increases with size of firm but at a diminishing rate. In each significant case the positive association between size and value-added per employee was offset by a significant negative association with value-added per net assets. This is consistent with capital intensity within these sectors increasing with size of firm. What makes these results particularly interesting is that in mechanical engineering and paper, printing, etc. we found that value-added per employee was significantly *higher* in the

---

[11] See, for example, D. J. Smyth, W. J. Boyes and D. E. Peseau, *Size, Growth, Profits and Executive Compensation in the Large Corporations* (Macmillan, 1975).

[12] To take an extreme example, metal manufacture, the coefficient on size in a regression of value-added per fixed assets on net assets size was -0.0009 for unquoted companies, and -0.00000045 for quoted. Only the former result was statistically significant. With assets measured in £000s, the implication is that an extra £1 million of assets would lead to a fall of 0.9 in value-added per fixed assets in the unquoted sector, but only 0.0005 in the quoted sector. These compare with averages of 3.755 and 3.377 respectively in the two sectors. As the range of company sizes is approximately from £2 million to £6 million of assets in the unquoted sector, and from £2 million to £16 million in the quoted sector, it clearly makes a great difference which coefficient we regard as appropriate for calculating the effect of size. Ideally we should estimate the size effect by pooling the samples. Unfortunately data problems precluded us from exploring this possibility.

unquoted than in the quoted sector. This must then be despite the smaller average size of the unquoted companies in these industries. The implication is that these are particularly efficient operations, especially since the comparisons of value-added per fixed'assets were also favourable to the unquoted firms.

Rates of return on net assets are not statistically significantly related to size within either the quoted or unquoted sector. However, it is worth recording that virtually all of the coefficients in the regressions were negative, but each was so small that it could not make a difference to our comparisons between the two sectors. Once again, the coefficients were larger in the unquoted sector, suggesting a non-linear relationship with size over the combined samples. Smyth *et al.*[13] examined the size-profitability relationship across the largest 500 and 1000 UK companies in the period 1970–3. They did not distinguish between sectors. They concluded that there was a statistically significant size effect, but that it was very small. For example, if the assets measure of company size is used, a ten-fold increase in size produces an average diminution of rate of return of only 0.016 per cent. In addition, their work showed that only about 6 per cent of the variation in company profits is explicable by size. Exactly the same result was found for an analysis of the largest 500 US corporations. These results are entirely compatible with our more detailed analysis, sector by sector.

We also examined the relationship between growth rates and size within the quoted and unquoted sectors by industries. The growth rates were calculated for the period 1973–5 for sales, employment and fixed assets. These were then regressed on the appropriate size variable at the beginning of the period. In the quoted sample we found no systematic association between size and growth. Few of the correlations were statistically significant and as many were positive as negative. This result contrasts strongly with those reported by Smyth *et al.* in their study of the largest 500 industrial firms. They found that smaller firms grew faster than large ones in the period 1971–3. This contrasted with previous findings (mainly relating to the 1960s) that large firms grow faster. The differences may well be caused by the trade cycle. For unquoted companies our data base enabled us to examine the relationship of initial employment and fixed assets to growth for the period 1973–5 as in the case of quoted companies. With one exception, few statistically significant relationships were found, but it is worth record-

---

[13] Smyth, Boyes and Peseau, *Size, Growth, Profits and Executive Compensation*, ch. 4.

ing that the majority of the coefficients on size variables in the regressions were negative. This suggests that if a relationship does exist it is likely to favour the growth of small firms. Our general conclusion is that the statistically significant differences in growth rates between quoted and unquoted companies, identified above, cannot be accounted for by differences in size; our favourable judgement on efficiency in growth of the unquoted firms stands.

The results obtained in Sections 6.4 and 6.5 are at once more detailed, more reliable and more striking than those derived from the *Business Monitor* series. The two are none the less quite consistent. Profitability appears higher in the unquoted sector, though the difference is rarely statistically significant; growth is higher and the difference frequently is significant; evidence on value-added supports the view derived from profit and growth data that the unquoted sector operates more efficiently. In general these differences cannot be explained in terms of the different average size of quoted and unquoted companies.

6.6 THE SMALL SAMPLE RESULTS

The analysis of efficiency in Section 6.4 suffers from the drawback of being restricted to a very short time-period. This may not be too serious in relation to value-added per employee and value-added per fixed assets because statistically significant deviations between their values for the quoted and unquoted sectors respectively are unlikely to vary widely from year to year. However profit and growth rates are likely to fluctuate much more as a result of random company-specific factors, and very short-run observations are therefore more suspect. We therefore re-examine these performance measures using an alternative longer-term data base. The analysis can also be extended to give some insight into company objectives.

For longer-term analysis sub-samples of quoted and unquoted companies were constructed as the basis of our third approach. By cutting down the coverage of our sample we can gain in terms of the detail available and the time-span covered. First, all those unquoted companies in the Jordan 1000 with significant operations in more than one SIC were ignored. Sixty were then selected at random from the undiversified companies, three being from each of twenty sectors. The company accounts of these sixty companies were then collated for the period 1966–79, and the data entered into a computerised data bank in standardised format.[14] One hundred and eighty companies were then selected at random from the Meeks data of quoted companies, nine from each of the twenty sectors, having eliminated all those for which a complete data set to 1975 was unavailable. This data bank was supplemented by figures for certain key variables for later years direct from company accounts.

This procedure introduces or retains at least two biases. First, the unquoted companies are large relative to the average size of unquoted companies. The effects of size, which have been examined already in relation to large-sample work must therefore be borne in mind, and are addressed explicitly below. Second, all diversified companies are excluded. This was done to improve the comparability of the quoted and unquoted companies, but runs the risk of distortion. Financing, risk-taking, associated returns and growth may all differ systematically for diversified companies, but there is no obvious reason to believe that these differences will be closely linked to a company's status. The gains from this procedure are therefore likely to outweigh any losses to a significant degree.

Five sectors were subsequently dropped from the analysis because there was an insufficient number of undiversified companies of one or other status with complete figures for the whole period.[15]

The main use of this new data base is to explore the financial characteristics of quoted and unquoted companies, and this is pursued in the next chapter. Here we focus again on profitability and growth to see what further insight is available. Table 6.7 gives fourteen-year average values for various measures of rates of return and for growth of capital employed for the sample quoted and unquoted companies for fifteen sectors. The first point to note from this smaller but much longer-term sample is that overall the average profit and growth rates are higher for unquoted companies than quoted ones. In terms of gross operating profit rates of return this pattern is observed in eleven of the fifteen sectors. Netting-out depreciation makes no difference to this, but netting-out interest payments as well reduces the number to ten. After deduction of tax, eight of the fifteen sectors reveal higher profit rates for unquoted companies.

Second, the average growth rate of unquoted companies is also substantially higher, this pattern again emerging in eleven of the fifteen

---

[14] The source of this data is Companies House, Cardiff.
[15] In some cases a further search could have circumvented this problem but would have extended the time taken and was not regarded as essential.

Sector	Gross operating profit rate§		Gross profit rate†		Profit rate net of depreciation		Profit rate net of depreciation and interest		Profit rate net of depreciation, interest and tax		Growth rate of capital employed‡	
	Q	UQ	Q	UQ	Q	UQ	Q	UQ	Q	UQ	Q	UQ
Food	20.9	17.9	21.9	20.0	14.7	12.0	13.6	11.9	8.3	6.3	25.1	110.0
Drink	16.9	30.6	17.5	31.8	15.0	26.1	14.1	26.1	8.6	13.3	11.7	15.8
Chemicals	22.7	25.7	23.7	27.4	16.7	20.6	15.8	20.4	8.3	12.5	12.1	15.5
Metal manufacture	18.5	42.2	19.2	44.1	13.3	36.8	12.7	36.8	7.7	19.1	7.9	22.9
Non-electrical engineering	20.9	14.9	22.2	17.8	16.4	10.4	15.8	10.2	8.8	13.8	14.3	10.0
Electrical engineering	31.0	21.6	32.4	22.9	26.1	15.2	25.2	15.0	13.7	7.6	15.8	16.4
Textiles	17.2	34.1	18.0	34.3	11.0	22.0	10.2	21.8	6.5	11.4	5.9	28.9
Leather, fur, etc.	27.8	37.5	28.2	37.9	22.1	33.0	21.5	33.0	31.1	17.2	14.6	15.3
Clothing, footwear, etc.	22.2	25.9	23.2	26.6	18.6	18.8	17.7	18.2	9.9	9.8	12.9	12.8
Bricks, pottery, etc.	27.2	31.1	28.2	31.4	19.5	22.5	18.7	21.4	11.4	10.8	15.4	23.3
Timber, furniture, etc.	22.1	28.9	23.1	29.0	17.8	23.9	17.2	23.2	9.9	12.8	9.8	18.4
Paper, printing, etc.	20.7	34.2	21.8	40.0	14.3	26.1	13.4	23.4	7.0	10.8	12.7	11.0
Construction	25.2	26.9	26.9	27.2	15.5	18.9	14.8	12.6	8.1	6.2	13.8	13.6
Transport, commun., etc.	29.6	25.3	30.7	27.4	20.8	14.4	20.0	11.5	12.7	8.6	9.7	51.1
Wholesale distribution	24.5	31.4	25.1	31.6	20.5	29.2	20.0	29.2	11.6	16.5	15.1	19.7
Average	23.2	28.5	24.1	30.0	17.5	22.0	16.7	21.0	9.7	11.1	13.1	19.6

* All figures are percentages.
† Gross profit equals gross operating profit plus non-trading income. All profit rates are expressed as a percentage of capital employed (net assets) and are on historic cost basis.
‡ The average growth rate of capital employed of unquoted companies excludes the outlying figure for the food sector.
§ Q: quoted; UQ: unquoted.

TABLE 6.8   Comparison of Three Data Sources*

(a) *Profit rates (net of depreciation)*

	Quoted		Unquoted		All companies†	
	Large sample	Small sample	Large sample	Small sample	Large sample	Small sample
Average, 1975	17.5	16.4	19.6	20.4	18.6	18.4
Average, 1966–79	—	17.5	—	22.0	—	19.8

(b) *Profit rates (gross operating rates)*

	Quoted		Unquoted		All companies	
	Business Monitor	Small sample	Business Monitor	Small sample	Business Monitor	Small sample
Average, 1971–7	22.0	24.2	25.2	28.1	23.6	26.1
Average, 1966–79	—	23.2	—	28.5	—	25.8

TABLE 6.8 (contd.)

(c) Growth rates (capital employed)

	Quoted		Unquoted		All companies	
	Business Monitor	Small sample	Business Monitor	Small sample	Business Monitor	Small sample
Average, 1971–7	13.1	14.6	16.3	19.1	14.7	16.8
Average, 1966–79	—	13.1	—	19.6	—	16.3

* All figures are percentages.
† These figures give the averages of the two sectors rather than the average across all individual companies, because the numbers of quoted and unquoted companies differ.

sectors. In two more the figures are almost exactly equal. In only one sector, non-electrical engineering, do the unquoted companies have both lower average growth and a lower gross operating rate. If profit rate is measured net of depreciation, interest and tax, then this is also true for clothing, footwear, etc. and construction.

No great weight can be attached to comparisons for any individual sector because of the small sample involved. Certainly statistical significance tests would not in general be passed at this level. Yet the fact that the figures pertain to a period of fourteen years and generate a very similar pattern in the great majority of sectors make the figures of background interest to our analysis.

Before reporting the main analysis it is worth comparing these overall figures with those obtained from our two earlier data sources. In general the three sets of data appear reasonably consistent. Averages for sectors appearing in both samples are shown in Table 6.8, together with the aggregate *Business Monitor* figures.

In terms of net profit rates, the small sample of unquoted companies is slightly more profitable (0.8 per cent) than the large sample; the discrepancy for quoted companies, though still small (0.9 per cent), goes the other way. This may reflect the fact that companies had to survive for the whole fourteen-year period to be included in the small sample. Given the greater variability of profits of unquoted companies,[16] they probably require a higher rate of return on average to avoid liquidation when conditions are depressed. In both groups average profits were higher over the whole period than in 1975, reflecting in part conditions in 1975, but also the secular decline in profits over this period. The difference between average profits over the period and profits in 1975 is greater for unquoted companies, reflecting the fact that profits of unquoted companies, though higher than those of quoted companies, declined faster over the period.

Comparison of profitability as between the *Business Monitor* cases and the small sample are also fairly close. The small sample is again more profitable both for quoted and unquoted companies, again reflecting the bias that it contains only companies who survived the whole fourteen-year period. Similar comments apply to the comparison of growth rates.[17]

---

[16] Standard deviation of post-tax profits equals 0.079 for quoted companies and 0.125 for unquoted companies.

[17] The large sample cannot be compared for growth rates as the measurement basis was different, i.e. employment, fixed assets and sales rather than capital employed.

The data on growth and profits were employed for two basic purposes. The first was to make further comparisons of profitability and growth as measures of efficiency. The sample comprises data for 180 companies for fourteen years. These data were pooled and an analysis of variance carried out, i.e. the data were examined to see whether variations in profitability and growth could be explained in terms of certain characteristics of the sample. In principle four different characteristics might be significant factors in determining the pattern of profitability and growth, and of interest in the present context. These are status (i.e. quoted or unquoted), sector, year and size.

The method employed in analysis of variance is to identify each characteristic that makes a statistically significant contribution to explaining the observed pattern of profits and of growth, in order of its importance. The procedure was carried out twice, first ignoring size, so that status, sectors and years could be listed in order of their contribution, and second, repeating the process but with size included. This second stage was itself split into two, the first stage using capital employed as a measure of size, the second stage using sales. The results are presented in Table 6.9.

These results reveal a number of interesting features. First, ignoring for the moment the possible impact of company size, for all four pre-tax measures of profitability the most significant characteristic is whether a company is quoted or unquoted. Depending on the measure of profitability used the average rate of return is higher in unquoted companies by the amounts shown in Table 6.10.

In each case the difference is statistically significant. Being unquoted makes a smaller difference to post-tax profits and in addition is only the fourth largest contributor to an explanation of the variance of profits. To the extent that unquoted companies pay out proportionately higher directors' remuneration, albeit because of their smaller relative size, these figures underestimate the higher profitability of unquoted companies.

With regard to growth, being unquoted is the second most important explanation, is again statistically significant and on average results in a growth rate 13.6 per cent p.a. higher than quoted companies. This figure will however be lower if the extreme figure for growth of unquoted companies in the food sector is omitted.

Certain sectors stand out as generally being more profitable for both quoted and unquoted companies, in particular leather, fur etc. (Sector 43); electrical engineering (36); wholesale distribution (81); and transport, communication, etc. (70). One sector stands out as being less

TABLE 6.9 Analysis of Profit and Growth Rates

Variable	Status	Sectors									
Block 1 – Size Excluded Block 2 – Capital Included Block 3 – Sales Included	(UNQ > Q)	21	23	26/7	31	33	36	41	43	44	46
Gross Operating Profit Rate	0.053								0.024		
Gross Profit Rate	0.055								0.018		
Profit Net of Depreciation	0.045						0.018	−0.075	0.040		
Profit Net of Depreciation and Interest	0.043						0.020	−0.072	0.045		
Profit Net of Depreciation, Interest and Tax	0.013						0.013		0.036		0.006
Growth Rate	0.136										
Gross Operating Profit Rate	0.067								0.020		
Gross Profit Rate	0.068								0.012		
Profit Net of Depreciation	0.052						0.023	−0.070	0.044		
Profit Net of Depreciation and Interest	0.052						0.011	−0.081	0.035		
Profit Net of Depreciation, Interest and Tax	0.017			0.010			0.013		0.035		0.005
Growth Rate	0.136										
Gross Operating Profit Rate	0.070								0.020		
Gross Profit Rate	0.072								0.011		
Profit Net of Depreciation	0.059						0.014	−0.079	0.034		
Profit Net of Depreciation and Interest	0.057						0.016	−0.076	0.038		
Profit Net of Depreciation, Interest and Tax	0.021			0.009			0.012		0.034		0.004
Growth Rate	0.136										

Notes: 1. The sectors indicated by numbers are identified in Table 6.4, apart from no. 41, which is Textiles.
2. Only differences which are significant at the 5% level are included in the table.

					Years												Size
47	48	50	70	81	67	68	69	70	71	72	73	74	75	76	77	78	K/S
														0.039			
														0.042			
				0.015						0.027				0.029			
				0.020			−0.024	−0.028		0.025				0.028			
			0.004	0.022						0.059				0.054			
									0.260	0.145							
		0.017					−0.031	−0.030						0.040			−0.023
		0.016					−0.030	−0.030						0.043			−0.02
				0.020			−0.025	−0.023		0.026				0.030			−0.014
				0.011			−0.026	−0.029						0.029			−0.012
			0.013	0.022			−0.017	−0.015	0.019	0.041			0.015	0.037			−0.008
									0.260	0.145							
							−0.033	−0.031						0.040			−0.009
							−0.032	−0.031						0.044			−0.009
				0.018			−0.027	−0.025		0.024				0.031			−0.008
				0.023			−0.030	−0.033						0.028			−0.008
			0.006	0.026			−0.018	−0.016	0.018	0.039			0.014	0.037			−0.005
									0.260	0.145							

TABLE 6.10   Differences in Profitability between Quoted and Unquoted Companies (Small Samples; Size Effects excluded)

Profit measure	Unquoted minus Quoted %
Gross operating profit rate	+5.3
Gross profit rate	+5.5
Profit net of depreciation	+4.5
Profit net of depreciation and interest	+4.3
Profit net of depreciation, interest and tax	+1.3

profitable, namely textiles (41). It may be noted that the relatively good performance of unquoted companies revealed in the current comparison cannot be explained in terms of their preponderance in highly profitable sectors. Our small sample standardises the number of quoted and unquoted companies in each sector, and the analysis of variance identifies the independent contribution of status and sector to the pattern of profitability. It may be added however that, with the notable exception of wholesale distribution, there are no indications from the large sample that unquoted companies are more preponderant in more profitable sectors. This is of significance in deriving the relative efficiency of the two classes of company from *aggregate* figures for the United Kingdom as a whole (see p. 147). The yearly differences clearly pick up cyclical fluctuations, with depressed profits in 1969 and 1979, higher levels in 1972 and again in 1976. Profits dip inbetween but the variation, at least in nominal profits, is not statistically significant.

In general the analysis explains relatively little of the overall variation in profits and growth.[18] This is to be expected however. A large set of factors to do with the efficiency, management and markets of each individual company will influence profitability and growth. Here we have attempted to separate out only that part of the explanation of profitability that relates to type of company, sector and year. Clearly this will only explain a small part of the total pattern, but the evidence suggests that the status of a company none the less has its own discernible effect amongst all the other influences.

As noted above, this analysis has so far ignored the size of companies as a factor influencing profitability and growth. When the exercise was repeated including size variables, further interesting results appeared. First, in no case did the ranking of status as a determinant change, nor

[18] Correlation coefficients varied between 0.27 and 0.29.

did it cease to be statistically significant. Second, size, whether measured by sales or capital employed, was itself significant and in a negative direction. The magnitude of the effect was however small. Table 6.11 summarises the impact of size. These results must be treated with more than usual caution. It is not necessarily surprising that size and profitability might be negatively correlated and such results have, as we have seen, been found before (see p. 164). But the relationship is unlikely to be linear over the whole size range of companies, and we have previously noted indications that it is not. Here we are examining companies over only one part of the size range, i.e. relatively large companies, and deriving an estimate of the impact of size on the presumption that the relationship is linear. It may of course be that over the whole size range a linear relation is a very good approximation, and certainly the relation identified here is statistically significant, but it would still be inadmissable to apply this correlation outside the size range of the sample, or even for sub-classes of size within the range.

It is of interest to note the differences to profit rates which being unquoted makes when variations in size are allowed for separately. This is shown in Table 6.12 and is the equivalent of Table 6.10 but allowing

TABLE 6.11 Effect on Profit Rates of an Increase of £10 million in Size

| | Size measure | |
| | Capital employed % | Sales % |
Profit measure		
Gross operating profit rate	−2.3	−0.9
Gross profit rate	−2.0	−0.9
Profit net of depreciation	−1.4	−0.8
Profit net of depreciation and interest	−1.2	−0.8
Profit net of depreciation, interest and tax	−0.8	−0.5

TABLE 6.12 Differences in Profitability between Quoted and Unquoted Companies (Small Sample; Size Effects Included)

Profit measure	Unquoted minus Quoted %
Gross operating profit rate	+6.7
Gross profit rate	+6.8
Profit net of depreciation	+5.2
Profit net of depreciation and interest	+5.2
Profit net of depreciation, interest and tax	+1.7

for size. In each case the difference is higher than before.

This appears at first sight a strange result. If smaller size increases profitability, then our unquoted companies, which though large for their class are on average smaller than the quoted companies with which they are compared, should demonstrate less superior profitability when this size effect is allowed for; i.e. separating out the advantage they have through being smaller would normally be expected to reduce their measured advantage purely from being unquoted. In fact the reverse occurs (though the effects, it should be noted, are very small). This could suggest some differences in the relation between size and profitability as between the two classes of company, or non-linearities in the relations. Some indications of this have been noted earlier with regard to the large sample of companies. However, an equally likely explanation arises from the fact that over the period studied, the growth rate of unquoted companies was much faster. They were therefore tending throughout the period to move into larger size classes with lower average profitability at a faster rate than quoted companies. This would tend to reduce the measured differences in profit rates attributable to status if the size effect is excluded. When allowance is made for the greater depression of profits of unquoted companies as a result of their more rapidly increasing size, the measured difference attributable purely to status is larger.

The inclusion of size as a discriminant makes no difference to the explanation of growth previously found, and is itself insignificant. This accords well with our previous results which found no relation between size and growth rate of companies (see p. 164).

Overall this analysis backs up and strengthens earlier results obtained from examining our large sample over a shorter time-period. Unquoted companies appear noticeably more profitable and faster-growing and the differences are statistically significant. This difference excludes any advantage which unquoted companies may have as a result of their smaller average size.

6.7 COMPANY OBJECTIVES

The figures for profits and growth can also be used to explore further the different objectives which quoted and unquoted companies may pursue.

The basic approach to this issue is that developed by Marris[19] and summarised in Figure 6.1. This represents the growth characteristics of a

[19] See R. Marris, *The Economic Theory of Managerial Capitalism* (Macmillan, 1963).

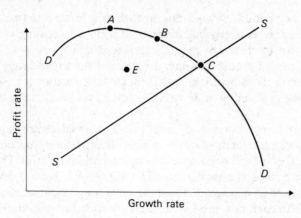

FIGURE 6.1   Company Growth

company whose shares are held by the public, i.e. a quoted company.[20]

The line *SS* in Figure 6.1 shows the growth of supply of funds along the horizontal axis as a function of the rate of return on capital along the vertical axis. In general terms it shows that the higher the rate of return, the more internal and external funds a company can generate for growth. For any given profit rate, a faster growth rate could be achieved by retaining more funds (paying fewer dividends) and/or borrowing more, and each of these would have the effect of pivoting the *SS* curve clockwise. There is however a limit to how far this can be pursued, as the lower dividends and greater gearing will generally depress share prices and increase the prospect of a takeover raid. This would threaten the senior management's position, and therefore places a limit on the growth obtainable on the supply side from any given profit rate.

The line *DD* shows the relation between the growth of demand for the company's products, measured on the horizontal axis, as a function of the rate of return. Initially the curve is upward-sloping, reflecting the fact that when growth rates are very low, some very profitable diversification may be foregone. The grasping of diversification opportunities will increase the growth rate of the company, but also improve its profit rate. Increasingly however other effects begin to operate. As a fairly general rule, faster growth of output of existing products will sooner or later come up against a combination of market saturation and

---

[20] A full derivation, explanation and critique of the model is to be found in Hay and Morris, *Industrial Economics*, ch. 9.

strong competition. Beyond this, growth at a faster rate than that at which the market is growing overall will become increasingly difficult. Faster growth therefore requires the development of new, though perhaps related products, which if successful can expand rapidly. But the faster the rate at which growth through diversification is pushed, the greater the probability of downward pressure on profit rates, for three reasons.

First, some combination of lower prices, more advertising and more research and development will help make diversification successful, but after some point will begin to reduce profit margins on sales. The faster growth is pushed, the greater this effect will become. Second, fewer and fewer resources, managerial, technical, marketing, research, etc., will be available to each new product as diversification becomes more rapid. The probability of error increases, which again will tend to pull down the rate of return, especially if output turns out to be significantly less than forecast. Third, faster growth will in the long term not only reduce managerial efficiency but entail faster recruitment of new personnel. This lowers the average level of experience and expertise, which will further jeopardise profit rates. Taken together these forces will eventually tend to create a negative relation between growth and profit rates, for firms operating as efficiently as their growth target permits. This last caveat is important. Clearly if a company is not using its existing resources with maximum efficiency, then it may well be sacrificing both profits and growth and be at a point such as E in Figure 6.1. An improvement in efficiency could move it to, for example, point B, generating improvements in both profits and growth. In practice many companies may directly experience this positive association as a result of changes in efficiency. But once at a point like B, or A or C, any further increases in growth can only be obtained by sacrificing some profitability.

At what point on the line DD will a company aim? If it seeks to maximise its rate of return on capital it will aim for point A, the peak of the DD curve. If it seeks to maximise growth then it will move as far down the DD curve as it can, consistent with not going to the right of the SS curve when the latter is as flat as possible, i.e. without creating unacceptable risk of takeover. In Figure 6.1 this is shown as point C. It can be shown[21] that a company wishing to maximise the valuation of its shares will in general select an intermediate point between A and C,

[21] See G. Heal and A. Silberston, 'Alternative Managerial Objectives: An Exploratory Note', *Oxford Economic Papers*, vol. 24, no. 2, July 1972, pp. 137–50.

indicated here by point *B*. In general the extent to which growth can be pursued beyond that indicated by point *B* depends on the reduction in profits from this level which owners will tolerate. As they will not freely sacrifice any profits, the scope for such growth will depend on the power of shareholders to limit managerial discretion, which in turn is a function of the extent to which shareholders are concentrated in a few hands and therefore more easily co-ordinated, and of the costs involved in discovering whether any realised profit rate is or is not below what could have been achieved by alternative management policies in the conditions prevailing. These hurdles to ensuring complete adherence to owners' wishes are generally termed enforcement costs.[22]

Tests of managerial motivation have examined whether companies controlled by salaried managers select point *C* and owner-controlled companies select either point *A* or point *B*. The argument for this is that salaried managers do not themselves gain from profits, provided these are at or above some minimum acceptable level necessary to make their positions secure from takeover or dismissal by shareholders. Rather they gain satisfaction from their salaries, status and power, each of which is related more to the size of their companies. Given that there are considerable costs attached to repeated switching between companies, these rewards are increased by pursuing growth-maximising policies. Owner-controllers however are presumed to receive the benefits of profits, either in dividends or in the form of increased valuation of their shareholdings. It has therefore been hypothesised that owner-controlled companies will have lower growth rates but higher profit rates.

Radice's test of this, to which reference has already been made (see p. 133), found that owner-controlled companies had higher profit rates *and* higher growth rates.

This suggests either that they were more efficient, or that the market constraints they faced were less tight, permitting their *DD* curves to be further to the right. These two possibilities are shown in parts (a) and (b) of Figure 6.2.

In both Figure 6.2a and 6.2b the line *SS* represents the minimum slope of the growth-of-supply curve consistent with an acceptable level of security from takeover. In all four comparisons (numbered 1–4) of management control (*M*) and ownership control (*O*) owner-controlled firms have higher growth and profit rates. In cases 1 and 2, the owner-controlled firms are more efficient at attaining the maximum growth–

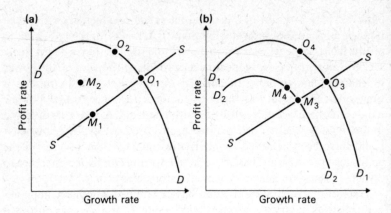

FIGURE 6.2 Interpretations of Differences in Profit and Growth Rates between Management- and Owner-controlled Companies

profit trade-off relation. In cases 3 and 4 they face a more buoyant growth-of-demand environment. Either explanation of Radice's results is possible. As he selected *large* owner-controlled companies, so that they would be equivalent in size to the management-controlled companies with which he was comparing them, he would have obtained a high number of particularly successful companies amongst his sample. This is because in general a company has to be very efficient or face very buoyant growth-of-demand conditions if it is to achieve large size without having to raise funds on the stock market and without therefore splitting up ownership and management control.

The difficulty in interpreting these results is that they do not give any unambiguous indication about motivation. In cases 1 and 3 both types of company are growth-maximisers; in cases 2 and 4 both are maximising the valuation of their companies. It is possible that the motivations hypothesised earlier do apply, e.g. O_4 and M_3, but also possible that the exact reverse applies, e.g. M_4 and O_3. To complicate the picture further, work by Llewellyn in the United States suggests that as much as five-sixths of the total remuneration of senior management is in fact related directly or indirectly to profitability, in the form of dividends on their own shareholdings, bonuses, stock options, pension arrangements, etc., rather than to their salaries, suggesting that management-controlled companies might equally well pursue profit or valuation-maximising strategies as owner-controlled companies.[23] This

[23] W. Lewellyn, 'Management and Ownership in the Large Firm,' *Journal of Finance*, vol. 24, May 1969, pp. 299–322.

only relates to salary however. The pursuit of status, related perks and power, are much more closely related to size and may constitute more powerful motivations.

Our interview programme, reviewed in the last chapter, suggested a rather different picture. We may recall from that chapter that although fourteen of the nineteen companies were unambiguously owner-controlled, only five paid significant dividends, over half tried to keep their share valuations as low as possible, no owner-manager had actually sold shares to raise capital (though they may well have raised personal loans on the security of their shares), and profit-related bonuses were an unimportant source of income. As far as direct interview information can reveal, the majority appeared to pursue growth subject to a security or profit constraint, with very few oriented to profit or valuation maximisation. Indeed profitability and share price considerations were seen as characterising *quoted* companies. Only to the extent that further growth entailed an eventual tax liability which could not be met was it not the main objective for most of the companies interviewed. It must be seriously questioned therefore whether owner-controlled firms which we here equate with our unquoted ones do pursue notably different objectives to quoted ones which are under the day-to-day control of salaried managers.

Our data can throw a little light on this issue. First, the general pattern of growth and profit figures are similar to those of Radice. That is, unquoted companies exhibited higher profit rates and higher growth rates. In addition it has been seen that this relation is not the result of differences in the size of the companies selected. Figure 6.3 shows the

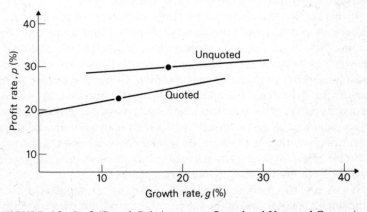

FIGURE 6.3   Profit/Growth Relations across Quoted and Unquoted Companies

average growth/profit (gross operating profit) for quoted and unquoted companies and also the line that best fits the individual growth/profit points across all companies in each group. (One unquoted company in the food sector with an exceptionally high growth rate has been excluded. Its inclusion would accentuate the comments made but it has been excluded in order to indicate that the analysis is not at all dependent on the extreme value in that sector.)

The equations of the lines shown in Figure 6.3 are:

$$\text{Quoted} \qquad p = 0.197 + 0.263 \, g$$
$$(18.33) \ (5.61) \qquad \bar{R}^2 = 0.28$$

$$\text{Unquoted} \qquad p = 0.278 + 0.072 \, g$$
$$(30.58) \ (0.56) \qquad \bar{R}^2 = 0.11.$$

From this it may be noted that the relationship for the unquoted companies is higher and flatter. The effect of growth rates on profit rates is statistically insignificant for unquoted companies, and the relation explains very little of the pattern of profitability. Separate tests showed that the two gradients were not statistically differentiable. Furthermore company status was not a discriminant in an analysis of the variance of the ratio of the divergence of profitability from its mean to the divergence of growth from its mean. We cannot separately observe both the growth-of-supply and growth-of-demand relations, so we cannot conclude that the data are inconsistent, with quoted companies being growth-maximisers and unquoted companies being profit-maximisers. But there is no evidence here to support that assignment of objectives, not is there any evidence that the growth of unquoted companies is more constrained by their profitability than unquoted ones.

If it is correct that there are no major differences in the underlying pattern of profit/growth preferences of quoted and unquoted companies, then it still remains an open question whether the objective is growth maximisation subject to a profit/security constraint, or the more traditional profit or valuation maximisation. However given the strong reason for believing that quoted companies controlled by salaried managers pursue growth maximisation, and given the strong indications of a similar type of motive (albeit for different reasons) indicated in our own extensive interviews, there are grounds for thinking that analytically the Marris-type growth-oriented paradigm represents the general case for both quoted and unquoted companies.

If correct, this finding is quite far-reaching. It suggests a more fundamental reappraisal of the validity of the profit-maximising motive still generally presumed with regard to company objectives; analysis of enforcement costs becomes a central aspect of our understanding of industrial economic behaviour; if differences of objectives between quoted and unquoted companies are smaller than previously thought, then differences in constraints, particularly financial constraints, assume a central role in evaluating the behaviour and performance of unquoted and quoted companies. The efficiency of the stock market as a supplier of funds and monitor of performance becomes a crucial issue, and it is to this that we turn in the next chapter.

6.8 CONCLUSIONS

In this chapter we have compared the objectives and performance of quoted and unquoted companies in some detail. Three different data sources were used and in each case unquoted companies generally exhibited faster growth rates and higher profit rates. There were also indications that they used their capital and labour resources more efficiently. With regard to motivation there is no indication to support the view that unquoted companies have a different set of preferences as between profit and growth from that of quoted companies. In fact the data are consistent with the interview evidence that unquoted companies are likely to be as growth-oriented as quoted ones, though to some extent for different reasons.

The performance differences revealed do not appear to reflect any characteristics of the companies examined, e.g. size or sectoral disposition, other than their status as quoted or unquoted companies. This suggests that the differences relate directly to those characteristics that stem from being unquoted. These are of two types: first, the ownership/control nexus which influences the managerial behaviour of unquoted companies, and second, the absence of short-term constraints on managerial behaviour via a market in the company's shares. The first of these was considered in some detail in Chapter 5. We now go on to look at the financial aspects of unquoted companies, as a guide to the second characteristic.

7 Financial Characteristics of Quoted and Unquoted Companies

7.1. INTRODUCTION

This chapter sets out to explore systematic differences in financial characteristics between quoted and unquoted companies. In the process it attempts to identify the financial constraints which the two groups face, the efficiency with which they obtain finance and the implications for overall performance and policy.

Three different types of observation of financial characteristics are made, these being dictated by the information available. The first compares the flow of funds and certain balance-sheet ratios of the two groups as derived from the *Business Monitor* M3 series. This source, to which reference has already been made (see pp. 143–5), gives the aggregate balance-sheet and profit-and-loss accounts for large samples of UK-owned quoted and unquoted companies for the period 1971–7.

The second approach is to examine our small sample data base (see pp. 165–6), to identify statistically significant differences in the financial structure of the individual companies comprising that data base. Finally we use the same source to investigate some simple models of the financial flows of the two groups.

Numerous inferences are drawn in this chapter about the financial behaviour of unquoted companies, some tentative, some more definite. Where possible these inferences are related back to our interview evidence in Chapter 5, but it is perhaps important to note at the beginning one major conclusion which emerges at several points. The evidence collected by the Bolton Committee, which was summarised in Chapter 3, suggested some notable differences between small and large companies. For example, small companies generally had a smaller proportion of fixed assets in their balance-sheet, and used very little long-term debt. They relied on retentions to finance expansion, and had very low pay-out ratios. Our conclusion in this chapter is that these features, identified by Bolton as typical of small companies, are in fact more accurately ascribed to unquoted companies, whatever their size. It is the differences in ownership and control patterns, and in the relation of companies to the financial market which represent the crucial determinants of the differences identified by the Bolton Committee, rather than size.

7.2 AGGREGATE FINANCIAL CHARACTERISTICS

(a) *Flow of funds*

Using the *Business Monitor* series we have chosen to set out the evidence on the flow of funds through quoted and unquoted companies in the form of flow diagrams. These are given in Figures 7.1 and 7.2 for four representative years 1971, 1973, 1975 and 1976. These give us a chance to consider different business conditions, and to detect any changes over the period of analysis.

Figures 7.1 and 7.2 trace the flow of funds through the companies per 100 units of income (gross profit, after payment of short-term interest). A certain proportion of this income is immediately applied to meet liabilities incurred of tax, dividends and interest on long-term loans. The residue is retained within the company (retentions therefore include depreciation as well as retained earnings). New issues of equity or debentures, and additions to short-term credit (mainly bank borrowing) are added to retentions to give total funds at the disposal of the company. The three main uses are then the purchase of new fixed assets, acquisitions and the building up of current assets (stocks and work-in-progress especially). Acquisitions financed by issue of new equity have been netted-out from both sources and uses of funds, since they do not affect the cash flow *within* the firm as it previously existed. The aim of the analysis is to trace what happens to company income in terms of these items.

A number of salient differences between quoted and unquoted companies are apparent from inspection of Figures 7.1 and 7.2. For every £100 of profit, the unquoted company sector pays slightly less tax than quoted companies, though the difference is not marked. A major difference occurs in payments to dividends, loan interest, etc., where quoted companies pay out about twice the level of unquoted per £100 of profit. The consequence is that in every year the unquoted sector retains

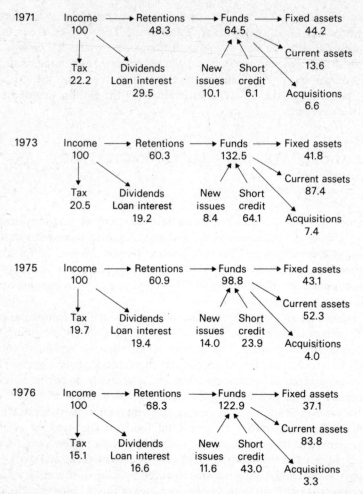

FIGURE 7.1 Business Monitor Analysis: Flow of Funds, UK-controlled Quoted Companies

a substantially higher proportion. The other sources of funds are new issues and short-term credits. Short-term credit is clearly related to the acquisition of short-term (current) assets. Thus in 1971 firms in both the unquoted and quoted sectors made relatively small additions to short-term assets; and this was paralleled in both sectors by low short-term borrowing. By contrast 1973 and 1976 were both years in which firms were building up substantial stocks, and this was matched by an increase

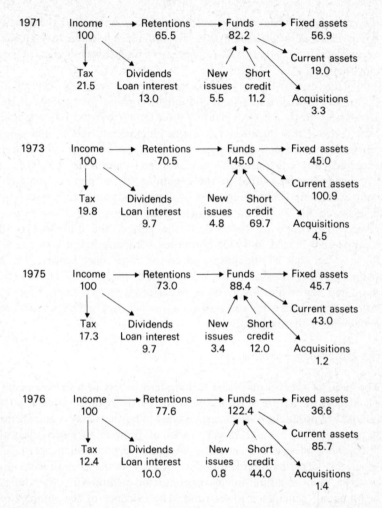

FIGURE 7.2 Business Monitor Analysis: Flow of Funds, UK-controlled Unquoted Companies

in borrowing. 1975 represents an intermediate case but reflects the same linkage of short-term assets and credits. As expected the quoted sector makes much more use of new issues as a source of funds. In 1971 and 1973, this did not compensate for their higher payment in dividends and loan interest, but towards the end of the period of analysis, it was doing so. Thus in 1971 and 1973 unquoted companies had more funds at their disposal (per £100 of gross profits) than quoted, but in 1975 the quoted companies had rather more funds. The difference however was entirely accounted for by higher short-term credit to finance their higher level of stockbuilding.[1]

On the uses-of-funds side of the analysis, there are no major differences between quoted and unquoted companies in respect of short-term assets. Both sectors evidently follow the same pattern through the trade cycle. On acquisitions, as might be expected, the quoted companies are more active, though not as active as might have been expected. (But note that acquisition financed by new issues is excluded.) This evidence shows that at the beginning of the period, unquoted companies were committing more of their gross profits to new capital assets, and the 1971 figures suggest a substantial difference in this respect. However, by the end of the period, the differences had disappeared: indeed in 1976 the quoted company figure was a little higher than that of the unquoted sector. That may however be a temporary feature. For most of the period under consideration the unquoted sector did devote more of its profit to new capital assets. Alternatively it may represent part of a trend change in the comparative behaviour of the two sectors.

(b) *Basic balance-sheet ratios*

The ratio of short-term assets to long-term assets in a firm is partly dictated by the nature of the business and partly by the physical capital intensity of production. Thus certain types of business may require firms to maintain on average larger stocks of product to cover cyclical fluctuations in sales. A vertically integrated production process will generate a larger requirement of current assets in the form of work-in-progress. A more capital-intensive production method will, other things being equal, generate a lower ratio. The evidence of the samples of quoted and unquoted companies is that the unquoted sector has the higher ratio, 2.0 compared to 1.7 for quoted companies in 1977. This difference was evident throughout the period 1971–7.

For a given short-term/long-term ratio on the asset side of the balance-sheet, the ratio of short-term to long-term liabilities is evidence of the company's desire to match short and long on both sides of the balance-sheet. Clearly a company which borrowed short to finance long-term assets would be taking a risk: borrowing long to finance short-term

[1] This may well have been influenced by the granting of stock relief in 1975.

assets would also involve risk. Matching the structures would be a risk-averse policy. The evidence shows that the ratio of short-term liabilities to long-term liabilities for quoted companies in 1977 was 0.65, compared to 0.80 for unquoted. This difference almost precisely mirrors the difference on the asset side, reported above. Hence both the quoted and unquoted sector were financing about one-third of their short-term assets from long-term funds. There is no difference in their risk position in this respect.

However a very significant difference between the two samples is apparent in gearing, measured either as the ratio of long-term debt to shareholders' equity, or as the ratio of long-term debt to net assets. The evidence is given in Table 7.1.

Whichever measures are taken it is evident that long-term borrowing is a much smaller part of the liabilities of unquoted than of quoted companies.

The ratio of long-term borrowing to total net assets falls for both samples of companies. This indicates that both sectors were becoming more reliant on short-term borrowing over the period (reflecting an increase in liquidity on the asset side), but within a reduced total of long-term funds, quoted companies' reliance on long-term debt, rather than shareholders' equity (new issues or retentions), was increasing.[2] Also in Table 7.1 we show the cost of debenture finance as implied in the long-term interest payments made by companies in the two samples. It is apparent that unquoted companies were paying more than quoted, though the difference is not particularly large. There are two possible explanations of this result. The first is that all companies, whether quoted or unquoted, enter the market for funds on roughly the same terms, though some risk premium is added to the cost of an unquoted company's borrowings, reflecting its smaller size. Then the discrepancy in gearing ratios is explained in terms of different demands for loans between the two sectors. The unquoted sector could borrow more at the given rate, but chose not to do so, because of the lower implicit cost of retentions. The second explanation is that firms in both sectors face rising interest costs with increased gearing, but that the supply of funds is more elastic to the quoted sector. Then the lower gearing ratio of unquoted companies is explained by their unwillingness to incur interest costs at the margin higher than those of the quoted sector. This would

---

[2] The stock market collapse in the middle of the period will have been an important factor here.

TABLE 7.1 Gearing and Cost of Debt Capital: Quoted and Unquoted Companies, 1971–77

Date	Long-term borrowing Shareholders' funds		Long-term borrowing Total net assets		Rate of interest on debentures	
	Quoted	Unquoted	Quoted	Unquoted	Quoted	Unquoted
1971	0.26	0.13	0.21	0.11	6.8	6.6
1972	0.30	0.11	0.21	0.09	6.7	7.3
1973	0.30	0.10	0.21	0.08	7.2	8.2
1974	0.28	0.12	0.19	0.07	7.6	8.4
1975	0.29	0.11	0.18	0.08	8.0	10.1
1976	0.25	0.10	0.16	0.07	8.0	9.2
1977	0.22	0.09	0.16	0.06	8.3	9.0

particularly be the case where a quoted and an unquoted company were competing in the same product market.

Analysis of the structure of short-term liabilities in overdraft finance, trade credit, etc. showed that there were no differences between the quoted and unquoted sector in this respect.

7.3 ANALYSIS OF DIFFERENCES IN FINANCIAL BEHAVIOUR: BALANCE-SHEETS

The small sample data enables us to look further at the differences in financing conditions of quoted and unquoted companies and consider the likely impact. Various separate but related types of observation may be made, the first of which focuses on company balance-sheets. The data comprise standardised balance-sheets for 180 companies for each of fourteen years. Analysis of variance is again the method employed to see whether company status, sector and the year in question are statistically significant determinants of the observed pattern of balance-sheets items, all expressed as percentages of capital employed. The results are given in Table 7.2.

Looking first at the sources of long-term funds, certain differences between quoted and unquoted companies are immediately apparent. First, as one would expect, the proportion of issued equity is considerably smaller for unquoted companies, representing nearer one-fifth of capital employed against one-third for quoted companies. Reference to Figure 7.3 however, which shows the change in the composition of sources of long-term funds for the unquoted companies, indicates that this figure had been falling steadily over the thirteen years, and by 1978 was only around one-seventh of long-term finance. A similar trend decline, though at higher levels, is evident for the quoted companies as well (see Figure 7.4). The effect is sufficiently pronounced for it to show up as significant year by year for most of the period (see Table 7.2)

Offsetting this, capital and revenue reserves represent a substantially higher proportion of capital employed in unquoted companies. Figure 7.3 illustrates that this figure has been relatively stable over time, rising somewhat in the period 1969–73[3] but then falling away again and revealing no trend over the whole period. This stability is again noticeable for the quoted companies. Most striking, in view of the lack

---

[3] This effect is also significant on a year-by-year basis even when combined with quoted companies (see Table 7.2).

TABLE 7.2 Balance Sheet Analysis

Balance Sheet Analysis 1967–1976	Mean of Q	Mean of UNQ	Diff of Means	Diff Coeff-icient	Mean of all Cos.	Sectors 21	23	26/7	31	33	36	41	43	44
Issued Capital (Ordinary)									−4.6		+1.8	+8.2	+0.4	+3.4
	30.9	20.8	−10.1	−17.5	25.8	+2.9		+19.3	−1.5					−0.5
Issued Capital (Preference)											+4.7	+5.3		
	3.4	2.3	−1.1	−2.1	2.8				+0.8		−1.9	−1.8	+1.2	−1.3
Reserves								+9.5	+10.7	+4.2	+8.5	−7.1		+15.1
	50.3	61.8	+11.5	+24.0	56.0	−4.2			+3.4	+2.1			+4.8	
Deferred Taxation							+6.6				−1.8	+6.7	+3.3	
	5.2	9.0	−4.8	+2.2	7.1									
Long Term Liabilities									−7.8					
	10.3	6.8	−3.5	−7.2	8.5	+2.8	−8.9		−1.7	−1.6			−3.2	
Long Term Assets														
Fixed Assets								−25.3	−6.4			+40.8	−6.7	
	65.2	54.9	−10.3	(−12.5)	59.5	+14.5	+25.2			+2.3	−3.9	+7.5		
Trade Investments								−5.1	+8.5	−5.5	+9.0	−4.7	−2.1	−2.6 −1.6
	5.3	4.6	−0.7	(−0.7)	4.9			+4.6			+4.1	+3.3	+3.6	
Short Term Assets														
Stocks/ W.I.P.								+41.1		−21.0		−43.1	−14.1	−52.1
	45.3	65.2	+19.9	(+14.1)	55.6	−10.8			−34.9				−14.9	−6.9
Debtors								+10.7			−34.5			
	46.3	84.8	+38.5	+43.5	63.2	−7.7	−37.0				+10.1	+75.9	−16.8	+131.7 −5.5
Securities and Cash	7.6	11.4	+3.8	+2.3	9.5						+10.7	+4.5		
Minus Short Term Liabilities														
Short Term Loans											+4.7	−3.7	+13.0	+32.0
	15.4	22.1	+6.7	+23.3	18.2		−3.4						+18.5	+9.8
Creditors													+170.5	
	40.8	86.6	+45.8	+49.7	62.2	−7.8	−30.4	−56.8		+25.2			+8.1	+4.7
Dividends Payable											−4.4	−1.5	+1.0	
	3.3	1.8	−1.5	−2.2	2.5			+2.3			+2.1	−0.8		
Tax Payable								+10.7			−3.8			
	8.0	6.8	+8.8	+1.1	8.0						+2.1	−4.8	+2.1	

Notes:
(i) Figures in the first 5 columns are all percentages of capital employed.
(ii) Q indicates quoted companies
UNQ indicates unquoted companies
w.i.p. is work-in-progress
(iii) Diff. Coefficient gives the difference between quoted and unquoted companies as revealed by analysis of variance. A plus sign indicates that the value is higher for unquoted companies. While the results themselves were taken from an analysis of the data for all companies in all sectors pooled across all years, they were only regarded as significant if the usual statistical significance test validated status or a sector as a discriminant for a majority of years taken separately. On this basis all values were statistically significant except the three shown in brackets.
(iv) Figures do not always sum to 100 as a result of rounding.
(v) The analysis was repeated twice with different size variables also included. The only significant differences were as follows:

Size measured by Capital Employed
(a) Difference coefficient on stocks and w.i.p. falls from 14.1 to 5.2 and remains insignificant.
(b) Diff. Coeff. on short term loans falls from 23.3 to 20.8 and remains insignificant.

by Sales
(a) Diff. Coefficient on deferred taxation rises from 2.2 to 4.1 and remains significant.
(b) Diff. Coeff. on fixed assets falls from 12.5 to 9.0 and becomes significant.

46	47	48	50	70	81	67	68	69	70	71	72	73	74	75	76	77	78
	−21.5	−2.0	−1.0														
−2.0										−3.1	−3.5	−6.1	−8.3	−8.9	−10.8	−10.7	−10.6
+1.2		−0.5															
−1.8	+1.1		−1.7					−1	−1.1	−1.5	−2.1	−2.8	−3	−3	−3.3	−3.3	−3
+5.2		+6.2	−6.5	−4.9													
			+14.2		+2.9					+2.8	+2.8	+3.6	+4.4	+7.1			
+4.8																	
				−6.5	−2.3		−4.1	−4.2	−4.0	−3.5	−3.1	−2.0	+6	+9.5	+11.2	+11.4	+8.9
+3.9	+3.6		+8.5	+33.1													
	−3.0			−1.6	−3.7										−2.2		
	+32.0	−10.5			−5.0												
+29.4	−4.0	+22.1		+46.6												−11.7	−10.7
	−2.9	+14.8		−4.1													
+4.9			+5.8														
+22.2		+5.5	+77.2	+19.3													
−35.4		−36.4	+15.3	−50.8	+9,5									+8.0			
	+3.3	−10.2		+85.8													
−19.3	+8.1		+2.8	+4.8	+34.7					+8.6	+9.1					−16.8	−15.0
		+1.9	+9.3														
												+1.3					
+12.6	+5.1	+5.6															
					+25.2	−4.7											
	+7.6	−5.9	+88.6	+93.1													
			+42.4	+29.4											+10.4		
		+2.0		−4.1													
		−1.3				+1.6	+1.5	+1.4	+1.5	+1.7	+2.3	+0.3					
				−7.2	+1.9		+5.3	+4.8	+3.4	+3.1	+2.4	+3.2			−1.5	−2.1	−4.2	−2.9

(vi) The lower line in 'sectors' indicates statistically significant deviations of a sector's balance sheets from the average balance sheet for all companies. The upper line shows deviations of unquoted companies only in each sector. While the figures shown are significant on the pooled data basis, there are too few companies to test on an annual basis and this makes the figures unreliable. This upper row of figures should therefore be taken as suggestive only.

(vii) The figures in the year columns indicate significant deviations from the average balance sheet over the whole period, and therefore can reveal trends in balance sheets through time.

(viii) Long term gearing of quoted companies is much lower in this sample than in the Business Monitor data. This is almost certainly because all companies in the small sample are undiversified. As many quoted companies are diversified, and as this tends to reduce risk, we would expect the figures in the Business Monitor series to be significantly higher. As this factor tends to reduce the measured different between quoted and unquoted companies we have not sought to examine the issue further in our small sample work.

(ix) See page 160 for the names of the sectors.

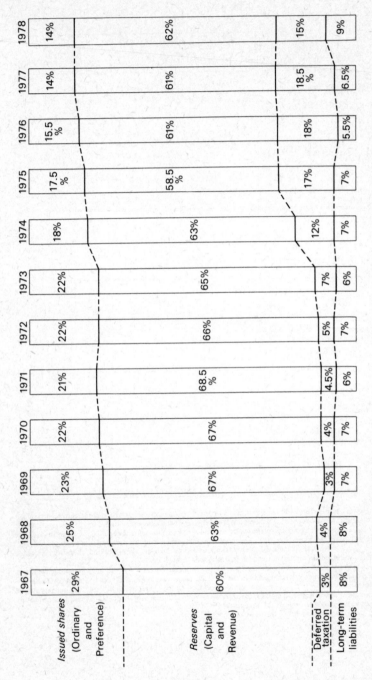

FIGURE 7.3 Change in composition of sources of long-term funds for sample of unquoted companies 1968–78

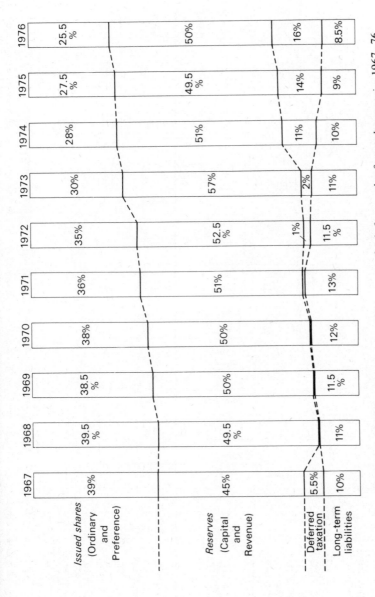

FIGURE 7.4 Changes in composition of sources of long-term funds for sample of quoted companies 1967–76

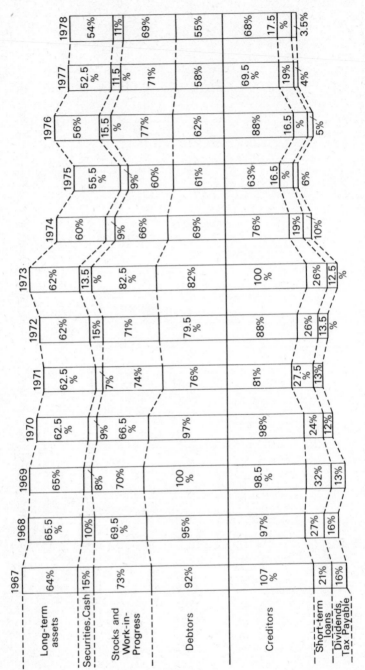

FIGURE 7.5 Changes in composition of use of funds for sample of unquoted companies, 1967–78

Note: All figures are percentages of capital employed. Total assets are shown above the line. Total assets minus short-term liabilities are shown below the line. Short-term liabilities may not equal 100 per cent due to rounding.

197

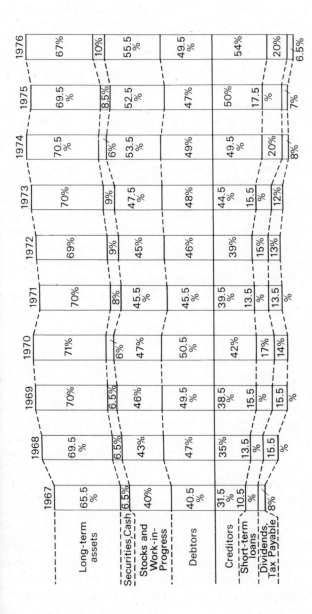

FIGURE 7.6   Changes in composition of use of funds for sample of quoted companies 1967–76

Note: All figures are percentages of capital employed. Total assets are shown above the line. Short-term liabilities are shown below the line. Total assets minus short-term liabilities may not equal 100 per cent due to rounding.

of access to the equity market, the unquoted companies have significantly lower long-term liabilities. This however accords with the
evidence of the interviews, and of our large sample analysis. The decline
in reliance on long-term borrowing by quoted companies noted in the
large sample again shows up (albeit on a different measure), but not with
regard to unquoted companies. Here the small sample does not reveal a
trend decline but a roughly constant position. The other source besides
reserves which is used more by unquoted companies and which
compensates for the lower utilisation of long-term funds is deferred
taxation. This has been growing in importance for both quoted and
unquoted companies[4] and is in fact the item which over time has
compensated for the decline in the percentage of issued share capital for
both groups (see Figures 7.3 and 7.4).

Turning to the uses of funds, three main characteristics stand out, as
can be seen by comparing Figures 7.5 and 7.6. These show the change in
composition of use of funds for the quoted and unquoted groups from
1967 to 1976 (plus two further years for unquoted companies), drawn on
the same scale and with all quantities expressed as a percentage of capital
employed. First the volume of both short-term assets and short-term
liabilities in relation to total capital employed is considerably higher for
unquoted companies. They have proportionately more stocks and
work-in-progress and much higher debtors' payments outstanding,
financed by more short-term loans and much higher creditors' liabilities.
Second, the behaviour of the two groups is quite different over time.
For the quoted companies the composition is fairly constant,
except for a clear growth in stocks as a percentage of capital employed,
financed by a growth in creditor liabilities. For the unquoted companies
there is little change in value of stocks as a percentage of capital
employed, but a very substantial reduction in both debtors and
creditors, and a smaller fall in long-term assets (fixed plus trade
investment).

A further difference is that short-term loans as a percentage of capital
employed show a trend rise for quoted companies, but a trend fall for
unquoted companies. The same is true for securities (financial assets)
and cash.

The overall effect of these changes is that while in 1967 the structure of
this side of the balance-sheet was markedly dissimilar between the two
groups, by the end of the period there had been a very substantial
convergence of their structures, with signs of further convergence

---

[4] This effect is also significant on a year-by-year basis (see Table 7.2).

continuing. One explanation for this is the behaviour of capital employed itself. While in nominal terms the quoted companies grew 203 per cent between 1967 and 1976, the unquoted companies grew 667 per cent. The unquoted companies were therefore becoming more similar in size to the quoted companies through the period.

To examine this the analysis of variance was repeated, with size, measured by capital employed, added as a discriminant. (The effect of the introduction of size on the difference coefficients in Table 7.2 are described in the notes to that table.) The results are summarised in Table 7.3 which shows the statistically significant changes which could be expected as a result of companies growing from the average size of the unquoted sample in 1967 to the average size in 1978.

The decline of all four major items in net short-term assets with size is apparent. The magnitudes are such that the observed decline in stocks and work-in-progress and short-term loans for unquoted companies over the period may entirely be due to size effects. The decline in debtors and creditors however is too large to be explained entirely by size, particularly when it is noted that both items were *increasing* for quoted companies despite their (albeit more modest) growth. It would appear

TABLE 7.3   Effects of Size on Composition of Use of Funds of Unquoted Companies, 1967–78

	Size measure – capital employed (%)
Issued capital (ordinary)	+ 3.0
Issued capital (preference)	− 2.3
Capital and revenue reserves	*
Deferred taxation	*
Long-term liabilities	*
Fixed assets	(− 2.2)[†]
Trade investments	+ 1.2
Stocks and w.i.p.	− 3.9
Debtors	− 13.4
Securities and cash	*
Short-term loans	− 5.3
Creditors	− 14.7
Dividends payable	*
Tax payable	*

* Size did not offer any measurable contribution to the explanation of balance-sheet composition.
† Brackets indicate a measured but statistically insignificant effect.

therefore that unquoted companies were experiencing a growing pressure to reduce their debtor and creditor items over the period in a manner which quoted companies did not experience, a conclusion which we will refer to again later.

The third point to be derived from Table 7.2 and the subsequent figures of annual data is that if the extra creditors financed by extra debtors of unquoted companies are both netted-out, the structure of the assets side of the balance-sheet is not dissimilar for the two groups, as shown in Table 7.4. On this basis, several remaining differences in the early part of the period had by 1975 disappeared. These include lower debtors, higher securities and cash, higher short-term loans and higher creditors. While 1976 accentuates some of these differences again, and reverses the position on short-term loans, Figure 7.5 reveals that 1976 was an exceptional year for the unquoted companies, with 1975 being much closer to 1977 and 1978. Only two differences still stand out after netting-out the extra trade credit of unquoted companies. These are the relatively larger figure for stocks in unquoted companies and the relatively smaller figure for fixed assets. At first it is tempting to explain this purely in terms of size, particularly as the discrepancy was diminishing a little as the relative size of the two groups came more into line over the period. With regard to stocks there may be some validity in this. It is seen from Table 7.3 that increased size does tend to reduce the ratio of stocks to capital employed, yet the figures for quoted companies rose despite their growth. Undoubtedly therefore the effect of inflation was tending to pull the figure substantially upwards. Unquoted companies, with their faster growth, then managed to offset completely the inflation-induced rise, thereby bringing the two groups closer together.

But with regard to fixed assets, this type of explanation is not readily available. There is no significant relation between size and the ratio of fixed assets to capital employed, and no evidence that the difference between quoted and unquoted companies was diminishing over the period.

It may be that this is simply a consequence of higher stock levels in unquoted companies over and above that caused by their average smaller size. This would be consistent with the higher creditor position either directly (higher stock-holding will encourage delay in payment for inputs) or indirectly (a higher creditor position is consistent with the same target ratio of current assets to liabilities if stocks are higher). It must also be recalled that the difference coefficient on fixed assets was not statistically significant (see Table 7.2). In other words the spread of individual figures around the averages was too broad to rule out that the

TABLE 7.4 Composition of Assets Side of Balance-sheet after Netting-out Procedure, 1967–76*

	1967	1968	1969	1970	1971	1972	1973	1974	1975	1976
(A) *Quoted companies*										
Fixed assets	39.8	38.6	37.8	37.4	38.3	37.3	37.1	36.6	36.4	34.2
Trade investments	3.2	3.3	2.7	3.3	3.1	3.5	3.0	2.8	2.6	2.9
Current assets:										
Stocks and w.i.p.	26.2	25.9	26.7	26.9	26.9	26.6	27.3	29.9	29.6	30.5
Debtors	26.6	28.3	28.8	28.9	26.9	27.2	27.6	27.4	26.4	27.2
Securities and cash	4.3	3.9	3.8	3.4	4.7	5.3	5.2	3.4	4.8	5.5
Minus current liabilities:										
Short-term loans	6.9	8.1	9.0	9.8	8.0	8.9	8.9	11.2	9.9	11.0
Creditors	20.7	21.1	22.4	24.1	23.4	23.1	25.6	27.7	28.2	29.7
Dividends payable	2.5	2.5	2.3	2.3	2.5	3.0	1.7	1.1	1.3	1.1
Tax payable	2.8	6.7	6.7	5.7	5.5	4.7	5.2	3.3	2.8	2.5
(B) *Unquoted companies*										
Fixed assets	30.7	31.8	31.3	31.2	31.1	28.7	27.9	30.4	30.2	26.4
Trade investments	2.6	2.3	2.3	2.1	1.6	2.0	2.3	2.2	2.0	1.9
Current assets:										
Stocks and w.i.p.	38.0	36.2	36.4	35.4	38.8	35.0	40.0	35.9	34.9	38.9
Debtors	21.0	24.5	25.8	26.9	23.8	27.0	23.3	26.6	27.9	25.0
Securities and cash	7.8	5.2	4.2	4.8	4.7	7.4	6.6	4.9	5.2	7.8
Minus current liabilities:										
Short-term loans	10.9	14.1	16.7	12.8	14.4	12.9	12.6	10.3	9.8	8.3
Creditors	28.9	25.5	25.0	27.4	26.4	31.2	32.0	30.4	29.1	38.1
Dividends payable	1.5	1.0	0.8	1.1	1.0	1.2	0.7	0.7	0.6	0.5
Tax payable	6.8	7.3	5.7	5.3	5.8	5.4	5.3	4.9	2.9	2.0

* All figures are expressed as a percentage of total assets.

differences arose from the chance selection of companies.

Having considered both the assets and liabilities sides it is interesting to consider the gearing position of the two groups of companies. If long-term liabilities are expressed as a percentage of capital employed, then unquoted companies are seen to be less geared, a point we have noted before from different sources. But if short-term loans are added, this discrepancy disappears and indeed is reversed slightly. Table 7.5 gives the values over the period.

While the gearing on this measure tends first to rise and then level out for quoted companies, it tends to rise but then fall away for unquoted companies, so that despite being noticeably higher at the start of the period, it is noticeably lower by the end.

The rationale for this measure is the evidence from the interviews that unquoted companies not only rely heavily on their bankers for finance, but that some proportion of nominally short-term finance is clearly recognised as term lending. The same may frequently be true for quoted companies, but this none the less suggests that to some extent any differences revealed by the long-term debt measure in part reflect only a different term-structure of debt. Given that this influences the measurement of capital employed Appendix 7.1. examines the distortion of measured rates of return that result, but finds them to be very small in comparision with the differences found between quoted and unquoted companies.

Further insight into the term-structure of assets and liabilities can be

TABLE 7.5 Gearing Ratios of Quoted and Unquoted Companies including Long- and Short-term Loans, 1967–76

| | Per cent of capital employed | |
	Quoted	Unquoted
1967	20.5	29.0
1968	24.4	35.2
1969	27.0	39.1
1970	29.0	31.0
1971	26.6	33.7
1972	26.5	33.3
1973	26.3	32.3
1974	30.1	26.1
1975	26.5	23.8
1976	28.3	22.0

obtained by aggregating, first, all short-term and, second, all long-term assets and liabilities for each class of company. Table 7.6 summarises the results for 1968, 1975 and the average over the whole period. This indicates a remarkably constant position for the quoted companies, with little change in the relationship of asset term-structure to liabilities term-structure. Approximately one-third of short-term assets are financed by long-term funds. For unquoted companies, the average figure over the period as a whole is somewhat lower, but there is a marked change during the eight-year period. The proportion of short-term assets financed by long-term funds almost doubles, and by 1975 is higher than for quoted companies.

It therefore appears that although unquoted companies generally have a shorter term-structure of both assets and liabilities, throughout the period considered they reduced their dependence on external debt finance, ran down their short-term debtor and creditor positions and, in the process, significantly lengthened the term-structure of their liabilities in relation to that of their assets. This was entirely due to changes on the liabilities side, with reserves playing an increasingly important part in their liability structure. This is of course consistent with their higher profitability.

Before summarising this first element of the investigation of financing it is worth commenting briefly on some of the sectoral differences that are revealed in Table 7.2. It must be stressed however that the top rows of figures for each balance-sheet item, which indicate the deviation of unquoted companies within each sector, are suggestive only. Bearing this in mind, it appears that four sectors in particular, drink, bricks, pottery etc., construction and wholesale distribution, contributed to the generally higher level of stocks in unquoted companies. The latter two are sectors where stocks are generally high, as the lower line indicates, but disproportionately so in unquoted companies. A similar pattern is observed for creditors in these two sectors, supporting the view expressed above that the two items may be related. However similar comments do not apply for the first two of these sectors, and the conclusion must remain tenuous. Focusing on the relation between debtors and creditors there are only three sectors, leather, fur, etc.; timber, furniture, etc.; and wholesale distribution, where both are higher in unquoted companies. In two more, they are both lower (mechanical engineering and paper, printing, etc.). Therefore to the extent that unquoted companies do systematically adopt higher debtor and creditor positions, this does not seem particularly sector-specific. A similar conclusion holds with regard to the inverse relation between fixed assets

TABLE 7.6 Comparison of Term-structure of Assets and Liabilities of Quoted and Unquoted Companies

		Using figures of % of capital employed		Using figures standardised for total assets = 1.0		Percent of ST assets financed by LT funds
		$\dfrac{ST^* \text{ assets}}{LT \text{ assets}}$	$\dfrac{ST \text{ liabilities}†}{LT \text{ liabilities}}$	$\dfrac{ST \text{ assets}}{LT \text{ assets}}$	$\dfrac{ST \text{ liabilities}}{LT \text{ liabilities}}$	
1968‡	Quoted	$\dfrac{96.5}{69.5}$	$\dfrac{64}{100}$	$\dfrac{0.58}{0.42}$	$\dfrac{0.39}{0.61}$	32.7
	Unquoted	$\dfrac{174.5}{69.5}$	$\dfrac{140}{100}$	$\dfrac{0.72}{0.28}$	$\dfrac{0.58}{0.42}$	19.4
1975	Quoted	$\dfrac{108}{69.5}$	$\dfrac{74.5}{100}$	$\dfrac{0.61}{0.39}$	$\dfrac{0.43}{0.58}$	31.1
	Unquoted	$\dfrac{136}{55.5}$	$\dfrac{85.5}{100}$	$\dfrac{0.71}{0.29}$	$\dfrac{0.46}{0.54}$	35.2
Average	Quoted	$\dfrac{99.2}{70.5}$	$\dfrac{67.5}{100}$	$\dfrac{0.58}{0.42}$	$\dfrac{0.40}{0.60}$	31.0
	Unquoted	$\dfrac{161.4}{59.5}$	$\dfrac{119.3}{100}$	$\dfrac{0.73}{0.27}$	$\dfrac{0.54}{0.46}$	26.0

* ST: short-term; LT: long-term.

† Longterm liabilities here include those to the owners of the company. Short-term liabilities include short-term loans, creditors, tax and dividends payable.

‡ 1968 and 1975 are chosen as they are typical of the earlier and later part of the period respectively (see Figures 7.3, 7.4, 7.5 and 7.6).

and stocks both as a percentage of capital employed noted above. Only drink, paper, and printing, etc. and wholesale distribution reveal this specific relation, while textiles reveals the reverse. Again therefore we must tentatively conclude that the effect is more generalised.

Overall, the main conclusions appear to be as follows. Unquoted companies make more use of reserves and deferred taxation to finance their operations and, as expected, rely much less on equity issue than quoted companies. In addition they make less use of long-term loans but this to a great extent appears to reflect only a different term-structure of debt. The most significant difference is the much greater use of debtors and creditors which they make, though this has been diminishing quite markedly over the period examined. In many respects the financial structure of the two groups was becoming more similar over time but this can only partly be explained by the growing similarity of their sizes over time. Abstracting from these effects, unquoted companies appear to carry higher levels of stocks as a proportion of capital employed and a lower level of fixed assets, and this cannot adequately be explained by size differences.

One further conclusion stands out most clearly from this comparison. Unquoted companies have much more flexible asset and liability structures, in that a much higher proportion of both are short-term. This cannot fully be accounted for by smaller size, particularly on the assets side. The persistently higher ratio of current to fixed assets is not easily explained. It might reflect lower efficiency in the control of stocks and work-in-progress on the part of unquoted companies. However this would imply still greater efficiency elsewhere in order still to permit significantly higher profitability overall. Alternatively, it reflects a less capital-intensive method of production in unquoted companies independent of any size effects. Coupled with the higher creditor and debtor positions and the shorter term-structure of debt, it suggests a general disposition on the part of unquoted companies to remain more flexible, more able to vary production quickly and less heavily committed by fixed asset installations. This is not inconsistent with certain other characteristics repeatedly discussed in interviews, namely the need for great flexibility and the desire for maximum independence of action. More centralised control can also be an important factor in achieving this flexibility. Organisations with more diffused management control and therefore less immediate adaptability will feel less resistance to long-term and largely irreversible decisons. In those organisations where relatively small numbers of owner-managers can make strategic decisions quickly, resistance to such decisions will be stronger. This view, often expressed both in general and specific terms in interviews, appears to find some support in the balance-sheets of unquoted companies.

On the liabilities side, the shorter term-structure reflects the greater dependence on bank borrowing, which is still predominantly short-term. It might also reflect that unquoted companies are viewed by the banks as more risky, or again that the companies prefer to retain high flexibility of their liabilities. The former explanation is consistent with the higher variability of profits of unquoted companies, albeit around a higher average level, but it must be recalled that few of the companies interviewed ever felt constrained either by lack of bank finance or by the terms on which it was offered. It may well be simply that the preferences of unquoted companies fit more easily with those of commercial banks as suppliers of predominantly short-term (but generally renewed) debt finance.

7.4 ANALYSIS OF DIFFERENCES IN FINANCIAL BEHAVIOUR: THE FLOW OF FUNDS

Flexibility of finance is an important consideration for most companies, but the overriding issue is whether they face an overall financing constraint. This is central to the comparison of quoted and unquoted companies. Does lack of access to the capital market place unquoted companies at a disadvantage? Analyses of balance-sheets alone can offer relatively little evidence. Certain pointers are however available: unquoted companies were able to operate with much higher creditors and debtors per unit capital employed than quoted companies. Total borrowing was also higher per unit capital employed. More significant, they were able to achieve much higher growth rates through relatively greater use of reserves and deferred taxation, and despite a substantial contraction in their creditor and debtor position over the period. Most striking, although they remained more profitable throughout the period, their dependence on external debt finance fell markedly from being above that of quoted companies to below it. This indicates that higher reserves were substituting for debt finance rather than being used as a basis for raising more debt. This in turn suggests that unquoted companies were not in general experiencing any substantial finance constraint.

A more definite view can be obtained by utilising data from our sample companies' profit-and-loss accounts in conjunction with the balance-sheet data. This allows us to focus more directly on the flow of funds through the two classes of company. The method employed is based on that used by Dhrymes and Kurz[5] to investigate the interrelation of various company financial flows. Their approach is first replicated fairly closely for the two separate groups of companies. A modified version is then developed, in the light of the information so far gained about the distinctive characteristics of unquoted companies, and this alternative also tested.

The first approach commences from the assumption that the sources of long-term funds, namely net profit plus depreciation, new borrowing and new equity issues will equal the use of funds for investment and to pay dividends.[6] If we presume that net profit plus depreciation are already determined, and that new equity finance is over the longer term the balancing item which covers any shortage of funds from other sources, then we have three financial decisions to examine: the investment decision, the dividend decision and the new borrowing decision. Each will in part depend on the others, but each will also be a function of other characteristics of companies. All will in principle be influenced by company profitability; investment will depend on growth prospects and potentially on the extent to which the tax system discriminates in favour of retained earnings. In addition the ability to pay dividends may be a function of the liquidity of a company, as measured by net current assets. The depreciation provision can be an important determinant of the supply of long-term funds, and may well therefore influence both investment expenditure and the raising of new long-term debt. Finally, existing long-term gearing may influence the extent to which a company will raise further long-term debt. These relationships are incorporated in the set of equations tested, which are presented in Tables 7.7 and 7.8[7].

The sets of equations were run as a simultaneous system using two-stage least squares for the quoted companies and for the unquoted companies.

The regressions were run on pooled annual cross-sectional data for the years 1970–6. There are severe limitations to this approach and the

[5] P. Dhrymes and M Kurz, 'Investment, Dividend and External Finance Behaviour of Firms', in R. Ferber (ed.), *The Determinants of Investment Behaviour* (National Bureau of Economic Research, 1967) pp. 427–67.

[6] See Dhrymes and Kurz, 'Investment, Dividend and External Finance Behaviour' for a more detailed exposition of the approach.

[7] Several other variables, most notably interest rates, were also examined. None however appeared significant in any equations in any tests and they have therefore been dropped.

TABLE 7.7 Flow-of-Funds Analysis: Stage 1

	Constant	$\frac{I_t}{S_t}$	$\frac{D_t}{S_t}$	$\frac{\Delta B_t}{S_t}$	$\frac{\pi_{t-1}}{K_{t-1}}$	$\frac{S_t - S_{t-2}}{S_t}$	$\frac{DEP_t}{S_t}$	$\frac{NCA_t}{S_t}$	T_t	G_{t-1}
(A) Unquoted companies										
$\frac{I_t}{S_t}$	0.012 (0.95)		−1.65 (1.71)	0.789 (8.34)	0.043 (2.33)	−0.001 (0.05)	2.25 (5.55)		−0.035 (2.02)	
$\frac{D_t}{S_t}$	−0.015 (1.3)	0.182 (4.23)		−0.201 (4.39)	0.045 (3.80)			0.066 (0.69)	0.022 (1.89)	
$\frac{\Delta B_t}{S_t}$	−0.038 (0.55)	−0.180 (0.08)	−0.466 (0.11)		0.307 (0.07)		0.038 (0.29)			0.376 (0.59)
(B) Quoted companies										
$\frac{I_t}{S_t}$	0.017 (0.79)		−1.81 (3.43)	−1.79 (2.20)	0.162 (1.49)	0.077 (1.55)	2.71 (3.65)		0.010 (1.79)	
$\frac{D_t}{S_t}$	−0.039 (4.48)	0.191 (4.40)		−0.382 (2.30)	0.136 (3.01)			0.064 (4.05)	0.049 (0.97)	
$\frac{\Delta B_t}{S_t}$	−0.021 (2.46)	0.109 (3.55)	−0.763 (2.60)		−0.087 (0.77)		−0.378 (2.68)			0.097 (3.34)

Explanatory notes

1. *Symbols:*

   I Investment
   D Dividends
   ΔB New long-term borrowing
   π Profits
   K Capital employed
   S Sales
   DEP Depreciation allowance
   NCA Net current assets
   T Tax discriminant variable (see below)
   G Long-term gearing
   t year t.

2. The systems were run cross-sectionally for each individual year from 1970 to 1976 as a means of exploring variations in the parameters over time. These results are not reproduced as in general the explanatory power of the equations was weak.

   The signs of the independent variables were generally stable over time, but not their values, nor was there a high degree of significance of parameter values on annual data. Overall the data limitations were regarded as rendering intertemporal inferences invalid. Pooling of data over time can provide a better insight into financial behaviour but is also subject to considerable limitations, in particular that the stochastic characteristics of the data are inadequate. The results are therefore no more suggestive.

3. All equations are deflated by sales in an attempt to remove spurious correlation as a result of variation in company size.

4. The tax discriminant variable is $1 - m/1 - s$ where m is the estimated effective marginal rate of taxation on the shareholders (persons, insurance companies, pension funds and charities) and s is the standard rate of tax, this equalling the first element of company taxation: see M. King, *Public Policy in the Corporation* (London, 1977) appendix A. It therefore measures the additional disposable income that shareholders would receive if one unit of retained earnings were distributed, and is an indicator of the extent to which the tax system discriminates in favour of (above unity) or against (below unity) distributions.

results are therefore suggestive only.[8] Within this limitation several features of the results deserve comment.

The majority of constants are, as would be hypothesised, insignificant. Two however are significant. Inspection of annual tests suggests that with regard to debt financing this indicates a tendency for quoted companies to reduce gearing over time, and this is consistent with the previous analysis of this chapter; but this explanation cannot be applied to the dividend equation, and the proper interpretation of this latter result is unclear.

It should next be noted that the debt equation for unquoted companies is completely uninformative, no variables being significant. However this is to be expected in that, as we have seen, unquoted companies make relatively very little use of long-term debt finance. In particular, if variations in long-term debt are minor, and often no more than the consolidation of rolling short-term debt, then few significant results can be expected.

Looking next at the interrelation of investment, dividend and debt behaviour, several points of interest appear. First, considering only significant variables, the signs of the parameters are the same for both groups except in one case. Whereas investment is positively related to new long-term debt for unquoted companies, the relation is negative for quoted ones. The former cannot be interpreted as showing that unquoted companies explicitly finance a part of their investment programme through new debt finance; that relation is identified in the debt equation. Rather it suggests that a lengthening of the term-structure of corporate debt of unquoted companies leads to a higher level of investment, reflecting a possible constraint on asset structure imposed by a relatively short term-structure of liabilities. This would apply both cross-sectionally and over time.

The negative relation running from new debt financing to investment in quoted companies indicates an overriding effect of business conditions and cash flow. When the latter are weak, quoted companies tend to raise more debt and cut investment. In more buoyant conditions, despite more expansionary investment plans, debt finance can be run down. If we now look at the reverse relation, i.e. the effect on the borrowing decision of an increase in investment, there are again differences. For quoted companies there is, as expected, a positive and significant effect. For unquoted companies the effect is insignificant, reflecting as argued previously, the rather different role of long-term debt in unquoted companies.

---

[8] See footnote 2 to Table 7.7.

Looking at the relation running from investment to dividends, the basic pattern is similar for both groups of company. Higher investment occasions higher dividends; but the reverse relation is negative for quoted companies and insignificant for unquoted ones. To interpret this it should first be made clear as a general statement that if we consider the case of an exogenously determined change in one of the financial variables, then, *ceteris paribus*, the relation between two sources or two uses variables will be negative, but the relation between a source variable and a use variable will be positive. If we consider a change in one of these variables *in response to* an exogenous flow-of-funds change, e.g. net profit, then we would normally expect the relations specified above to be reversed. For example, while higher investment, *ceteris paribus*, will tend to lower other uses of funds, higher investment as a result of higher profits is more likely to be associated with rising expenditure on other uses of funds. Against this general framework, the results suggest that investment and dividends respond positively with cash flow for both groups of companies, but while dividends have no significant effect on investment in unquoted companies, they have a significant negative effect in quoted ones. Given the relatively minor role of dividends in unquoted companies the former is in line with our expectation. The latter result is at first sight surprising. It is however consistent with the original results of Dhrymes and Kurz[9] and is interpreted by them as showing that investment and dividends compete as uses of funds. From our general statement above we infer that this is so if companies wish to vary their dividends policy (or their investment policy) exogenously. Given the well-established view (following Lintner[10]) that dividends are in fact heavily dependent on profitability, this suggests that investment in unquoted companies, despite being more heavily financed by internally generated funds, is less directly influenced by availability of internal finance than in quoted ones. In other words most investment in unquoted companies is financed from retentions, but there are sufficient funds at the margin, either from retentions or elsewhere, for investment plans to be sheltered to some degree from fluctuations in cash flow.[11]

Looking at the relation running from borrowing to dividends, this is

[9] Although single-equation methods gave positive correlations, simultaneous-equation system results gave negative ones, as a result of separating out the positive reverse causation.

[10] J. Lintner, 'Distribution of Incomes of Corporations among Dividends, Retained Earnings and Taxes', *American Economic Review*, Papers and Proceedings, vol. 46, 1956, pp. 97–113.

[11] This will to some extent reflect the lower ratio of fixed to current assets of unquoted companies.

negative for both groups. This appears plausible, suggesting that both types of company increase their borrowing and cut dividends in more depressed periods. At first sight it is surprising to find the relation to be significant for unquoted companies in view of what was discovered about the determinants of both dividend and borrowing decisions. The result may reflect the seriousness with which a longer-term debt structure is viewed, but it is not clear that this is consistent with our interpretation of the debt/investment relation. The reverse relation from dividends to debt is, as expected, insignificant for unquoted companies and negative for quoted ones.

Turning to the independent variables in the system, further points of interest arise. Past profits have significant positive effects for both groups as expected, but are unrelated to the raising of new debt. While both groups exhibit positive coefficients in their investment equations for lagged profits, this is significant only for unquoted companies. This goes against our earlier view that investment in unquoted companies is heavily financed internally but not greatly limited by this source. We therefore return to this issue again below. Past growth of sales is insignificant for both groups. The measure of the effect of past growth as an indicator of expected growth is however very crude, and further analysis of this influence is required. Depreciation allowances as a source of funds have a strongly positive and significant effect on investment for both groups as expected. They do however have a significant negative effect on new long-term borrowing for quoted companies, suggesting that the latter offers an important source of long-term funds only for quoted companies when other sources are squeezed. Further differences are revealed when the role of net current assets, as a measure of liquidity, is examined. This has no effect on the dividends paid by unquoted companies and this is again consistent with the evidence previously presented on their dividend behaviour. In contrast, liquidity is a significant factor in the payment of dividends by quoted companies, reflecting the greater importance of these payments in the financial flows of quoted companies.

Turning to the tax discrimination variable, neither the relation to investment nor to dividends was found to be significant for quoted companies. It was however negative, as expected, and significant for investment by unquoted companies, and positive and barely significant for dividends. This suggests that the tax system is a partial deterrent to the payment of dividends by unquoted companies, as was indicated in our interviews, but probably not in the case of quoted companies, where the dividend decision is much more remote from the shareholder. The negative relation to investment again hints at the importance of retained earnings for financing the investment of unquoted companies. Finally the effect of existing long-term gearing was found to be insignificant for unquoted companies; for quoted ones there was a positive and significant relation with new borrowing. If companies are viewed as having an optimum gearing ratio, then the relationship should be negative. If however companies tend normally to adopt rather conservative gearing ratios, raising them when their other sources of funds appear inadequate in relation to uses, then a positive correlation might reflect that those with poor cash flow positions faced progressively weaker financial conditions, both across quoted companies and over time. This is consistent with the negative relation between lagged profits and new borrowing for quoted companies, though the relation was not itself found to be a statistically significant one.

Overall the results are suggestive only, but none the less permit two types of inference. First, much of the distinctive character of unquoted companies' financial behaviour is borne out: the lack of relation of long-term debt to other financial variables (whereas the links are significant for quoted companies), the much weaker indications of any competition between investment and dividends, and some (but only some) signs of a stronger role of internal funds in determining investment levels. Second, there are some indications that access to external borrowing and external equity give quoted companies easier access to finance for investment but that this weakens the effect of the previous year's profits, and does not remove the greater competition for funds between competing uses. Yet it is difficult to conclude that this reflects greater demand for investment funds by quoted companies in view of their lower profits and slower growth.

The most important question to ask is whether these results have anything to suggest concerning the financial characteristics most likely to produce efficient investment expenditures. Quoted companies have the pressure of a capital market test for at least a proportion of their investment but appear more constrained by other uses of funds. Unquoted companies do not face that test so directly but none the less have to achieve high returns if they are to maintain their investment programmes. There are no obvious indications that investment by unquoted companies suffers through not having access to the stock market, and this, coupled with the higher return which they make, raises at least some doubts about how well the stock market works in providing funds and enforcing their efficient use.

The test described above largely replicated the work of Dhrymes and

TABLE 7.8 Flow of Funds Analysis: Stage 2

	Constant	$\dfrac{I_t}{S_t}$	$\dfrac{D_t}{S_t}$	$\dfrac{\Delta B'_t}{S_t}$	$\dfrac{\Delta R_t}{S_t}$	$\dfrac{\Delta C_t}{S_t}$	$\dfrac{\Delta W_t}{S_t}$
Unquoted companies							
$\dfrac{I_t}{S_t}$	0.163 (0.99)		−3.73 (0.75	0.828 (1.27)	−4.85 (0.81)	1.52 (0.45)	−1.43 (1.61)
$\dfrac{D_t}{S_t}$	0.043 (2.32)	−0.247 (0.73)		0.197 (0.43)	−1.29 (9.87)	0.427 (0.19)	−0.389 (1.60)
$\dfrac{\Delta B'_t}{S_t}$	−0.186 (0.59)	1.17 (1.34)	4.19 (0.49)		5.47 (2.32)	−1.66 (0.33)	1.60 (0.43)
$\dfrac{\Delta R_t}{S_t}$	0.033 (2.97)	−0.193 (0.79)	−0.774 (9.87)	0.153 (1.48)		0.329 (1.05)	0.300 (0.59)
$\dfrac{\Delta C}{S_t}$	−0.01 (0.00)	−0.191 (0.50)	0.845 (1.86)	0.386 (0.91)	0.865 (4.31)		0.416 (0.89)
$\dfrac{\Delta W_t}{S_t}$	0.109 (1.54)	−0.621 (0.59)	−2.53 (1.01)	0.491 (2.40)	−3.27 (1.60)	1.00 (0.92)	

Quoted companies

$\dfrac{I_t}{S_t}$	-0.043 (1.20)		3.24 (2.98)	1.02 (2.90)	0.468 (0.39)	1.66 (5.45)	-0.832 (1.07)
$\dfrac{D_t}{S_t}$	0.014 (1.73)	2.298 (3.01)		-0.310 (2.71)	-0.148 (0.42)	-0.493 (2.42)	0.245 (0.96)
$\dfrac{\Delta B_t^r}{S_t}$	0.414 (1.25)	0.941 (2.93)	-3.09 (2.71)		-0.467 (0.42)	1.57 (2.89)	-0.817 (1.22)
$\dfrac{\Delta R_t}{S_t}$	0.039 (0.79)	0.684 (2.58)	-2.35 (0.62)	-0.74 (0.62)		-1.12 (0.94)	0.845 (1.97)
$\dfrac{\Delta C_t}{S_t}$	0.029 (1.45)	0.590 (5.70)	-1.96 (2.58)	-0.520 (1.78)	-0.246 (0.47)		-1.01 (0.24)
$\dfrac{\Delta W_t}{S_t}$	-0.039 (0.74)	-0.941 (1.16)	3.01 (2.23)	1.05 (1.31)	0.655 (2.98)	1.57 (1.19)	

See notes to Table 7.7.

Kurz to see whether unquoted companies stood out as behaving in a distinctively different manner from quoted ones. In the light of all the evidence so far presented it is possible to hypothesise a modified financial system designed to bring out more explicitly the differences between the financial behaviour of quoted and unquoted companies. One of the major contrasts in balance-sheet analysis was the greater proportional significance of short-term assets and liabilities for unquoted companies. The flow-of-funds analysis was therefore repeated, but adding in short-term loans to long-term ones, and introducing new equations for creditors, debtors and stocks/work-in-progress.[12] The system this generates is too elaborate, given our data, to test fully, but it was able to throw some further light on the interrelation of the various sources and uses of funds identified. The interlinkage of the six variables was examined by the instrumental variables procedure, using the same independent variables as before as instruments. The results are shown in Table 7.8.

In general terms the parameters were much more significant for the quoted than the unquoted group, suggesting a much higher degree of variability in the unquoted group. This makes it inappropriate to examine the system for detailed information, but one interesting characteristic of the results as a whole is worth noting. We have seen that if cash flow generated by business operations changes, then we would expect sources and uses of funds identified in our equations to be negatively correlated, but positively so if companies attempt to change their planned expenditures in the face of unchanging business conditions. We also saw that there was conflicting evidence on whether the heavy dependence of unquoted companies' investment on retentions and depreciation was constraining. Looking at the pattern of positive and negative correlations in our results, the quoted and unquoted samples do in this respect exhibit very different behaviour. In general the quoted companies fit the first pattern, with reduced cash flow being met by greater use of other sources and curtailment of uses (and the opposite for increased cash flow). In fact nineteen of the thirty parameter signs fitted this pattern, eleven of them being significant. Only four of those not fitting the pattern were significant. In very sharp contrast only three of the thirty signs fitted this pattern for unquoted companies and none were significant. Twenty-seven of the thirty were positive as between sources and uses or negative as between two sources or two uses, though only five of them were significant.

[12] Dhrymes and Kurz originally included inventory investment in their formulation but excluded it when they came to estimate their equations.

Clearly this final test is again tentative. Yet the difference in the pattern of linkages between sources and uses is quite striking, for it does suggest that to a much greater extent unquoted companies were varying not only their dividends independent of their cash flow position but also their short- and long-term assets and liabilities. Quoted companies in contrast were varying them much more in response to changes in cash flow brought about by variations in business conditions.

Even if this conclusion were firm it leaves open the precise interpretation. It may be that unquoted companies remain much more firmly within their financial constraints, and this would be entirely consistent with their desire for security in the face of generally higher commercial risk, and their desire for flexibility and independence of action; or it may reflect easier access to funds as a result of the greater security which their shorter-term asset structure can provide for lenders; or it may reflect easier access because of their higher profitability. In practice probably all three factors are important. We have found both the latter two differences to be statistically significant, and the first emerges repeatedly in the evidence on motivation. If however we bear in mind the faster growth of unquoted companies, it seems unlikely that they were systematically avoiding any financial pressure simply by curtailing their operations to a level comfortably inside the constraint. This is particularly so when it is recalled that their growth appeared relatively unconstrained by their profitability. We believe therefore that overall the result tends to support the view that unquoted companies were not facing any more acute financial constraint as a result of their lack of access to the stock market. If this had been a problem then we would have expected the pattern of correlations to be reversed, with quoted companies having more scope to pursue chosen financial policies despite fluctuations in cash flow. In fact this appears to be a characteristic of the unquoted companies.

7.5 CONCLUSIONS

Overall there are marked differences in the financial behaviour of quoted and unquoted companies which go considerably beyond those directly resulting from access to the stock market. Unquoted companies not only are found systematically to raise far fewer funds from new equity issue but also from long-term debt. At the same time they tend to hold much higher levels of short-term assets in relation to their capital base but only slightly lower fixed assets. Heavier use of three types of finance make this possible: creditors, short-term loans and reserves. The result is a much more flexible financial structure with only very limited long-term commitments to external shareholders or to lending institutions. While such characteristics are partly a function of size, this is true to only a limited extent. Rather they reflect, as we have seen before, the need for the owner-managers to retain fairly immediate control of their assets when no ready market for those assets exists.

Statistical examination of the flow of funds through companies tended to confirm earlier conclusions as to the different characteristics of dividends and long-term borrowing of unquoted companies. Considering all the interrelations between various sources and uses, the results suggest two main conclusions. First, that while unquoted companies finance more of their investment internally they are less constrained by fluctuations in internal funds. This may partly reflect conservative financing policies but mainly indicates easy access to funds, notably short-term ones, because of their higher profitability and shorter-term asset structure. Second, absence of access to the stock market does not appear to put unquoted companies at a financial disadvantage; in fact they appear more rather than less able to pursue chosen financial policies in the face of fluctuations in internally generated cash flow. While considerably more work needs to be done in this area, we believe these results to be interesting indicators of the efficiency of the financing of unquoted companies.

APPENDIX 7.1 THE STRUCTURE OF COMPANY LIABILITIES, AND CALCULATIONS OF RATES OF RETURN

This Appendix uses some of the results reported in Chapter 7 on the differences in financing and balance-sheets of quoted and unquoted companies to explore the implications for the profit-rate comparisons that were made in Chapter 6. In particular we examine the possibility that differences in the term structure of liabilities imparts an upward bias to the calculated rates of return of unquoted companies in comparison with those for quoted companies.

The difficulty arises from the definition of profit in company accounts. Invariably this is calculated after all current costs of operations, *including* the interest on short-term loans such as overdrafts. The amount of short-term interest paid is seldom reported, and would be difficult to estimate as the amount of overdraft is likely to fluctuate through the year.

Given that the figure for profit before payment of short-term interest cannot be obtained, the convention is to calculate profit rates on the basis of capital employed (net assets), which is the sum of fixed assets and current assets *minus* current liabilities. By definition, this can also be calculated as the sum of the long-term liabilities of the company since:

Shareholder capital *plus* reserves *plus* long-term loans = Fixed assets *plus* current assets *minus* current liabilities.

The purpose in choosing this valuation of capital employed is to treat numerator and denominator alike by deducting interest on current liabilities from the numerator, and current liabilities from the denominator.

In symbols, the rate of return, which was calculated in Chapter 6, is given by:

$$R = \frac{\pi - i \cdot CL}{TA - CL}$$

where R is the rate of return
π is the profits *before* deduction of interest
i is the interest rate on current liabilities
CL is current liabilities
TA is total assets, fixed plus current.

The source of the bias referred to above can now be explained. Suppose two firms have the same ratio of profits before interest to total assets (π/TA), but that one finances those assets with more short-term liabilities. Then there is a possibility that deducting interest ($i \cdot CL$) from the numerator, and current liabilities (CL) from the denominator, will systematically bias the returns upwards in a firm with more current liabilities. Hence comparisons of rates of return, R, will be misleading. Specifically, the analysis of balance-sheets in Chapter 7 has shown that unquoted firms rely much more heavily than quoted firms on short-term (current) liabilities to finance their operations. Could the bias explain the superior rates of return reported for unquoted companies in comparison with quoted companies in Chapter 6?

Unfortunately we cannot, for reasons already alluded to, circumvent the problem by measuring π/TA directly, the reported profits are of the form ($\pi - i \cdot CL$) and we do not have figures for $i \cdot CL$. Hence all we can do is to explore the likely magnitude of the bias.

We write the measured rates of return to quoted (R_Q) and unquoted (R_{UQ}) companies as follows:

$$R_{UQ} = \frac{\pi - i(CL + \Delta CL)}{TA - (CL + \Delta CL)}$$

$$R_Q = \frac{\pi - i \cdot CL}{TA - CL}$$

ΔCL is the difference in current liabilities between unquoted and quoted companies.

It is easy to derive the difference in rates of return:

$$R_{UQ} - R_Q = \frac{\pi - i \cdot TA}{TA - CL} \times \frac{\Delta CL}{TA - CL - \Delta CL}$$

It is evident that for positive ΔCL (unquoted were more reliant than quoted companies on short-term liabilities), $R_{UQ} - R_Q$ is positive if $\pi > i \cdot TA$. Now π is simply total assets *times* the gross return on assets (g). Hence the condition can be written as $g > i$. One would normally expect average returns on assets to exceed the short-term cost of borrowing. So the existence of the bias is confirmed and we must explain its likely magnitude. This is most easily achieved by rewriting the expression:

$$R_{UQ} - R_Q = \left[\frac{\pi}{TA - CL} - \frac{i \cdot TA}{TA - CL} \right] \frac{\Delta CL}{TA - CL - \Delta CL}$$

$$= \left[\frac{\pi - i \cdot CL}{TA - CL} - \frac{i(TA - CL)}{TA - CL} \right] \frac{\Delta CL}{TA - CL - \Delta CL}$$

$$= \left[\frac{\pi - i \cdot CL}{TA - CL} - i \right] \frac{\Delta CL}{TA - CL - \Delta CL}$$

This expression may be evaluated as follows:

$\dfrac{\pi - i \cdot CL}{TA - CL}$ is the quoted companies' rate of return, R_Q. Table 6.8 gives a value of 23.2 per cent as the average for the small sample of quoted companies for the period 1966–79.

i is the interest rate on short term finance, which is mainly bank overdrafts. In the period 1966–79 the rate varied roughly between 10 and 20 per cent, starting quite low and rising throughout the period. Hence the bracketed term in the above expression probably lies between 3 and 13 per cent with a mean of about 8 per cent.

$\dfrac{\Delta CL}{TA - CL - \Delta CL}$ can be derived approximately from Table 7.2. However, it is not appropriate to use the average differences in short-term liabilities between unquoted and quoted companies as given in the third column of the table. This is because much of the difference arises from the fact that unquoted companies in the sample have higher short-term assets as a percentage of capital employed as well as higher short-term liabilities. To allow for possible distortions from the latter alone would be incorrect. As we have seen, to a considerable extent the shorter-term structure of unquoted company liabilities is matched by their shorter-term asset structure. The appropriate figures from which to calculate ΔCL are therefore those in Table 7.4, where higher short-term liabilities matched by higher short-term assets have been netted out for unquoted companies. Over the ten years the average value of short-term liabilities *minus* the equivalent figure for quoted companies as a percentage of capital employed for unquoted companies calculated from Table 7.4 is 12.6 per cent.

Hence we calculate that $R_{UQ} - R_Q$ lies in the range 0.4 to 1.6 per cent. Since the differences in operating profit rates reported in Tables 6.10 and 6.12 are 5.3 per cent (size effects not considered) and 6.7 per cent (size effect accounted for), the calculated bias is quite insufficient to explain those differences.

Before leaving this issue, there is a further theoretical point that warrants note. The profit rate as defined for our calculation is widely used as an indication of company profitability and performance, since it represents the returns on long-term funds committed to the company. If it were possible to increase significantly the apparent profitability of a company simply by increasing the proportion of short- to long-term liabilities, it is hard to imagine that this would not be done. It seems far more plausible to imagine that the financing pattern adopted by firms is in fact optimal for them. This has been examined to some extent in the body of Chapter 7. While, therefore, it is important to remember that specific measures of profitability are to some extent arbitrary and subject to limitations as indicators of performance, it would be wrong to infer that over the long term their value can be undermined through purely financial rearrangement of companies' balance-sheets.

Index